IN THE SMALLER SCOPE
OF CONSCIENCE

In the Smaller Scope of Conscience

The Struggle for National Repatriation Legislation, 1986–1990

C. TIMOTHY McKEOWN

THE UNIVERSITY OF
ARIZONA PRESS

TUCSON

THE UNIVERSITY OF ARIZONA PRESS

www.uapress.arizona.edu

Library of Congress Cataloging-in-Publication Data

McKeown, C. Timothy, 1955–
   In the smaller scope of conscience : the struggle for national repatriation legislation, 1986–1990 / C. Timothy McKeown.
      p. cm.
   Includes bibliographical references and index.
   ISBN 978-0-8165-2687-1 (hardback)
   1. Human remains (Archaeology)—Repatriation—Law and legislation—United States.   2. United States. Native American Graves Protection and Repatriation Act.   I. Title.
   KF8210.A57M38   2013
   344.73'09—dc23   2012017149

Publication of this book is made possible in part by the proceeds of a permanent endowment created with the assistance of a Challenge Grant from the National Endowment for the Humanities, a federal agency.

♻

Manufactured in the United States of America on acid-free, archival-quality paper containing a minimum of 30% postconsumer waste and processed chlorine free.

17   16   15   14   13   12   6   5   4   3   2   1

For decades, the skeletal remains of American Indians were removed from their burial sites, studied, catalogued, and relegated to the bins of museums and science. This legislation is about respecting the rights of the dead, the right to an undisturbed resting-place. It is a good bill, and long overdue. What we are saying to American Indians today, Mr. Speaker, is simply that your ancestors and their burial grounds are sacred, and will remain so.

In the larger scope of history, this is a very small thing.

In the smaller scope of conscience, it may be the biggest thing we have ever done.

Representative Morris Udall
October 22, 1990

Contents

Illustrations

Prologue

On November 28, 1989, President George H. W. Bush signed into law the National Museum of the American Indian Act (NMAI Act), which included provisions requiring the repatriation of human remains and funerary objects in the possession or control of the Smithsonian Institution. Almost a year later, on November 16, 1990, Bush also approved the Native American Graves Protection and Repatriation Act (NAGPRA). These two statutes together established a national framework for achieving three related goals. The first is the repatriation of Native American human remains, funerary objects, sacred objects, and objects of cultural patrimony, collectively defined as cultural items, in the possession or control of all federal agencies and institutions receiving federal funds. The second goal is the disposition of cultural items excavated or removed from federal or tribal lands. The third is the prohibition of commerce in certain Native American cultural items.

The federal repatriation mandate embodied by the NMAI Act and NAGPRA did not spring forth fully formed from the Senate or House of Representatives. Between 1986 and 1990, members of the 99th, 100th, and 101st Congresses considered sixteen different numbered bills including repatriation provisions, some with several versions. Each bill reflected the unique experiences of its sponsor and his staff, as well as a progressive refinement of the system of definitions and processes that would be applied to repatriation. Each bill also reflected the evolving confrontations, negotiations, and, eventually, agreements between the various constituent groups involved intimately in crafting the legislation. The story of that struggle is the subject of this book.

Why is such a legislative history important? "The less people know about how sausages and law are made," says the old adage, "the better they sleep."[1] Sausage making involves selecting ingredients, including various cuts of meat, spices, and seasoning; grinding the ingredients coarsely, then again to the desired consistency; and finally stuffing the ingredients into uniform casings. Law making involves identification of an end to be attained, mischief to be remedied, or purpose to be accomplished by a congressional sponsor; refining the relevant terms and processes through a series of drafts, statements, and hearings; markup by the sponsoring committee and issuance of a committee report; passage by the House and Senate; signing as a Public Law by the president; and finally, addition of the law to the corpus of the U.S. Code.[2] The old adage implies that some aspects of both sausage making and law making, if generally known, might result in anxiety, stress, or even depression, the common psychological causes of insomnia. What is not said is that while ignoring the culinary genesis of your meal may provide for restful nights, ignoring legislative history is done at one's peril. Sausages are generally forgotten soon after they are eaten. Statutes, on the other hand, remain guideposts for years, decades, and in cases like the U.S. Constitution, centuries. The specific combination of statutory text, reports, drafts, statements, and hearings leading to enactment provide each new generation with the references needed to apply a law to new situations.

My professional interest in the topic of legislative history began in late 1991, when I was hired by the National Park Service as team leader for national implementation of NAGPRA. One of my primary duties was to draft implementing regulations, including the main body of regulations promulgated in 1995 at 43 CFR §10, and various reserved sections of that part published in 1997, 2003, 2007, and 2010. Over this nearly two-decade period, I immersed myself in the text of the NAGPRA statute and those documents readily available to and relied on by the legislators in passing the bill to understand the meaning of specific words, phrases, or provisions.

The standard work on the history of the NAGPRA legislation was done by Jack F. Trope from the Association for American Indian Affairs and Walter R. Echo-Hawk from the Native American Rights Fund shortly after the bill was enacted.[3] The authors were intimately involved in negotiating NAGPRA's final language, as they had been with the language of the NMAI Act the year before. However, their forty-two-page article covers the series of bills and actions that ultimately led to passage of the NMAI Act and NAGPRA in just four pages, the rest of the article being devoted to background information and a review of NAGPRA's provisions. There is no similar article on the genesis of the repatriation provisions of the NMAI Act.

This book has a broader focus. Early on in my tenure with the National Park Service, I realized that the two statutes were inextricably linked, with many provisions in NAGPRA marking the logical evolution of procedures set forth initially in the NMAI Act. The history of the two statutes needed to be told together. A legislative history typically starts with the enacted statute and uses a relatively narrow range of specific congressional documentation to understand the legislative intent of each provision. Chapters 1 through 7 flip this around, starting instead at the beginning of the legislative process to explore the issues in need of legislative remedy; chronicling the actions of lobbying groups; documenting the introduced bills, congressional hearings, and reports over several Congresses; and ending with the enacted statutes. This history of the legislation also relies on a wider range of sources, beyond just the bills themselves and related committee and hearing reports prepared prior to passage, to include handwritten meeting notes, emails, faxes, postenactment recollections, even sticky notes—basically any and all relevant information—to better understand the varied and conflicting intents of congressional members and staff, executive branch officials, and Native American, museum, and archeological lobbyists involved in this legislative process. Chapter 8, on the other hand, assumes a more traditional approach to legislative history, applying rules of statutory construction to clarify the congressional intent regarding specific provisions of the statutes and how they have been applied, and on occasion misapplied, in various judicial opinions and executive actions.

The research underlying this book was conducted over two decades and involved many institutions and individuals. The focus is on the evolution of legislative text over time, so much of the primary documentation was derived from libraries and archives, including the Billie Jane Baguley Library and Archives of the Heard Museum, Phoenix, Arizona; Seeley G. Mudd Manuscript Library, Princeton University, Princeton, New Jersey; National Anthropological Archives, National Museum of Natural History, Suitland, Maryland; Smithsonian Institution Archives, Washington, DC; Main Library Special Collections, University of Arizona, Tucson, Arizona; George Bush Presidential Library and Museum, College Station, Texas; Center for Legislative Archives, National Archives, Washington, DC; and Special Access and FOIA Staff, National Archives, College Park, Maryland.

The documents only tell so much of the story. I was also interested in documenting the unwritten context of the various bills that were developed. Applying my training as a linguistic anthropologist, I conducted interviews with a number of the principal congressional staffers involved in the development of the NMAI Act and NAGPRA, using an interviewing approach that emphasizes the identification of semantic categories, relationships, and cases to document the insider's perspective on the legislative process.[4] Marie Howard, professional staff for Chairman Morris Udall, Committee on Interior and Insular Affairs, with primary responsibility for passage of H.R. 5237, graciously provided insights into the processes and issues involving in passing the bill, and Patricia Zell, staff director and chief counsel; Eric Eberhard, minority staff director and counsel; and Steven J. W. Heeley, deputy minority staff director, Senate Committee on Indian Affairs, provided similar understanding of the parallel efforts in the Senate. Jack Trope, counsel for the Association for American Indian Affairs; Suzan Shown Harjo, executive director of the National Congress of American Indians and later president of the Morning Star Institute; Karen Funk, legislative analyst, Hobbs Straus Dean & Walker LLP; Keith Kintigh and Vin Steponaitis, representing the Society for American Archaeology; Dan Monroe and Martin Sullivan, representing the American Association of Museums; Tom King, representing the Advisory Council for Historic Preservation; and Robert McCormack Adams, secretary of the Smithsonian, all shared their recollections of the intense negotiations between their respective groups that ultimately resulted in agreements. Colleagues at the National Park Service likewise provided useful insights, including the late Muriel Crespi and Douglas Scovill, as well as Francis McManamon, Ruthann Knudsen, Patricia Parker, Richard Waldbauer, and Sherry Hutt. Special thanks to my friends and colleagues who read the final manuscript and helped improve its accuracy and clarity, including Patricia Zell, Martin Sullivan, Jack Trope, James Nason from the Burke Museum in Seattle, and Larry Zimmerman from Indiana University–Purdue University Indianapolis.

Finally, I acknowledge the passing of several individuals who served critical rolls in conceptualizing, formulating, and implementing the NMAI Act and NAGPRA:

Reuben A. Snake (Winnebago): 1937–1993
William Tallbull (Cheyenne): 1921–1996
Representative Morris K. Udall: 1922–1998
Patrick H. Lefthand (Kootenai): 1938–1999
Edward Kanahele (Hawaiian): 1942–2000

Jan Hammil Bear Shield (Mescalero Apache): 1947–2001
Rachel C. Craig (Inupiaq): 1930–2003
Maria D. Pearson (Yankton Sioux): 1932–2003
Representative Charles E. Bennett: 1910–2003
Michael S. Haney (Seminole): 1947–2005
Nelson Wallulatum (Wasco): 1926–2010

May they all rest in peace.

The Struggle for National Repatriation Legislation
1986-1990

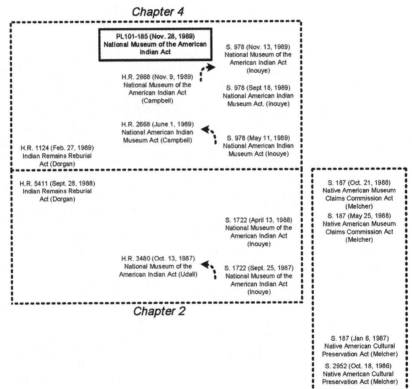

Chapter 4

PL101-185 (Nov. 28, 1989)
National Museum of the American Indian Act

S. 978 (Nov. 13, 1989)
National Museum of the American Indian Act (Inouye)

H.R. 2668 (Nov. 9, 1989)
National Museum of the American Indian Act (Campbell)

S. 978 (Sept 18, 1989)
National American Indian Museum Act. (Inouye)

H.R. 2668 (June 1, 1989)
National American Indian Museum Act (Campbell)

S. 978 (May 11, 1989)
National American Indian Museum Act (Inouye)

H.R. 1124 (Feb. 27, 1989)
Indian Remains Reburial Act (Dorgan)

H.R. 5411 (Sept. 28, 1988)
Indian Remains Reburial Act (Dorgan)

S. 187 (Oct. 21, 1988)
Native American Museum Claims Commission Act (Melcher)

S. 187 (May 25, 1988)
Native American Museum Claims Commission Act (Melcher)

S. 1722 (April 13, 1988)
National Museum of the American Indian Act (Inouye)

H.R. 3480 (Oct. 13, 1987)
National Museum of the American Indian Act (Udall)

S. 1722 (Sept. 25, 1987)
National Museum of the American Indian Act (Inouye)

Chapter 2

S. 187 (Jan 6, 1987)
Native American Cultural Preservation Act (Melcher)

S. 2952 (Oct. 18, 1986)
Native American Cultural Preservation Act (Melcher)

Chapter 1

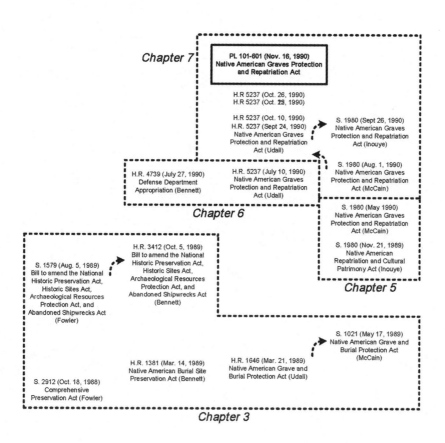

Chapter 7

PL 101-601 (Nov. 16, 1990)
Native American Graves Protection
and Repatriation Act

H.R 5237 (Oct. 26, 1990)
H.R 5237 (Oct. 22, 1990)

H.R 5237 (Oct. 10, 1990)
H.R. 5237 (Sept 24, 1990)
Native American Graves
Protection and Repatriation
Act (Udall)

S. 1980 (Sept 26, 1990)
Native American Graves
Protection and Repatriation
Act (Inouye)

H.R. 4739 (July 27, 1990)
Defense Department
Appropriation (Bennett)

H.R. 5237 (July 10, 1990)
Native American Graves
Protection and Repatriation
Act (Udall)

S. 1980 (Aug. 1, 1990)
Native American Graves
Protection and Repatriation
Act (McCain)

Chapter 6

S. 1980 (May 1990)
Native American Graves
Protection and Repatriation
Act (McCain)

S. 1980 (Nov. 21, 1989)
Native American
Repatriation and Cultural
Patrimony Act (Inouye)

Chapter 5

H.R. 3412 (Oct. 5, 1989)
Bill to amend the National
Historic Preservation Act,
Historic Sites Act,
Archaeological Resources
Protection Act, and
Abandoned Shipwrecks Act
(Bennett)

S. 1579 (Aug. 5, 1989)
Bill to amend the National
Historic Preservation Act,
Historic Sites Act,
Archaeological Resources
Protection Act, and
Abandoned Shipwrecks Act
(Fowler)

S. 1021 (May 17, 1989)
Native American Grave and
Burial Protection Act
(McCain)

H.R. 1381 (Mar. 14, 1989)
Native American Burial Site
Preservation Act (Bennett)

H.R. 1646 (Mar. 21, 1989)
Native American Grave and
Burial Protection Act (Udall)

S. 2912 (Oct. 18, 1988)
Comprehensive
Preservation Act (Fowler)

Chapter 3

Introduced bills   House/Senate bill number (date
                          introduced) Bill title

Enacted bills   Public Law number (date
                          enacted) Statute title

                          Parallel House/Senate bills

CHAPTER ONE

Tallbull's Quest

The wooden cabinets were clearly a custom job—fourteen drawers stacked floor to ceiling, each with a tarnished brass pull and a faded yellow label written in flowing long-hand script, cabinet after cabinet on both sides of the dimly lit hallway. The famous anthropologist Aleš Hrdlička had designed the avocado-green cabinets (see figure 1.1) in the early part of the twentieth century to hold his expanding collection. The old Cheyenne man adjusted his glasses, stunned at the sheer magnitude of collections around him.

William Tallbull was born in 1921 in Muddy Creek, Montana.[1] Raised by his grandparents on the rural Northern Cheyenne reservation, he spoke the Cheyenne language fluently. During World War II, he served in Europe as a member of the Army Air Corps, but he returned to the reservation afterward to hold a variety of government positions, including election to the Tribal Council. He retired in 1972 after thirty years of public service and dedicated the rest of his life to increasing the public's awareness of Native American cultures and beliefs. As part of a delegation of tribal religious leaders, he found himself among Hrdlička's cabinets seeking a pipe in the collection of the Smithsonian's National Museum of Natural History in Washington, DC.

Tallbull was also a member of the Dog Soldiers, one of the ancient Cheyenne warrior societies entrusted with the protection of the two sacred covenants given to the Cheyenne people by the Supreme Deity. *Mahuts*, the four sacred arrows, were given to the Cheyenne at Bear Butte in South Dakota. *Is'siwun*, the sacred buffalo hat, was given, along with the sun

1

Figure 1.1 The green cabinets that held human osteological specimens at the Smithsonian National Museum of Natural History.

dance, to the Suhati people who later merged with the Cheyenne.[2] The Dog Soldier Society, along with the Fox, Elk, Shield, and Bowstring Societies, are responsible for ensuring that the rituals surrounding these objects were carried out properly.[3] Each society maintained an assortment of other objects that were needed to carry out its ceremonial obligations.

The Cheyenne believed the pipe in the Smithsonian's collection had once been the most significant part of a "chief's bundle" carried by Chief Tall Bull. In 1869, Chief Tall Bull and other members of the Dog Soldier Society captured two German women in Kansas and were being pursued across the prairies by the army. Colonel Eugene Carr and his troops came upon the Cheyenne camp near Summit Spring, Colorado. In the ensuing attack, Chief Tall Bull was killed and all of the Cheyenne lodges were sacked. A bundle consisting of the pipe with a red stone bowl and long wooden stem (see figure 1.2), a Dog Soldier rattle, a greasewood pipe tamper, and sweet grass, all contained in a buffalo wool bag, was taken from Chief Tall Bull's lodge. The bundle was a critical part of the ceremony in which members reaffirmed their commitment to the society, and its loss

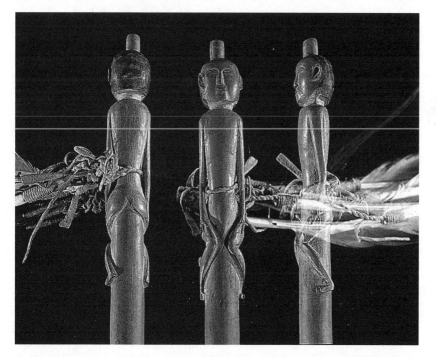

Figure 1.2 The carved stem of the Tall Bull pipe (triple exposure). #78-15883, Department of Anthropology, Smithsonian Institution.

led to a split among the Dog Soldiers and demoralized the Cheyenne people. An army record of the seizure helped William Tallbull, after years of effort, track down the pipe that had been in his paternal grandfather's care to the Smithsonian.[4] After reviewing Tallbull's documentation, a Smithsonian employee led him over to a drawer. "Here is the pipe that is referred to in the record."[5] The Cheyenne religious leaders were overjoyed to finally touch the wooden pipe stem for which they searched so long. The red stone bowl was missing.[6]

A chance inquiry by one of the other Cheyenne led the Smithsonian employee to pull out another of the green drawers. "A Kiowa," explained the staffer as a jumble of bones was revealed in the carefully designed drawer, long enough to hold a femur, deep enough to accommodate a human skull.[7] Hrdlička was the premier physical anthropologists of his day, collecting the crania and skeletons of thousands of individuals between 1903, when he joined the staff of the Smithsonian, until his death in 1943.[8] His seven-volume *Catalogue of Human Crania in the U.S. National Museum* meticulously documented the collection that lay silently surrounding the Cheyenne.[9] The elation at having found the Tall Bull pipe after years of searching was shattered by the stark realization that they were standing among the remains of tens of thousands of Native American dead collected from graves and battlegrounds. "The chiefs were quite alarmed because we had been sitting there all day with those restless spirits," reported Clara Spotted Elk, a fellow Cheyenne and legislative assistant to Democratic Senator John Melcher from Montana. "We really beat it out of there."[10] Tallbull and the other Cheyenne went immediately to Melcher's office. "I told him of my concern, the concern of Indian people," Tallbull recalled of this meeting with Melcher, "and he said 'I'll do all I can.'"[11]

The Bones Bill

In 1986, Melcher was four years into his second six-year term in the Senate, after serving eight years in the House of Representatives. A silver-haired World War II veteran and former veterinarian, the farm state Democrat was regarded as somewhat of a maverick in Congress. Conservatives criticized him for supporting increases in food stamps, overseas food aid, and congressional salaries, and liberals found fault with his support of increased spending on nuclear arms and staunch prolife stance on abortion. With 6 percent of the Montana population identified as Native American,

Melcher took an active interest in Indian issues, serving as chair of the Senate Select Committee on Indian Affairs from 1979 before becoming its ranking minority member when the Republicans took control of the Senate in 1981. His efforts were returned with strong support at the polls from Montana counties with large Native American populations.[12]

Drafting of the so-called Bones Bill began shortly after Melcher met with the Cheyenne delegation.[13] An undated draft was circulated in August 1986 under the title Native American Archeological Resources and Development Protection Act. An alternative title appears to have been the Bridge of Respect Act.[14] While drafting of the bill continued, Melcher contacted the Library of Congress and arranged to provide tape duplicates of early wax cylinder recordings of tribal religious songs in the library's collections to each of the seven Montana tribes (see figure 1.3).[15]

On the last day of the 99th Congress, Melcher formally introduced his bill, now called the Native American Cultural Preservation Act, to "protect Native American rights to the remains of their dead and to sacred objects, and to create Native American cultural museums."[16] "The museums

Figure 1.3 Northern Cheyenne tribal member and traditional religious leader William Tallbull accepting tape duplicates of Cheyenne wax cylinder recordings and other materials from Senator John Melcher of Montana on behalf of the Federal Cylinder Project and the American Folklife Center during a ceremony at the Library of Congress on September 29, 1986.

say 'we own the stuff,'" Spotted Elk said in discussing the new bill. "The Native American tribes are saying 'no, you can't own human remains.' It is a classic example of two cultures clashing."[17] Spotted Elk said that the bill had been introduced with the hope that it would act as a bridge between Indian groups and educational institutions. Melcher acknowledged that there was clearly no opportunity for Congress to consider any measure introduced on the last day of the session, but he explained that he wanted something in writing so that he could solicit comments before introducing another version when Congress reconvened in January 1987.[18]

The difficulties encountered by the Cheyenne in locating the Tall Bull pipe, as well as their revelation of the large number of Native American human remains stored in the green cabinets at the Smithsonian Institution, were clearly reflected in the bill. Melcher's solution to the paucity of information on Native American collections that was generally available to Indian tribes was to require each museum that either received federal funds or participated in federally funded programs to prepare a provenance (history of ownership) of all Native American artifacts under its control, including sacred artifacts and skeletal remains.[19] The definition of "sacred artifact" used in the bill would clearly include items such as the Tall Bull pipe that were used for the conduct and observance of Cheyenne religion.[20] Each museum would submit its provenance to the Native American Center, a new bureau that would be established under the Regents of the Smithsonian Institution to determine the ownership "to the fullest extent possible, of all Native American artifacts that had been acquired or collected by the Federal government or with the assistance of Federal funds."[21]

Melcher recognized that there was considerable controversy regarding the title to, preservation of, and contemporary disposition of Native American skeletal remains and sacred objects.[22] To help resolve these matters, his bill would establish a Native American Museum Advisory Board composed of fifteen voting members to be appointed by the president, including six Indian elders, spiritual leaders, or traditional cultural authorities; one Native Hawaiian elder and spiritual leader; two anthropologists or archeologists; two museum representatives; two members of the House of Representatives; and two members of the Senate.[23] Following formal acknowledgment of a dispute,[24] any Indian tribe, Native Hawaiian organization, or museum could request assistance from the board.[25] The board would initiate an investigation to verify that Native American skeletal remains or sacred artifacts were involved and, if they were, mediate negotiations between the disputing parties.[26] If mediation was unsuccessful, the board was authorized to formulate a compromise settlement balancing the interests of Indian tribes or Native Hawaiian organizations in repatriation and the museums' interests in preserving and maintaining access for further study and research on skeletal remains and sacred artifacts.[27] Any museum that failed to carry out the compromise settlement risked being ineligible to receive any federal funds or benefits for two years.[28] Indian tribes or Native Hawaiian organizations identified as being responsible for the failure of a compromise agreement risked being ineligible to receive any federal historic preservation funds for two years.[29] Board determinations would be final and not reviewable by any court.[30]

The Native American Museum Advisory Board was explicitly modeled on the Indian Claims Commission, established forty years earlier to hear and determine certain types of claims brought against the United States on behalf of Indian tribes, bands, or other identifiable groups of American Indians. The Indian Claims Commission was authorized to hear claims in law or equity arising under a broad range of congressional, judicial, and executive precedents.[31] Theoretically, an Indian tribe could have filed a tort claim with the commission for violation of sepulcher of a Native American buried on federal lands or for sacred objects that had been obtained by a federal agent through fraud, duress, unconscionable considerations, or less than fair and honorable dealings. In reality, virtually all of the 600 cases heard between 1946 and 1978 dealt with situations in which the claimant had been paid less for land than its fair market price.[32] The Native American Center in Melcher's bill likewise had a parallel in the Investigations Division authorized under the Indian Claims Commission Act. The Investigations Division was charged with making a complete and thorough search for all evidence affecting each claim, including documents held by the courts and executive agencies, and providing it to the commission, as well as the interested Indian tribes and federal agencies.[33] Unfortunately, the Investigations Division was never adequately staffed or funded, and the task of generating information was shifted to the litigants, resulting in time-consuming and costly hearings and the nagging possibility that some of the early dismissals and small awards were due to differential access to experts.[34] Melcher was intimately familiar with the Indian Claims Commission Act, participating in its reauthorization in 1972 and 1976 as well as its termination in 1978.

Melcher also included amendments to bring the Archaeological Resources Protection Act (ARPA) into conformance with his bill. ARPA was enacted in 1979 to protect archaeological resources and sites on public and Indian lands for the benefit of the American people.[35] Unlike the earlier Antiquities Act that applied to a more generic category of antiquities found on public lands,[36] ARPA's definition of "archaeological resources" specifically applied to graves and human skeletal material[37] and went on to stipulate that all such items found on public or tribal lands would remain the property of the United States.[38] Melcher's proposal would have amended ARPA to require federal land managers to consult with the culturally affiliated Indian tribes or other communities or groups to determine the disposition of graves, human skeletal remains, or sacred artifacts excavated on public or Indian lands.[39] The graves, skeletal material, or sacred artifacts would be maintained in place or stored in a secure and respectful manner while their disposition was being determined and subjected to only such study as the consulted parties permitted. If an agreement on disposition has not been reached within eighteen months, the federal land manager was directed to seek mediation from the Native American Museum Advisory Board.

Once the Senate adjourned, Melcher wasted no time in soliciting comments on his proposed bill. In a November 10 letter, he asked for reactions and comments to S. 2952.[40] "I was absolutely shocked to find out that the Smithsonian had a bunch of bones stored away in the attic," Melcher told a reporter for a November 16 article. "It was most offensive to me. I think it is highly disrespectful to treat the dead as curios and is contrary to the values I hold dear. Do we want to dig up George Washington and hang up his bones in the Smithsonian for scientific study? I think people would be outraged if we did."[41]

As promised, Melcher introduced a slightly revised version of his bill on the first day of the 100th Congress in 1987. He reported that comments to S. 2952 were very positive.[42] As a result, S. 187 was nearly identical to the earlier bill; the only substantive difference between them concerned the administration of the Native American Center that the new bill established under the Native American Museum Advisory Board instead of under the Regents of the Smithsonian Institution.[43] Melcher described the proposed bill as absolutely essential to deal with a shameful problem.[44] "I think it is a shame on our country, on our people as a whole, that we have not corrected this problem," continued Melcher. "I believe respect is due, dignity is due, and now is the time to do it." He explained that he had reserved the number S. 187 because he hoped it would be one of the first bills passed in 1987.

Melcher's efforts to provide a mechanism to return skeletal remains and sacred objects to the Cheyenne and other tribes were not supported by everyone. "Argument on reburial of excavated bones expected to heat up," warned a headline in the *Arizona Republic*.[45] The article quoted the chair of the local university anthropology department explaining that the issue of repatriation had been around forever, but there was a growing recognition among tribes that they can dictate what happens on reservation land. "We've got a divided camp," offered an archeological consultant, explaining that although many archeologists understood the Indians' sensitivities, "when there's reburial, that's data lost forever." A physical anthropologist put it much more bluntly. "No living culture, religion, interest group, or biological population has any moral or legal rights to the exclusive use or regulation of ancient skeletons."

Prepared to Arrange for the Return

On February 20, 1987, the Senate Select Committee on Indian Affairs held a hearing on Melcher's bill that was now cosponsored by Senators Quentin Burdick from North Dakota, John McCain from Arizona, and Bill Bradley from New Jersey. Senator Daniel Inouye from Hawaii, the select committee's new chair, opened the hearing by adding his name as a cosponsor.[46] Inouye—another World War II veteran—began his involvement in Indian affairs in 1978 when Senate Majority Leader Robert Byrd suggested that the Japanese American senator from a state with no federally recognized Indian tribes accept a position on the Select Committee on Indian Affairs.[47] "At that point," Inouye recalled, "my knowledge of Indian affairs was one degree above nil." With the help of committee staffer Patricia Zell, Inouye studied American Indian history and let tribal leaders know that he would carry their agenda forward. Now, as committee chair, Inouye delayed the scheduled witnesses to invited Melcher to speak.

> Thank you very much, Mr. Chairman. The bill incorporates, by law, procedures to return the skeletal remains and sacred artifacts to the families, bands, and tribes of Native Americans. The present situation is this. The skeletal remains of Native Americans are stored in museums in this country and abroad. In this country alone we have no idea of how many skeletal or sacred religious artifacts might be in museums, but we do know that in the Smithsonian alone there are 18,000 specimens of remains.[48]

The number of Native American human remains at the Smithsonian was not generally known until the year before. In responding to a request from the National Congress of American Indians,[49] the acting director of the National Museum of Natural History estimated that the Smithsonian held about 14,000 American Indian skeletons from the contiguous United States.[50] Following a series of telephone calls, letters, and meetings,[51] the chair of the Anthropology Department at the National Museum of Natural History sent tribal representatives a state-by-state listing of 13,010 Native American remains from the forty-eight contiguous states.[52] The approximately 4,000 human remains removed from sites in Alaska were considered separately. Suzan Shown Harjo, executive director of the National Congress of American Indians (NCAI), cited the figures in her written testimony to the House Interior Appropriations Subcommittee on March 6, 1986. When the figures were pointed out to him by a staffer, Representative Sidney Yates interrupted Harjo. "I haven't known about the Smithsonian skeletons. Did you know about it before now?" Harjo answered affirmatively. Yates was incredulous. "How come you didn't tell us?"[53]

Harjo had begun working with a coalition of Native American people in 1967 to establish state and federal repatriation policies. One of the results was the American Indian Religious Freedom Act of 1978, which affirmed U.S. policy to protect and preserve for American Indians their inherent right of freedom to believe, express, and exercise traditional Native American religions, including the use and possession of sacred objects.[54] NCAI representatives began meeting with Smithsonian Secretary Robert Adams in 1985 to discuss the care, treatment, and exhibition of Native American human remains and cultural items. The inventory of Native American human remains in the Smithsonian collections was eventually made available to tribal attorneys and NCAI members. The size of the Smithsonian collection of Native American human remains only became known to the general public with the May 20, 1986, *Washington Post* article titled "Indian Bones: Balancing Research Goals and Tribes' Rights."[55] In testimony to the House Committee on Interior and Insular Affairs, Jan Hammil, director of American Indians Against Desecration, estimated the number of Indian bodies in university, museum, and laboratory collections to be between 300,000 and 600,000[56] (see figure 1.4).

"Now," Melcher continued rhetorically, "how did they get there?" He answered his own question.

Well, in the early stages of this country, when we—those of us who are not Native Americans—were battling and conquering Indians, there was returned and collected—collected, first of all, and returned to

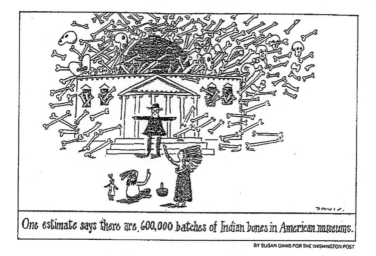

One estimate says there are 600,000 batches of Indian bones in American museums.

BY SUSAN DAVIS FOR THE WASHINGTON POST

Figure 1.4 Graphic by Susan Davis, accompanying article by Henry Mitchell, Sacred Ground and Bones of Contention, *Washington Post* (January 20, 1989).

Washington—by the Army itself innumerable skeletal remains. The Army had a museum that they were collecting them in. Some were picked up from battlefield; some were actually picked up from graves.[57]

Melcher was referring to the Army Medical Museum, established in 1862 to document the effects of war wounds and disease on the human body. All Union Army medical officers were initially directed to send the museum all specimens of "morbid" (pathological) anatomy, along with projectiles and foreign bodies removed from the bodies and explanatory notes.[58] The assembled collection was eventually published in the six-volume *Medical and Surgical History of the War of the Rebellion (1861–1865)*.[59] In 1867, museum curator George A. Otis contacted army medical officers in the western territories and urged them to send Indian specimens to expand the museum's collection.[60] Melcher introduced into the hearing record copies of two handwritten responses received by Otis. One letter accompanied crania recovered from the graves of two named Sioux hung by the army in 1860. The second letter was sent with the skull of another named Sioux and included a detailed description as to how it had been surreptitiously acquired from a fresh grave.[61] In May 1898, 2,206 Native American skulls were transferred from the Army Medical Museum to the Smithsonian, with a second transfer of 674 skeletal items in 1904, the year after Hrdlička was appointed to the Smithsonian staff.[62] "Of course," Melcher continued, "remains were also obtained by archaeologists."

> In general those are older remains, gathered for study to piece together the millennium of our unknown beginning. We do not intend in any way to interfere with this study and science in the bill; rather, the bill would permit the living to prove the identity of their ancestors and set up the procedure for the return of those bones and skeletal remains, once they have been proven to belong to a family, band, or tribe of Native Americans.[63]

Melcher's statement tied together two important facets of his proposed bill. The first was that in fashioning its compromise settlements, the Native American Advisory Board was required to accommodate both the repatriation interests of Indian tribes and Native Hawaiians and the interests of museums in further study, research, and preservation.[64] How such compromises would be accomplished was left to the members of the board. The second facet was that although the board would consider claims for Native American skeletal remains of any member or ancestor of a member of an Indian tribe[65]—with ancestry based in part on the discovery of the remains on lands historically occupied by a claiming Indian tribe or Native Hawaiian organization[66] or on "cultural affiliations"[67] (the latter an as yet undefined term)—the study of "older remains" (also undefined in the bill) would not be affected. In questioning one of the witnesses, Chairman Inouye reiterated this point when he explained, "we're not talking about remains from the Neanderthal period or the Mesozoic period; we're talking about the rather recent past . . . we're talking about 100 years ago, 50 years ago."[68]

"Now," Melcher continued,

> on the sacred artifacts taken from Native Americans, it must be understood that these are important for religious ceremonies. They are a mainstay of the Native Americans culture, both in the past and in the present and, we would assume also, in the future. The ceremonial nature and the religious beliefs of Native Americans are tied to these sacred artifacts. So when they can be identified, it's important that they be identified now and the procedures of return set in motion. We will hear testimony today, Mr. Chairman, from one of the Northern Cheyenne who will have a startling story, a true story, to tell us how one of the sa-

cred artifacts, extremely important to the Northern Cheyenne, was discovered to be in the Smithsonian.[69]

Finally, Melcher introduced into the record a handwritten note from the Friends Committee on National Legislation, an organization dedicated to bringing the peace and justice concerns of the Religious Society of Friends (Quakers) before Congress, thanking him for his leadership in introducing S. 187 to address issues of religious freedom and tribal self-determination.[70]

Although Senate procedure typically allows a representative of the executive branch to appear as a hearing's first witness, Chairman Inouye started by introducing William Tallbull, who updated the committee on the status of various Cheyenne sacred items and human remains then in museum collections. Tallbull told the committee about his grandfather's bundle that was still in the Smithsonian collections and how its continued absence was causing the Dog Soldier Society to lose membership. Three days before the hearing, the Smithsonian forwarded photographs of several Cheyenne objects in its collections, including the Tall Bull pipe, to William Tallbull through Senator Melcher's office.[71] He also spoke of a hide strap, marked to indicate the number of sweet grass burnings to be offered during the Sacred Arrow ceremony, taken from the *Mahuts* covenant holding the four sacred arrows and now in a Cody, Wyoming, museum.[72] An initial request to return the hide strap was rebuffed by the former museum director. However, it was believed that a new museum director might be more receptive.[73] "I believe it is my duty, as a warrior society member," Tallbull stressed, "to try every means possible to fulfill that ritual with its return."[74] Last, Tallbull told the committee of his quest to recover the bodies of the victims of the infamous Fort Robinson outbreak. In late 1878, a group of Northern Cheyenne under the leadership of Dull Knife was captured by the 3rd Cavalry and held at Fort Robinson in northwestern Nebraska. On the night of January 9, 1879, the Cheyenne broke out of their barracks and fled into the dark. Over the next two weeks, most of the escaped Cheyenne were either recaptured or killed and reportedly buried in a mass grave. Tallbull learned that the bodies were actually put on a train and sent to medical schools for study. "I have not been able to locate the remains of those people," Tallbull concluded, "but the search goes on."[75]

The first government witnesses spoke on behalf of the Advisory Council on Historic Preservation (ACHP), a nineteen-member panel combining representatives of federal, state, and local governments and members of the preservation community to review the effect of federal undertakings on historic properties and advise the president and Congress on historic preservation matters.[76] Acting ACHP Executive Director John Fowler explained that although the council had taken no formal position on the particulars of Melcher's bill, the council previously acknowledged a need to make ARPA more flexible to deal with the reburial of human remains.[77] Fowler felt that the absence of a clear national policy on the excavation and disposition of human remains hindered the ACHP's ability to research acceptable compromises between the scientific needs of the archeological community and respect for Native American cultural and religious interests. Inouye's follow-up questions regarding the amount of time necessary for the scientific study of human remains were fielded by ACHP senior archeologist Thomas King.[78]

The next witness was Mark Leone, chair of the government affairs committee of the Society for American Archaeology (SAA). The SAA was founded in 1934 as a forum for integrating the views and interests of professional archeologists and members of the public interested in the pre-European occupation of North America.[79] Part of that forum included archeologists and physical anthropologists working at various federal agencies. In 1985, an archeologist in the Bureau of Land Management's Washington office briefed the SAA Executive Committee on the state office's new policy requiring the reburial of human remains found on agency lands in Wyoming, encouraging the society to contact the state director regarding its concerns.[80] Likewise, a Smithsonian scientist briefed the SAA Executive Board when the state-by-state listing of Native American remains was sent to the tribes.[81] The SAA convened a conference on reburial issues in Chicago.[82] The society's 1986 Statement Concerning the Treatment of Human Remains opposed federal legislation to establish uniform standards for the disposition of human remains and instead advocated case-by-case consideration of the scientific importance of the material, the cultural and religious values of the interested individuals or groups, and the strength of their relationship to the remains in question.[83]

The last witness was Smithsonian Secretary Adams.[84] Adams started by outlining the scope and depth of the Smithsonian collections of human skeletal remains, which he describes as one of the largest such collections in the world, consisting of nearly 33,000 entries, of which more than 18,000 were Indians from North America.[85] He estimated that 3,500 of these Native American remains represent periods since 1492, and 45 sets of remains were of named individuals.[86] Under questioning from Melcher, Adams conceded that the provenance (place or source of origin) of a considerable proportion of the collection was incomplete and was thus of very limited use to science.[87]

Melcher wondered if perhaps a commission with some judicial powers patterned on the Indian Claims Commission might be a better method to resolve these issues than the board described in the bill. Adams concurred that a commission with at least some judicial powers might be helpful.[88] He then questioned Melcher on the applicability of the Indian Claims Commission model, because in that case the U.S. Treasury stood behind every settlement reached by the commission. Conversely, many Native American skeletal remains and sacred artifacts are in the hands of private collectors. Melcher felt that the current situation was embedded in the common law and that the Indian tribes had very strong rights.[89]

Adams estimated that preparing a provenance of all Native American skeletal remains, sacred artifacts, and other artifacts held by the Smithsonian's National Museum of Natural History would cost approximately $3.78 million, with $30–35 million to verify provenience records in the nation's other museums. In addition, Adams estimated that between $500,000 and $1 million would be required solely for the transfer of Smithsonian records to a national computer network.[90] Melcher estimated that the time span for all of this to take place would be about twenty years.[91]

In closing his testimony, Adams touched on the issue of the Tall Bull pipe, which he confirmed was still in the Smithsonian collections.[92] "Our curator made it plain then," continued Adams, referring to the Cheyenne's previous visit to the Smithsonian, "and we make it plain again today, that we are prepared to arrange for the return of that material." He went on to explain that over a year earlier the Smithsonian promised to meet the expenses of a properly chosen Cheyenne group to come to Washington. "I can assure you that it is not the position of the Smithsonian that we are going to hang on to what we've got and resist performing what is clearly a socially responsible and constructive act, of helping that society to sustain itself in this difficult time we now face."[93]

Patricia Zell, who served as general counsel to the Senate Select Committee on Indian Affairs at the time, identified the February 20, 1987, hearing as pivotal in setting the future direction of repatriation in Congress. One of the critical events was Adams's testimony regarding the 18,500 Native American remains in the Smithsonian's collections. "That came as quite a shock to Senator Inouye," recounted Zell.[94] From that point on, Inouye and the committee pursued the notion of repatriation in two separate directions, one focusing on the Smithsonian and the other dealing with federal agencies and museums.

An editorial in the *Fresno Bee* lauded Melcher's efforts as an attempt to lay to rest a sad remnant of U.S. history.[95] The paper commended Melcher's willingness to negotiate the specific terms of the bill, as well as his refusal to compromise on three principles: (1) ensuring the return of any body for which living relatives can prove direct line of descent; (2) providing that grave goods that were illegally obtained must be reinterred; and (3) creating a process for the tribes to recover sacred artifacts that were essential to the practice of their religions. "That all amounts to something less than what many Native Americans consider appropriate, but it's certainly the right place to begin."

During 1987, Melcher was busy sponsoring or cosponsoring sixty-one other measures, including amendments to the Indian Health Care Improvement Act[96] and a resolution recognizing the contribution of the Iroquois Confederacy to the U.S. Constitution and the continuing government-to-government relationship between the United States and Indian tribes.[97] A November 9, 1987, story in the *Chicago Tribune* reported that Melcher intended to introduce a new version of his repatriation bill early in 1988. Melcher said that most members of the Senate Select Committee on Indian Affairs were outraged that boxes of human remains were sitting around museums and thought there was strong support for his bill.

The Native American Museum Claims Commission Act

After careful consideration of the testimony presented at the February hearing fifteen months before, Melcher introduced a substitute version of S. 187 on May 25, 1988. The findings section of the amendment expanded on the earlier version to include specific reference to the policy of protecting Native American religious practices and beliefs affirmed in the American Indian Religious Freedom Act.[98]

Three categories of objects were now covered by the revised bill: skeletal remains, ceremonial artifacts, and grave goods. The "sacred objects" of the earlier bill were replaced with "ceremonial artifacts," defined as any item devoted to a Native American religious ceremony by an Indian tribe, Native Hawaiian group, or an individual member of such tribe or group which is necessary for the ongoing observance of religious ceremony or ritual by the tribe, group, or its members.[99] The new category, "grave goods," was defined as any object that was found in the grave of a Native American or otherwise directly associated with the skeletal remains of a Native American.[100]

The definition of "Native American" was expanded to include individuals who are Alaska Native, Aleut, and Eskimo, as well as Indian and Native Hawaiian.[101] Conversely, the category of "Native Hawaiian" was narrowed in the new bill by requiring such individuals to be citizens and residents of the state of Hawaii. Hawaiian descent could be demonstrated by genealogical records, *kupuna* (elder) or *kama'aina* (long-term community residents) verification, or birth records of the state of Hawaii.[102] Melcher narrowed the applicability of his revised bill by excluding those tribes terminated by federal law after 1940, although state-recognized Indian groups and federally recognized Indian tribes still had standing to file a petition with the board. The definition of Native Hawaiian organization was deleted completely.

Instead of the previous seventeen-member Native American Museum Advisory Board, the new bill would establish a three-member Native American Museum Claims Commission to resolve disputes between museums and Indian tribes and Native Hawaiian organizations over certain objects in museum collections. The three commission members were to be appointed by the president with the advice and consent of the Senate.[103] At least one member of the commission was required to be Native American.[104] No more than two members could represent the same political party.[105]

In apparent response to criticism of the earlier penalty scheme that was based on ineligibility to receive federal funds, the new bill authorized the commission to impose a fine of up to $500 for each day of noncompliance following issuance of a written notice of noncompliance.[106] The bill also made commission decisions appealable to the federal District Court.[107]

Earlier provisions establishing the Native American Center and amending ARPA were deleted from the new version of S. 187, presumably to narrow the focus of the bill to a set of core principles and reduce the overall cost of implementation.

In submitting his substitute for S. 187, Melcher stated that all Americans should be outraged that museums have been systematically collecting bones and ceremonial artifacts as "scientific curios." He felt that Indian tribes would not object to some study of Native American human remains if some value to humankind could be demonstrated, but he questioned the necessity of museums hoarding hundreds of thousands of Native American human remains once scientific study was finished. With religious practice already protected by the American Indian Religious Freedom Act, Melcher felt that Congress must take existing policy a step further to assist Indian tribes in retrieving objects essential for the ongoing conduct of Native American religion. "It is time to ensure that Native Americans are accorded the same protection as other Americans receive," explained Melcher. "It is an issue of common human dignity and respect."[108]

The Senate Select Committee on Indian Affairs convened a hearing on the second version of S. 187 on July 29, 1988.[109] Senators Inouye and Melcher were joined at the hearing by Senators Frank Murkowski from Alaska, Tom Daschle from South Dakota, and Daniel Evans from Washington.

Three separate panels appeared before the committee. The first consisted of Dean Anderson, deputy under secretary of the Smithsonian; Michael Fox, director of the Heard Museum in Phoenix, Arizona; and Cheryl Ann Munson, chair of SAA's government affairs committee.

Anderson opened his statement by recalling the previous testimony of Secretary of the Smithsonian Adams at the February 20, 1987, hearing. "At that time," recounted Anderson, Adams "acknowledged the good intentions behind the legislation, but suggested then, as we would now, that it is probably unnecessary and in any case still premature."[110]

Anderson continued by offering the committee information regarding the approximately 33,000 human remains held by the Smithsonian. Anderson estimated that 18,300 human remains, or approximately 55 percent of the entire collection, were Native American. Another 17 percent of the entire collection consists of the remains of black or white Americans, and 28 percent includes remains from Asia, Africa, Europe, and elsewhere.[111] Of the Native American collection, Anderson stated that fourteen human remains could be identified by name, fewer than the forty-five identified by Secretary Adams at the February 20, 1987, hearing. Anderson estimated that the tribal affiliation of another 606 human remains had been identified.[112] Approximately 4,100 of the Native American remains were of individuals who lived since Christopher Columbus's first voyage in 1492,[113] which represented a 17 percent increase over the figure given by Adams.

Following Anderson's presentation, Senator Inouye reminded him that although the current population of the United States was in excess of 240 million individuals, only 1.4 million, or less than 1 percent, were Indians.

"Don't you think we should increase our black and white collections?" asked Inouye. Anderson's response that "we're attempting to, Mr. Chairman," drew laughter.[114]

Somewhat less lighthearted was the grilling Anderson took regarding the Smithsonian's previous repatriation efforts. Anderson explained that five crania had been returned to the Modoc tribe in 1984. In November 1985, the Smithsonian sent letters to the chairs of the 225 federally recognized Indian tribes to inform them of the institution's skeletal collection. To date, nineteen inquiries had been received.[115] One of these was from the Blackfeet tribe. In response to their inquiry, Smithsonian officials located fifteen crania, some mandibles, a radius, an ulna, and one copper and nine iron bracelets in their collections.[116] All were identified as having been removed from a known Blackfeet cemetery in 1892 by army surgeon Z. T. Daniel, who subsequently recounted his activities in a letter transferring the remains to the Army Medical Museum. "I collected them in a way somewhat unusual: the burial place is in plain sight of many Indian houses and very near frequent[ed] roads. I had to visit the country when not even the dogs were stirring. After securing one [skull] I had to pass the Indian sentry at the stockade gate which I never attempted with more than one [skull], for fear of detection. On stormy nights," Daniel continued, "I think I was never observed going or coming by either Indians or dogs, but on pleasant nights—I was always seen but of course no one knew what I had under my coat . . . The greatest fear I had was that some Indian would miss the heads, see my tracks & ambush me, but they didn't."[117] The Blackfeet remains were subsequently transferred from the Army Medical Museum to the Smithsonian. In February 1987, Blackfeet tribal representatives asked the Smithsonian to verify that the remains were indeed Blackfeet because in 1892 there were open hostilities between the Blackfeet and many of their neighbors, and to bury Blackfeet with their enemies would be sacrilegious. The Smithsonian also made casts of the bones for further study.[118] Having made the verifications, the remains were scheduled to be transferred to the Blackfeet in August 1988 (see figure 1.5).

Inouye was incredulous at Anderson's response. "Would I be correct in stating," he asked, "that in the last fifty years the Smithsonian has returned twenty-one skeletal remains to Indian tribes?"

"If one were to add together that which will happen next month," Anderson responded, "I believe that's correct, Mr. Chairman."

"I find it distasteful," summarized Senator Melcher, "to have the Smithsonian say, on one hand, we're in favor of [the intent of the legislation] and

Figure 1.5 Members of the Blackfeet tribe of Montana pass a pipe as part of a ceremony marking repatriation of the remains of their ancestors by the Smithsonian National Museum of Natural History. From left to right, the members are Ken Weatherwax, Gordon Belcourt, Mike Swims Under, Buster Yellow Kidney, Marvin Weatherwax, Tom Whitford, and Curly Bear Wagner. Harriet Skye of the National Museum of American History is also shown. Many of the remains came from a Blackfeet cemetery by individuals collecting for the Army Medical Museum and were transferred to the Smithsonian Institution in 1898. SIA #88-16362.15. Used with permission of the Smithsonian Institution Archives.

on the other hand say we don't think it's necessary. The question of whether it's necessary or not is not one for the Smithsonian or some other museum; it's for Congress to decide. Surely, Mr. Anderson, if it were your grandparents or great grandparents that were involved, you would feel that your family had some rights to reclaim the remains, would you not?"

"Yes, indeed," responded Anderson, "and we are actively—"

"Thank you," Melcher cut him off.

Michael Fox, director of the Heard Museum in Phoenix, testified on behalf of American Association of Museums. He recognized Native American concerns regarding repatriation as legitimate but did not feel the proposed amendment answered those concerns. Fox considered that several provisions of the amendment would be costly and burdensome to museums, to Native Americans, and to the federal government. He felt the proposed commission would alienate the two communities, placing the relationship between museums and Native Americans in an adversarial context.[119] Fox also objected to having only three people on the commission[120] and thought that six months would not be long enough for museums to document their collections.[121]

As an alternative to legislation, Fox proposed an immediate and intense year-long dialogue on the identification, use, care, and ownership of Native American materials. Patricia Zell later recalled that Melcher and others on the committee were skeptical of Fox's proposal. There was a perception among the senators that the museum, scientific, and Native American communities were "worlds and worlds apart on these issues," she explained, "and it didn't seem as though there was much promise of a dialogue yielding any consensus or meeting of the minds."[122]

The second panel consisted of William Parker representing the Northern Cheyenne Tribe and the Dog Soldier Society; Oren Lyons, faithkeeper of the Onondaga Nation; Vincent Johnston, also representing the Onondaga Nation; and Russell Hartman, representing the Navajo Nation.

Parker focused much of his testimony on the current status of the Tall Bull pipe, which had been discussed at the February 20, 1987, hearing. Parker indicated that the Northern Cheyenne Tribe understood Secretary Adams to say at that hearing that the pipe would be returned.[123] However, William Tallbull had recently received a letter from Adams indicating that the information available to the Smithsonian was not adequate to prove the pipe belonged to Tall Bull or that the pipe was the communal property of the Dog Soldier Society.[124] Research for Adams's letter had been ongoing for several months. The pipe had been donated to the Smithsonian four years after the Summit Springs engagement by Army Quartermaster General M. C. Meigs, following his return from an inspection of western military posts. In the accompanying note, Meigs indicated that the pipe was identified as Tall Bull's by his wife when she was interrogated after the battle and that scalp locks decorating the pipe stem were from whites killed by the Cheyenne in Kansas.[125]

Smithsonian curator William Merrill conducted a number of interviews with individuals knowledgeable of Cheyenne religion in preparing Adams's response to Tallbull's claim. Father Peter Powell, an Episcopal priest, historian, and honorary member of the Northern Cheyenne Tribe, told Merrill that nearly every Cheyenne society had a bundle that included a pipe, and it would have been appropriate for Chief Tall Bull, as the most prominent of the four headmen of the Dog Soldier Society, to have been the keeper of the society's bundle. Powell believed that Tallbull had clearly established himself as a direct descendant of Chief Tall Bull and that individuals in Oklahoma or Denver were distant descendants at best. According to Powell, stories of the loss of the pipe at Summit Springs were well known among the Cheyenne. The missing pipe had not been replaced, and the Dog Soldier Society rituals had survived among the Northern Cheyenne only as attenuated fragments of oral tradition. William Tallbull was trying to revitalize the Dog Soldier Society among the Northern Cheyenne. "If he says it would be used in society ceremonies," said Powell regarding the claim for the pipe, "that can be relied upon."[126]

Merrill also spoke with John Moore, an anthropologist who had worked among the Southern Cheyenne in Oklahoma. Moore was not aware of the pipe, but he did know William Tallbull, whom he considered a respected traditionalist, religious leader, and a good guy. However, Moore did not think that Tallbull was a descendant of Chief Tall Bull because most of the Dog Soldiers who survived Summit Springs were believed to have escaped south to Oklahoma. Although Moore thought that any legitimate heirs to the Tall Bull pipe would be affiliated with the Southern Cheyenne, he also considered that the Northern Cheyenne, particularly William Tallbull, would be better keepers of the pipe. "If it came south," Moore speculated, "it would be placed in the museum, not used in ceremonies."[127]

In the June 29, 1988, letter to William Tallbull, Secretary Adams described the information the Smithsonian had been able to acquire as containing significant gaps and being inadequate to prove where the pipe was obtained or whether it was the communal property of the Dog Soldier Society. Adams invited Tallbull to provide any additional information that might allow the Smithsonian to trace the history of the Dog Soldier Society from Summit Springs to the Northern Cheyenne Reservation and explain how the pipe was essential to the society's religious practice.[128]

"Now, Mr. Anderson," Senator Melcher called out to the Smithsonian under secretary,

> there's no amount of testimony that the Smithsonian could conjure and inundate this committee with that could demonstrate that you've acted in good faith. Might I note that while Bill Tallbull, now seventy-five, is still alive so he can participate in the ceremonies that the tribe has every summer where the pipe is an important object. [He] may well die before the pipe is returned. The arbitrary decision by the Smithsonian that the demonstrated evidence is not conclusive is the best argument that I know of for a legal procedure to resolve these issues.[129]

Vincent Johnson, from the Onondaga Nation, told the committee that he had just returned from a site in Kentucky where ten people paid a farmer $10,000 to excavate archeological sites in his cornfield. Johnston estimated that they dug 400 holes and plundered over 1,100 Native American graves. Onondaga involvement helped ensure passage of a new Kentucky law regarding excavation of Native American graves.[130]

The final panel consisted of John T. Vance, former chairman of the Indian Claims Commission, and Walter Echo-Hawk Jr., staff attorney with the Native American Rights Fund.

Vance, who assisted Melcher in drafting the new version of S. 187, described the bill as setting forth a procedure to provide a more equitable way to correct a long-standing irritant to all Native Americans. He was astounded that Native Americans were forced to petition Congress to regain proper custody of the mortal remains of their ancestors.[131] Vance contrasted this situation with the ongoing efforts to return the bodies of soldiers lost in Vietnam. He considered Melcher's bill a way to expedite the process and grant equity in a way superior to a complicated legal trial.[132]

Echo-Hawk, who had recently published an extended essay on assessing competing legal interests in Native American cultural resources,[133] supported the bill, with several recommendations, including extending coverage to both private institutions and individuals. He also recommended that commission membership should be at least 50 percent Native American. Echo-Hawk also criticized both the Antiquities Act and the Archaeological Resources Protection Act, which had been interpreted to mean that Native bodies and graves in fact "belong" to the federal agencies as their "property." He identified these statutes as a significant departure from the body of U.S. common law and violative of both the Equal Protection Clause and the Due Process Clause of the U.S. Constitution.[134]

Although Echo-Hawk did not refer in his testimony to any specific interpretation of the Antiquities Act or the Archaeological Resources Protection Act, he was probably referring to an April 22, 1988, memorandum from Bill Horn, assistant secretary for Fish and Wildlife and Parks. In response to a growing number of requests from Indian tribes to relinquish certain museum collections recovered from archeological sites located on land owned or controlled by the Department of the Interior, Horn wrote to other assistant secretaries within the department to inform them that legal counsel advised that collections recovered from federal lands between 1906 when the Antiquities Act was enacted and the 1979 passage of the Archaeological Resources Protection Act could not be relinquished without the written approval of the secretary of the Smithsonian Institution, and then only to another museum where they must be accessible to the public.[135] The legal advice seems to have been a memo from a departmental field solicitor in Santa Fe, New Mexico, responding to an inquiry from National Park Service (NPS) Regional Director John Cook.[136] The provision requiring Smithsonian concurrence prior to relinquishment of collections was not included in the Antiquities Act itself but was added by regulation in December 1906.[137] "In discussing this matter with Smithsonian officials," NPS Assistant Director for Archeology Bennie Keel wrote in a separate memorandum to Cook, "they have indicated to us that they are eager to divest themselves of this responsibility. They also have indicated that they have declined to comment on the one request received to date."[138]

Immediately following the July 29, 1988, hearing, Smithsonian Under Secretary Anderson, William Merrill, and several other Smithsonian staff met with Northern Cheyenne Chairman Parker, NARF's Walter Echo-Hawk, and Clara Spotted Elk from Senator Melcher's office to discuss the possibility of the Smithsonian loaning the Tall Bull pipe to the Dog Solder Society.[139] Anderson agreed to send the pipe to Montana with a Smithsonian representative the following week for use by the Dog Soldier Society members in ceremonies associated with the Sun Dance. Parker, Echo-Hawk, and Spotted Elk acknowledged that the loan would have no bearing on the Smithsonian's consideration of William Tallbull's repatriation claim. The next week, a Smithsonian representative boarded a flight to Montana with the pipe stem in a hastily constructed shipping container. The pipe was used in a ceremony with the Dog Soldier Society providing a new stone bowl and a pouch of native tobacco. The pipe, bowl, and tobacco were then returned to the Smithsonian.

On September 7, 1988, the Department of Justice (DOJ) offered its opinion of S. 187, concluding that "as presently drafted, the bill presents significant constitutional problems" and "were the bill in its present form to be presented to the President for his signature, the Department would strongly urge that it be disapproved."[140] Of central concern was the standard to be used by the commission in adjudicating rights. The DOJ felt the bill's direction that the commission "issue orders of the right to possess items which are the subject of such claims" in accordance with "the facts disclosed in the investigation" provided no federal rule of decision or specification of what kind of facts would be necessary to support such a determination. Conversely, if, as the DOJ assumed, the rights at issue were governed by state law, members of the commission would have to be appointed for life tenure consistent with the requirements of Article III of the U.S. Constitution. The Congressional Research Service disagreed, pointing out the statement in the bill's preamble that "there is no Federal law to facilitate the resolution of disputes which arise when Native Americans claim skeletal remain[s], ceremonial object[s] or grave good[s] held by a museum or other institution" as evidence that Congress was creating a new federal right and not just creating a federal forum for adjudicating state causes of action.[141]

On September 23, 1988, the Senate Select Committee on Indian Affairs unanimously recommended a third version of S. 187 and reported the bill to the full Senate on October 21, 1988, the last day of the 100th Congress. The new version further narrowed the definition of Indian tribe to what the committee report called the "standard Federal definition"[142] by excluding state-recognized Indian groups.[143] Instead of the previous three-member Native American Museum Claims Commission, the new bill would establish a five-member commission to resolve disputes between museums and Indian tribes and Native Hawaiian organizations over certain objects in museum collections. At least two members of the commission were required to be Native American.[144] Two others were required to be practicing archeologists, anthropologists, or museum professionals.[145] The first four members were to recommend a candidate for the fifth member to the president.[146]

Why Are You Doing This to Us?

In a *Harper's Magazine* article, Douglas Preston, a former writer and editor at the American Museum of Natural History in New York, summarized some of the congressional activities over the previous three years related to repatriation. Preston argued that for much of the past century, anthropologists and museum professionals were the only forces working to protect or at least save what remained of Native American society and culture. Many Indian tribes turned to the museums during the 1970s and 1980s when they sought to revive their traditions. Preston found it ironic that the traditional defenders of Native American rights and culture were now under attack by the very people they had been devoted to observing, researching, and caring about.[147] His characterization was somewhat overdrawn, because, while some tribal advocates staunchly proposed the repatriation and reburial of all Native American human remains and some academics argued that all such remains should be considered the nation's patrimony and permanently preserved in museums, others on both sides sought the middle ground.

Preston also found it ironic that Native Americans received some of their strongest support from what he described as white, right-wing, Christian fundamentalists, who traditionally opposed Native American rights. It is unclear from Preston's article to whom he was referring because the only religious group that had become openly involved in the repatriation discussion was the Friends Committee on National Legislation, which had provided written support to an earlier version of Melcher's bill. If in fact Preston was referring to the Friends Committee, he clearly misunderstood the theology, politics, and diversity of the Society of Friends. Repatriation would be relatively inexpensive, he explained, and "can be used, and has been, to bash the liberal, elitist Eastern museum and scientific establishment—always a crowd pleaser."[148] As a result, Preston proposed, western politicians in chronic trouble with Indian tribes, such as Senator Melcher, could support repatriation legislation without alienating their white conservative support.

Back home in Montana, Melcher's political situation was somewhat more complicated than Preston's characterization. In campaigning for the Republican challenger, Vice President George H. W. Bush described Melcher, avowedly prolife and a champion of prayer in public schools, as "nothing less than a hard-core liberal." The Republican Senatorial Committee had targeted the Montana race for a series of negative TV ads.[149] The week before the election, President Reagan pocket vetoed a Montana wilderness bill that Melcher long championed.[150] Melcher was defeated at the polls on November 8, 1988.[151]

As the Smithsonian's Dean Anderson had predicted at the hearing in July 1988, Blackfeet elders accompanied the remains of sixteen individuals from the Smithsonian collections back to the reservation. However, the transfer was not without controversy. "The Smithsonian wanted to ship them back to us by parcel post," said Curly Bear Wagner, the tribe's cultural director, shaking his head. "It just shows they don't understand what they've got."[152]

Melcher's legacy in S. 2952 and S. 187 was to establish a set of principles and a working vocabulary for resolving issues related to the disposition of certain Native American items in federal agency and museum collections. His primary focus was establishing an autonomous body—the Native American Museums Claims Commission—to assist in resolving disputes between Indian tribes and Native Hawaiian organization and the federal agencies or museums that held Native American skeletal remains, grave goods, and sacred objects. The commission was explicitly patterned on the Indian Claims Commission and would have been able to enforce its decisions on both museums and Indian tribes. Membership of the committee, which started with seventeen individuals, decreased significantly and became less politicized in the later versions of the bill. Definitions were developed for "grave goods" and "sacred objects," with the latter term undergoing significant revision in the various versions of the bill. "Skeletal remains" were not defined. Both Indian tribes and Native Hawaiian organizations were recognized as having standing to make claims for such items, with the definition of Indian tribe being ultimately revised to be consistent with the federal standard, excluding both state-recognized and terminated Native American groups. The definition of Native Hawaiian organization, initially included, was deleted in the later versions of the bill.

Preston reported that Senator Inouye intended to reintroduce Melcher's bill in the next Congress.[153] "In all my years of working in and around museum people," Preston concluded, "I have never seen anything like the uneasiness this issue inspires. One curator, on hearing the subject of my phone call, blurted out, 'Oh my God.' And an eminent physical anthropologist, after a long and unresponsive interview in which he repeatedly denied there was a problem, suddenly broke off and said: 'Why are you doing this to us?'"[154]

CHAPTER TWO

The Green Boxes

Legislation to establish the National Museum of the American Indian had its inception with the response to a question at the February 20, 1987, hearing on the Native American Cultural Preservation Act. Smithsonian Secretary Robert Adams's testimony to the Senate Select Committee on Indian Affairs regarding what turned out to be 18,584 Native American human remains in the National Museum of the Natural History elicited swift reaction as Indian tribes around the country called for their repatriation. In response to the tribal initiative, committee chairman Daniel Inouye began to explore the feasibility of establishing a memorial to the American Indian on the National Mall that could serve as a permanent resting place for those human remains that were not the subject of ongoing scientific inquiry. Inouye was advised that the last remaining site on the National Mall was reserved for use by the Smithsonian.[1] Inouye announced his proposal at the congressional awards banquet of the National Congress of American Indians.[2]

To Preserve This Great Collection

Hearing of Inouye's interest in establishing a memorial to the American Indian that might include a museum on the National Mall, Barber Conable, former chair of the board of trustees for the Museum of the American Indian, Heye Foundation, invited him and Smithsonian Secretary Adams to visit the museum's facilities in New York City. The Heye Foundation had been established in 1916 to maintain the enormous collection of Native American artifacts accumulated by George Gustav Heye. Heye had begun collecting Indian artifacts as a hobby in 1897, when, while working for the railroad, he acquired a leather shirt from a tribal laborer in Kingman, Arizona.[3] As a collector, Heye has been described as an "omnivorous and compulsive consumer of Indian material from North and South America."[4] He was notorious for seeking out Indian communities and buying everything available for sale. "When Heye sent someone to a village," reported Senator Patrick Moynihan, "he bought everything."[5] Heye also employed some of the leading anthropologists in the country and sent them on collecting expeditions throughout the Americas.[6] He made fifty-three trips to Europe to track down and purchase other Native American artifacts. He obtained hundreds of Native American human remains from graves throughout the Americas. Moynihan viewed the comprehensive nature of the Heye collection as its primary scientific value, because "for purposes of a study, if you have everything, then you know what the range of things is instead of just going in and getting the best pieces."[7]

By 1906, Heye's collection had grown large enough to require rented storage space in New York City, and by 1910 the overflow filled three halls at the University Museum in Philadelphia.[8] Heye's collecting activities were not without controversy. In 1914, he was convicted and fined for removing human remains from the Munsee Cemetery near Montague, New Jersey. On appeal, the New Jersey Supreme Court found that although Heye's actions may have "violated the laws of decency and morality," his excavations were not for the purpose of dissection, sale, or mere wantonness, and thus did not violate the specific restrictions of state law.[9] The death of his mother in 1915 left an inheritance that allowed Heye to increase his collecting activities.[10] His collection ultimately totaled over one million pieces and constituted one of the three largest collections of North American artifacts in the world.[11] In 1916, he established the Heye Foundation as a charitable trust to create and maintain a museum in New York City.[12]

The Heye Foundation was not completely immune to requests for repatriation, particularly when public opinion and political pressure were involved.[13] In the 1920s, a Hidatsa elder was induced to sell the Water Buster clan bundle and its associated shrine for $160 to a Presbyterian minister, and Heye eventually added the items to his collection. Clan members initiated efforts to reclaim the bundle, starting with personal overtures, which, when rebuffed by the museum, escalated to stories in the *New York*

Times and *Washington Post* and a meeting with President Franklin Roosevelt. The bundle was returned to the tribe in 1938, with CBS, NBC, and Movienews covering the event. The shrine and associated offerings, possibly intentionally miscataloged by Heye himself, remained in the museum's collection for another fifty years.[14]

The Heye Foundation endowment ultimately proved insufficient to cover the museum's operational expenses, and Heye supplemented the endowment with personal funds during his lifetime. In 1956, most of the foundation's substantial collection of Native American human remains was transferred to the New York University College of Dentistry.[15] Heye died the next year, and the Museum of the American Indian was forced to seek private resources to supplement the endowment. Some objects in the collection were sold. Despite these efforts, the museum continued to have significant difficulties in obtaining sufficient resources to meet its needs. Starting in 1977, the board of trustees engaged in negotiations with the General Services Administration, American Museum of Natural History, and Ross Perot to provide a more satisfactory and secure future for the Heye collection.[16] Locations in Nevada and Indiana were also considered.[17] Adams and Inouye's April 1987 tour of the Museum of the American Indian and their meeting with representatives of the board of trustees was the latest of these efforts. The thought of acquiring the Heye collection for the Smithsonian was appealing to Adams, who considered it to be of "monumental significance."[18] Inouye was stunned, shocked, and nauseated by the deplorable conditions in which the collection was kept.[19] "The first thought that came to my mind upon concluding my tour was 'how obscene!'" recalled Inouye of his visit to the museum's Bronx warehouse. "Priceless, sacred items placed in corrugated boxes. Items that would find a place of honor in any of the world's great museums, are found on shelves and not even labeled."[20] "Then and there, I decided that something had to be done to preserve this great collection."[21]

Negotiations commenced between the Smithsonian and the Heye Foundation to establish a National Museum of the American Indian. At one point during the negotiations, Inouye was invited to tour the National Museum of Natural History in Washington. The tour went smoothly until the end, when Inouye began to look agitated. "What about the green boxes?" he finally asked his host, who seemed not to comprehend the question. "You know what I mean," continued the senator. "Why didn't you show me the green boxes with the skulls and skeletal remains in them?" Melcher had talked with Inouye after the Northern Cheyenne discovered Hrdlička's cabinets. "Well, uh," stammered the Smithsonian host, "we didn't know they interested you or we certainly would have made time on this tour."[22] "With all of the meetings that the senator had had with the Smithsonian prior to his visit to the National Museum of Natural History," explained Patricia Zell, who accompanied Inouye on the tour, "it should have been very clear to all concerned that the senator had a keen interest in the Native American human remains that were in the Smithsonian's possession." Appearing to be unaware of the senator's often expressed and serious concerns about the remains was not the best way to handle the situation. If anything, it served to heighten his concern that the Smithsonian was not being totally forthcoming. "He returned to the Senate more committed than ever to find out why."[23]

The National Museum of the American Indian Act

On September 25, 1987, Inouye, along with twenty-eight cosponsors, introduced S. 1722, the National Museum of the American Indian Act, to establish a museum within the Smithsonian to educate the public about the culture and achievements of Native Americans. Most of the bill concerned establishment of the museum itself, but Title II called for the Smithsonian to determine the geographical and tribal origin of all skeletal remains of Indians and Alaska Natives in its control within five years.[24] All skeletal remains that could not be identified as having been associated with a specific Indian tribe or group of Alaska Natives or acquired from a specific archeological or burial site were to be interred in a memorial at a site on the National Mall.[25] The secretary of the Smithsonian was directed to consult with Indian tribes and groups of Alaska Natives to develop proper interment ceremonies.[26] Inouye's bill gave standing to "Indian tribes," the definition of which included both those Indian groups and Alaska Native villages currently recognized by the United States, and nonfederally recognized Indian groups, including those terminated by federal law after 1940,[27] and unspecified "groups" of Eskimo, Aleut, Alaska Indian, Inuit, or Inupiat.[28]

Inouye's proposal received a cool reception from the Smithsonian staff. In a memo to his fellow curators, linguist Ives Goddard called for vigorous resistance to the construction and maintenance of a memorial crypt and the permanent physical removal of items from the national collection, which he viewed as irrevocably antithetical to the museum's mission of increasing and diffusing knowledge.[29]

On the same day S. 1722 was introduced, the Smithsonian responded to a request to rebury some human remains in the green boxes. The initial letter from the Larsen Bay Tribal Council was sent in July. The council, representing an Alutiiq village on Kodiak Island, off the south coast of Alaska, sought redress from the museum for "a wrong that was committed years ago when ancient village sites were plundered in the name of archaeology."[30] Aleš Hrdlička had spent the summers of 1932, 1934, 1935, and 1936 at Larsen Bay, excavating the Uyak site.[31] The Tribal Council demanded the immediate return of all skeletal remains, burial objects, and artifacts from the Uyak site. Adrienne Kaeppler, chair of the museum's anthropology department, responded on September 25, National Indian Day, indicating that there was no evidence that the modern people of Larsen Bay were related to the more than 800 human remains from the Uyak site. She also suggested that Hrdlička had the permission of local residents to excavate at the site.[32]

On October 13, 1987, Congressman Morris Udall from Arizona and five cosponsors, including Ben Nighthorse Campbell from Colorado, introduced H.R. 3480, which was nearly identical to Inouye's S. 1722. Joint hearings of the Select Committee on Indian Affairs and the Committee on Rules and Administration were held on November 12 and 18, 1987, to consider S. 1722 and another bill. Inouye opened the November 12 hearing by recalling the 1868 order by Army Surgeon General Madison Mills to all field officers to collect Indian crania, as well as several others of the "sad and tragic chapters" in Indian history. "Medical officers in your departments understand the importance of collecting for the Army Medical Museum specimens of Indian crania and of Indian weapons and utensils so far as they may be able to procure them," explained Mills's order. "The Surgeon General is anxious that our collection of Indian crania, already quite large, should be made as complete as possible and that we should preserve, likewise, illustrations of the weapons of the fast disappearing tribes."[33]

"Today we are here to begin a new chapter in the history of the relationship between the United States and the Indian Nations," urged Inouye. "Today we will consider legislation that will finally provide a resting place for those skeletal remains of North Americans that were taken from the battlefields and robbed graves to be sent to Washington."[34] Inouye also pointed out that although Washington was often referred to as the "city of monuments," with over 150 statues in the U.S. Capitol Building alone, there was not one to honor American Indians.[35]

Testimony generally supporting the transfer of control of the Heye collection to the Smithsonian was received from representatives of the Smithsonian; Museum of the American Indian, Heye Foundation; National Capital Planning Commission; and several Indian tribes. Representatives of New York City and state, as well as Senator Moynihan and Representatives D'Amato, Rangel, and Weiss voiced strong opposition to Inouye's proposal.[36] The New York delegation supported establishment of a display and storage facility for the museum at the old U.S. Customs House in lower Manhattan. "This is the precise spot where in 1624 a group of Canarsie Indians paddled over from Long Island and sold Manhattan to the Dutch," explained Senator Moynihan, "thus commencing a long practice along Wall Street of selling things that don't belong to you."[37] On October 1, 1987, Weiss introduced an alternative to S. 1722 in the House of Representatives that did not include repatriation provisions.[38]

"Obviously, Congressman Weiss has twenty-six cosponsors," offered McCain. "Have the Native Americans been asked their opinion on this issue?"

"No," responded Weiss, "we have not consulted with any except the governmental people."[39]

McCain responded that Native American desires would be key in deciding the future of the two museums. "It is a practice on the Indian Affairs Committee," continued McCain, "certainly under this chairman, that we don't take action unless the Indians are fully consulted and are in agreement with the actions that we take."[40] McCain recommended that Weiss initiate consultation with tribal representatives. John Gonzales, president of the National Congress of the American Indian, later commended Senator McCain for this statement.[41] The New York delegation left after their testimony, a fact not lost on Lionel John, executive director of the United South and Eastern Tribes. "It didn't surprise me that they all left before the Indian people had a chance to tell them our side of the story."[42]

The New York delegation was largely silent on Title II of the bill, which would require the Smithsonian to determine the geographic and tribal origin of the Native American skeletal remains in its control and inter those that could not be identified in a memorial on the National Mall. Earlier in the year, however, Representative D'Amato had used the ongoing discussions regarding repatriation to warn against any association between the Museum of the American Indian and the Smithsonian[43] (see figure 2.1).

Secretary of the Smithsonian Adams assured the committees that the Smithsonian was sensitive to the interests of native people. He recognized that descendants have an unquestionable claim on the remains of their known ancestors. However, he was suspicious that any single policy or

Figure 2.1 Hy Rosen, American Indian Museum Must Move to Museum of Natural History, *Albany Times-Union* (May 22, 1987), A-15. Used with permission of the *Albany Times-Union*.

legislation could resolve issues related to the disposition of the Native American human remains in the National Museum of Natural History collection. "The difficulties multiply as we shade off from certainty to uncertainty. At what point," he asked, "do the claims of possible descent weaken until the claims of the advancement of scientific knowledge outweigh them?"[44] Adams made it clear that the Smithsonian was opposed to Title II of S. 1722.[45]

In his written testimony, Adams offered four reasons for the continued maintenance of the Smithsonian's collection of skeletal remains. The first focused on the importance of skeletal information in documenting patterns of human diseases and health. Adams offered several examples. Studies of the bone density of American whites and Eskimos have documented surprising differences in the occurrence of osteoporosis—a weakening of the bone due to loss of calcium—due in part to the high-protein, high-fat, but calcium-deficient Eskimo diet.[46] Studies of degenerative joint disease, a major debilitating condition in aging populations, have documented significant differences between past and present populations.[47] Past populations show more disease in the upper limbs, whereas the legs of modern urban populations were more commonly afflicted. The occurrence of osteoporosis in multiple joints was rare in prehistoric populations but more common in modern groups.

Adams's second reason focused on predicting how health and economic factors affect demographic patterns in contemporary human populations.[48]

The third reason for maintaining the Smithsonian's skeletal collection was that they enabled studies of human behavior and social and political history. Adams cited one study that showed that early agriculturists in Kurdish Iraq were more similar to Iranian and Indo-European populations than to Natufian and more recent Arab groups.[49] Another study of dental traits in Sudanese archeological populations showed genetic continuity through more than a thousand years despite cultural changes evidenced in the archeological sequence.[50] Other studies of dental genetic distances have been used to chart the progressive distinctiveness of American Indian groups from Asian and Pacific Island populations from an estimated date of separation.[51]

Last, Adams considered the Smithsonian's collections of human skeletal remains critical to assisting law enforcement officials in identifying missing persons and victims of foul play. He reported that the FBI had recently submitted the remains of a young adult male for investigation. Smithsonian anthropologists were able to positively identify the missing person and assist in the prosecution and conviction of the assailant.[52]

Adams concluded that Title II of S. 1722 was inconsistent with both the Smithsonian's historic mandate for the increase and diffusion of knowledge and with the precepts of modern scientific inquiry. He also questioned the assumption inherent in section 203(b) that the institution, in consultation with Indian tribes, could somehow develop an intertribal, ecumenical, archetypal burial ceremony that would have general support.[53]

Written testimony from the National Congress of American Indians (NCAI) took issue with Adams's statement. "The Smithsonian claims that it needs a collection of human remains to study important matters that benefit living people, including us. In several meetings this year, the Smithsonian Secretary could not tell us what those studies might have been, but we note that some few were mentioned in his testimony last week. Now that these studies have been completed," concluded the NCAI statement, "we urge the Committee to require the Smithsonian to quickly conclude its tribal identification and to report them to the tribes for their decisions regarding the disposition of their ancestors."[54]

The Society for American Archaeology (SAA) concurred with Adams's opposition to Title II of the bill. However, the SAA did support the proposed memorial if it only contained human remains with no scientific value.[55]

Oren Lyons, faithkeeper of the Onondaga Nation, objected to using "scientific value" as the basis for determining whether the remains should be reinterred. "There is a curious catch-22 with this process," offered Lyons.

> From what I understand, the value of remains for study depends immediately upon documentation. If there is no documentation for remains, then the remains become almost valueless in terms of study. So, it seems to me that the skeletal remains that can be identified would be the ones that would be of most value to be studied. [These] go home immediately, leaving this vast group that no one knows who they belong to and what sort of studies can be conducted. . . . The question of whose they are is certainly a standing question, but there is one thing that we do know. We know whose they are not, and they are not the Smithsonian's.[56]

NCAI's written testimony also questioned the propriety of allowing the Smithsonian to make decisions about which remains are of "scientific interest," and suggested that such a course would result in delaying tribal identification and reports to tribes to satisfy academic curiosity.[57]

Written testimony from the Association on American Indian Affairs (AAIA) reiterated Lyons's concerns, pointing out that decisions regarding the "scientific value" of Native American human remains rest largely with non-Indians who have "bitterly opposed Native Americans' attempts to change policies dealing with their ancestors' remains."[58] The AAIA recommended the bill require Native American religious concerns serve as the basis for such decisions.

John Gonzales, president of the NCAI, also thought that most Indian people would object to reinterment on the National Mall and suggested instead that some land off the Mall be set aside for that purpose.[59] Gonzales's accompanying written testimony pointed out that many more traditional Native Americans already would not visit certain parts of the Smithsonian because human remains were there.[60] He supported the idea of a memorial and living monument as the centerpiece of the National Museum of the American Indian. "Just as the Viet Nam Memorial is a powerful statement without being a burial ground," concluded Gonzales, "the American Indian monument can be a powerful tribute without being a mass grave."[61]

Robert E. Gresham, acting executive director of the National Capital Planning Commission, thought the proposed interment of skeletal remains on a site on the National Mall would set an unfortunate precedent, which could lead to other requests for burials in this very important area in the heart of the nation's capital.[62]

Gonzales recommended the bill be changed to require the Smithsonian to initiate a dialog with Indian people and provide each tribe with a complete inventory of all items related to that tribe's traditions and history. This listing would include both items currently in the Smithsonian collections as well as those transferred to other institutions. Gonzales urged the committees to require the Smithsonian to repatriate items to requesting Indian tribes. Unclaimed human remains were to be reburied.[63]

Lionel John, executive director of the United South and Eastern Tribes, expressed concern that S. 1722 was silent on the disposition of sacred and religious items. He urged that priority be given to the identification and return of sacred items to the appropriate Indian tribes and that at a minimum, spiritual leaders should be provided access to conduct the necessary ceremonial activities if agreement could not be reached regarding the disposition of sacred items.[64]

John was also concerned that S. 1722 failed to address the ongoing acquisition of human remains and funerary objects. He recommended strengthening federal laws with punitive provisions for people who engage in desecration of Indian burial sites. NCAI's written testimony also recommended changes to the Archaeological Resources Protection Act and identified the Smithsonian's statement that its collection of Native American skeletal remains were the "archaeological resources" of the United States as technically correct but socially offensive under any standard of human rights.[65]

In thanking John for his testimony, Inouye offered his own opinion. "I just couldn't help but think to myself," he stated, "that when Indian burial grounds are desecrated, it is anthropology, but if burial grounds of non-Indians are desecrated, it is called grave robbery."[66]

Lyons also brought up the necessity of resolving certain legal, ethical, and moral questions prior to the transfer of any collections from the Heye Foundation to the control of the Smithsonian. He explained that the Onondaga Nation had been involved in a long-standing battle with the Heye Foundation for the return of wampum and medicine masks.[67] "The possession and display of these sacred objects pose a moral and legal question to the Senate and Congress of the United States since the bill will remand these objects into the possession of a quasi-governmental institution."[68] Suzan Harjo, representing the board of directors of the Museum of the American Indian, pointed out that certain legal issues also needed to be resolved regarding the study of Native American human remains.[69] "Nowhere in the Constitution does it guarantee the scientific right of anthropologists and archaeologists to study Indian remains," offered Harjo. "It does talk about religious freedom, and the collection and display of human skeletal remains is violative of our religious freedom."[70]

Inouye finally queried the tribal representatives.[71] "I gather that all of you are of one mind as to the advisability of the establishment of a museum under the auspices of the Smithsonian on the National Mall. Are there any Indian tribes who are against this proposal that you are aware of?"

"As far as NCAI is concerned," responded John Gonzales, "in our meetings that we have held for the last one and a half years or so, we haven't heard any expression of any opposition to the concept."

"Would it be possible for the leadership of the Indian country to get together to come up with your recommended amendment to Title II on the interment or the burial or the disposition of skeletal remains?"

"Absolutely," replied Gonzales. "I think that question is a very sensitive one, and how each tribe deals with it is something that will have to be dealt with on a case-by-case basis."

"Are you suggesting that Title II be deleted from the measure?" Inouye finally asked.

"I would suggest not," replied Gonzales. "I believe that there are some solutions that can be developed. It is just a matter of getting the tribal leaders together and figuring out how best to deal with that matter. Some leaders may want to address that themselves."

"Mr. Chairman," interjected the chairman of the Yakima Nation, "I am Mel Sampson. If the question about deleting Title II means the remains would remain in the Smithsonian, I would say definitely not. Each tribe is unique in their concepts as it pertains to putting away the remains of one of our deceased. I think there is a way, given the proper time, that an adequate and feasible concept could be addressed."[72]

Absent an Agreement with the Smithsonian

Discussions among the various parties continued in the months following the hearing. On April 11, 1988, Senators Moynihan and Inouye announced that a compromise had been reached to accommodate the concerns of the New York parties.[73] The following day, Secretary Adams sent a letter to Inouye. "I can only reiterate my observations made verbally this morning that an association of the Smithsonian with this undertaking appears to be unwise and unworkable. The reasons for this negative judgment are related to problems associated with collections management, duplication of cost and facilities, museum operations, governance, and financing."[74] The disposition of the Smithsonian's collection of Native American skeletal remains was not specifically mentioned in this letter, although subsequent events soon revealed it was a major issue.

The Moynihan-Inouye compromise, formulated as an amendment in the nature of a substitute to S. 1722, was considered by the Select Committee on Indian Affairs on April 13, 1988, and ordered reported to the Senate.[75] The secretary of the Smithsonian was no longer required to determine the geographical and tribal origins of the skeletal remains of Indians and Alaska Natives in the collections of the National Museum of the Natural History. Instead, the entire Native American collection[76]— including the Native American skeletal remains—were to be transferred temporarily to the National Museum of the American Indian.[77] The remains would be held by the new museum pending determination of their disposition by Congress. Within one year, a nine-person task force was directed to conduct a study, in consultation with Native American traditional religious leaders, and make recommendations regarding disposition of the skeletal remains to Congress.[78] The task force's members were to be appointed by the president, three from nominees provided by the president *pro tempore* of the Senate, three from nominees provided by the speaker of the House of Representatives, and three of the president's selection.[79] Although the findings section of the amendment indicated that the new museum site "may" also contain a memorial to inter the remains of American Indians and Alaska Natives whose tribal affiliation was not capable of identification and whose remains are also unsuited for scientific inquiry,[80] the section where the monument was actually authorized did not mention the disposition of Native American skeletal remains.[81] The amendment also authorized the Smithsonian's Board of Regents to purchase, accept, borrow, or otherwise provide for the temporary or permanent acquisition of Native American objects and artifacts from other museums or private collections.[82] Though not specifically identified in the legislative text, this seems to have included the transfer of the sizable Native American collection of the Department of the Interior to the Smithsonian.[83]

On April 18, 1988, Adams wrote to Representative Wendell Ford, chairman of the House Committee on Rules and Administration, to reiterate his opposition of the proposed amendment of S. 1722.[84] He strongly objected to the amendment in the nature of a substitute and two additional amendments recently accepted by the Senate Select Committee on Indian Affairs. The same day, Inouye responded to the Smithsonian.[85] He agreed with Adams's characterization of the world-renowned status of the Smithsonian's Native American collection and suggested that the addition of the Heye Foundation collections would make it unsurpassed and unequaled the world over. Inouye acknowledged that development of a National Museum of the American Indian was "not a matter that excites my constituency, but I firmly believe that we must act to set aside the dark pages of our relations with the Indian people."[86] In response to the Smithsonian's opposition, Inouye announced at the April 19, 1988, mark-up of S. 1722 in the Committee on Rules and Administration that he would not seek Senate action on the bill until every effort had been undertaken to address Adams's concerns.[87] The amended bill passed by a recorded vote of seven yeas (including Inouye, Dennis DeConcini from Arizona, Moynihan, Brock Adams from Washington, Warner, Garn, and Ford) and two nays (Stevens and McClure).[88] On August 11, 1988, the Committees on Indian Affairs and Rules issued a joint committee report on S. 1722 to the Senate.[89]

Absent an agreement with the Smithsonian, Inouye began to explore other alternatives. He instructed his staff to develop a proposal that would establish the National Museum of the American Indian as an independent federal agency under the jurisdiction of the secretary of the Interior. The new agency would initially be headquartered in the U.S. Customs House in New York with another facility to be built later somewhere in Washington. Inouye presented his proposal to the trustees of the Museum of the American Indian and representatives of New York City and state. "His proposal allied some of the most powerful persons in the Senate," commented Roland Force, then director of the Museum of the American Indian. "It would allow for some of them to win. The Smithsonian would be the loser."[90]

Apparently in reaction to the failure of S. 1722 in the Senate, on September 28, 1988, Representative Byron Dorgan from North Dakota introduced H.R. 5411, the Indian Remains Reburial Act, to require the secretary of the Smithsonian to determine the tribal origin of all Indian and Native Hawaiian skeletal remains in the Smithsonian collections originating after 1600 AD.[91] Those remains would be transferred for the purpose of providing an appropriate final resting place on receipt of a written request from the appropriate Indian tribe or Native Hawaiian organization.[92] "Indian tribe" was defined to include both federally and state-recognized groups, as well as groups terminated after 1940 by federal law.[93] "Native Hawaiian organization" was defined as any organization recognized by governor of Hawaii as serving and representing the interests of Native Hawaiians.[94]

S. 1722, H.R. 3480, and H.R. 5411 allowed Congress to explore the issues initially raised in Melcher's earlier legislative efforts as they applied to the repatriation of the single largest collection of Native American skeletal remains. Inouye's and Udall's initial attempts called for the Smithsonian to determine the geographical and tribal origins of all Indian and Alaska Native skeletal remains within five years. Grave goods and sacred objects were not addressed. Skeletal remains identified as having been associated with a specific Indian tribe or Alaska Native group were to be repatriated. Tribes terminated by federal law after 1940 were explicitly recognized as having standing to repatriate skeletal remains. Native Hawaiian organizations were not recognized as having standing. Native American skeletal remains for which no Indian tribe or Alaska Native group could be associated were to be interred in a memorial on the National Mall. Following strong objections, the second version of Inouye's bill dropped the requirement for the Smithsonian to determine the geographic and tribal origin of skeletal remains in their collection. Instead, a nine-person task force was directed to develop recommendations regarding disposition of the skeletal remains. Congress would then determine their disposition. The earlier proposal to inter the remains on the National Mall was barely mentioned in the second version of the bill. After continued objections, Inouye finally agreed to postpone action on S. 1722. Dorgan's bill reestablished the earlier requirement for the Smithsonian to determine the tribal origin of all Indian and Native Hawaiian skeletal remains, at least for those collections originating after 1600.

While Secretary Adams clearly abhorred the idea of having to repatriate any of the human remains in the National Museum of Natural History's collections, he also had misgivings about expanding the Smithsonian's Native American collections. As tribal representatives passionately wished for the return of their dead, the idea of a single mass grave proved equally abhorrent. The contents of the green boxes remained intact and, Secretary Adams's promises to the contrary, Bill Tallbull was no closer to regaining his grandfather's pipe than he had been the day he first saw it in the drawer.

CHAPTER THREE

The Political Dynamics of Public Awareness

Senators Melcher's and Inouye's efforts during the 100th Congress had focused on the repatriation of collections of Native American human remains and other objects excavated long ago and then gathered in museum collections. It was only a matter of time before Congress began to address ongoing excavations of Native American human remains and funerary objects as well. Anticipating this prospect, the Advisory Council on Historic Preservation (ACHP) began to develop a policy for the treatment of human remains and grave goods that might be recovered during excavations on federal lands or federal "undertakings," meaning projects, activities, or programs either funded by or under the jurisdiction of a federal agency. Tom King, director of the ACHP's Office of Cultural Resource Preservation, circulated a draft policy statement as early as 1985.[1] At issue was a common interpretation of the Archaeological Resources Protection Act (ARPA), enacted in 1979, which defined "archaeological resource" as the material remains of past human life or activities that are of archaeological interest and at least 100 years of age, and explicitly included graves and human skeletal remains.[2] ARPA also authorized the secretary of the Interior to promulgate regulations regarding the ultimate disposition of archaeological resources,[3] but these were not included in the regulations published in 1984.[4] Some federal officials were interpreting the lack of regulations to mean that they were forbidden from allowing reburial of Native American human remains recovered from federal lands. The ACHP's final policy statement, adopted at a September 27, 1988, meeting in Gallup, New Mexico, made it clear that it did not believe Congress had intended the ARPA to prohibit federal land managers from reburying human remains and grave goods where reburial was otherwise appropriate. The ACHP directed its staff to prepare a draft amendment to ARPA giving federal land managers the clear flexibility to allow reburial to occur. A draft amendment was completed on October 5, 1988, revising section 4(b) of ARPA to explicitly allow human remains and other contents of graves to be reburied or transferred to Indian tribes or other groups for reburial.[5] The draft was distributed for comment to preservation officers of every federal agency and every state and to members of Congress.[6]

The Fowler Bill

One of the recipients of the ACHP draft was Senator Wyche Fowler from Georgia. Fowler had previously served five terms in the House before being elected to the Senate in 1986. Fowler's staff was working on a comprehensive bill to establish a National Preservation Agency, consolidating the ACHP with the National Register Programs from the National Park Service and the Cultural Properties Advisory Committee from the U.S. Information Agency. On October 18, 1988, Fowler introduced S. 2912, the Comprehensive Preservation Act.[7]

In Fowler's bill, one of the National Preservation Agency's responsibilities would be to develop a comprehensive policy on the reburial of human remains and grave-associated artifacts recovered on federal or tribal lands.[8] Fowler considered federal reburial policy a contentious question that raised difficult ethical, religious, scientific, and legal issues between and among Native Americans, the scientific community, and the government. Title IX of S. 2912 was intended to address the problem by reconciling the competing claims.[9] Unlike earlier bills, S. 2912 included a definition of human remains that included any human body or part thereof, whether in skeletal, fossil, unmummified, or other form.[10] Development of the reburial policy was to be guided by four principles. First, human remains and grave-associated artifacts not in danger of destruction should not be exhumed for research or training purposes. Second, human remains and grave-associated artifacts that did have to be exhumed could be subjected to nondestructive analysis before being reinterred according to state or local law or the wishes of the biological, cultural, or tribal groups associated with the deceased. Third, human remains and grave-associated artifacts with a demonstrated extreme significance in current or likely research could be subjected to destructive analysis and should not be reinterred until their research significance was exhausted. Last, human remains and grave-associated artifacts with a demonstrated cultural or religious significance of such magnitude that their analysis would impede the free exercise of religion by their biological or cultural descendants would be reinterred, with only such analysis as would not be inconsistent with their wishes. S. 2912 was read twice and referred to the Committee on Finance. The Senate adjourned on October 22, 1988.[11]

On March 6, 1989, the Society for American Archaeology (SAA) submitted comments on S. 2912.[12] The SAA pointed out both positive and negative aspects of establishing a National Preservation Agency, then provided lengthy comments on the proposed comprehensive policy on the reburial of human remains and grave-associated artifacts. The SAA preferred to address the disposition or repatriation of such items instead of their reburial. In the first principle, they recommended language that would allow for the exhumation of human remains and grave-associated artifacts for research purposes, though exhumation for training would remain banned. In the second principle, SAA recommended replacing the term "nondestructive analysis," which was not defined in the bill, with a phrase that would allow research, including excavation, analysis, and curation, as directed for unmarked graves or unknown individuals. They also recommended limiting the range of individuals who might direct the disposition of the human remains and grave-associated artifacts to descendants of the deceased instead of the associated biological, cultural, or tribal groups proposed in the bill. In the third principle, the SAA recommended reducing the threshold for additional research from the extreme significance of the human remains and grave-associated artifacts to their pertinence to current or likely scientific research. They also recommended language that would allow for the curation of such items in perpetuity for the benefit of present and future generations. For the fourth principle, the SAA recommended language that would limit claims for reburial based on the free exercise of religion to biological descendants, excluding cultural descendants as proposed in the bill. They also recommended language that would only allow the biological descendants to carry out their wishes if the security of the remains was assured. Last, the SAA proposed a fifth principle requiring decisions regarding the treatment and disposition of human remains and grave-associated artifacts to be made on a case-specific basis at the local level by the National Preservation Agency, archeologists, physical anthropologists, and the biological descendants of the deceased.

The Bennett Bill

With Melcher's departure from the Senate at the end of the 100th Congress, Clara Spotted Elk, Melcher's former staffer, became a private consultant representing Indian interests. One of her first activities was to publish an editorial in the *New York Times* on March 8, 1989, outlining a rationale for repatriation of what she estimated were 600,000 Native American human remains in federal agency and museum collections.[13] Spotted Elk offered that although many tribes were willing to accommodate some degree of study of Native American human remains—provided that it was for a limited period of time and would benefit Indian people or humankind in general—Indians would not accept grave robbing and the continued hoarding of their ancestors' remains. "What would happen if the Smithsonian had 18,500 Holocaust victims in the attic?"[14] She predicted that American Indians would continue their efforts to repatriate their ancestors despite few resources and little money.

A week after Spotted Elk's letter appeared in the *New York Times*, Representative Charles Bennett of Florida introduced H.R. 1381—the Native American Burial Site Preservation Act—to establish a national system for dealing with the discovery and excavation of Native American human remains. Bennett had long been interested in archeology and had cosponsored the Archeological and Historic Preservation Act of 1974 with Senator Frank Moss from Utah. The so-called Moss-Bennett Act provided for the preservation of historical and archeological data from federal or federally assisted or licensed programs.[15] Bennett specifically acknowledged the role of recent press reports in motivating him to introduce the new bill, singling out a *National Geographic* article documenting the carnage at the Slack Farm site near Uniontown, Kentucky.[16] In 1987, Slack Farm was one of the last relatively undisturbed Late Mississippian settlement sites in the Midwest. The farm's owners accepted $10,000 to allow ten individuals to dig the site. The diggers used a tractor to clear away the village midden, then shoveled out at least 650 graves, scattering human remains across the site and taking the pots and funerary ornaments to sell on the antiquities market.[17] The situation at Slack Farm had previously been brought to congressional attention when Vincent Johnson of the Onondaga Nation had testified before the Senate Select Committee on Indian Affairs in 1988.[18] The March 1989 issue of *National Geographic* provided photographic evidence of what "looked for all the world as if a lowflying squadron of bombers had just swooped over on a practice run."[19]

H.R. 1381 was also motivated by a situation in Bennett's home district. He explained that there were a number of outstanding grave mounds on very expensive private real estate in northeast Florida.[20] "Not only did the *National Geographic* article stimulate me to think in this field," Bennett later explained, "but also the sadness that I felt when I saw some of these great mounds being chopped down, and not even properly archaeologically studied as they were taken down, with very expensive residences put on top of them. It was a chilling experience for me to see."[21]

Bennett felt that the protection of Native American burial grounds was more than just a matter of safeguarding archeological resources but also involved civil rights and protection of religious freedom. "Many of us have 'Rest In Peace' inscribed on the graves of our loved ones," he explained in summing up his reasons for introducing H.R. 1381. "Unfortunately, as a Nation we have failed to accord the same respect to the graves of Native Americans, our chief predecessors. Congress should put an end to both shameless grave robbing and unauthorized academic excavation by enacting legislation to protect the burial grounds of Native Americans."[22]

The findings section of Bennett's bill—which was almost as long as the entire rest of the bill—explicitly placed his effort on the foundation provided by the American Indian Religious Freedom Act of 1978. The bill also found that there was an extensive and growing vandalism of American Indian burial grounds and that there was an interstate market in American Indian remains and artifacts.[23] Bennett's bill precluded excavation or removal of the contents of any Native American burial site without a state permit.[24] The purview of Bennett's bill was extremely broad. Each state could permit the excavation or removal of items from a Native American burial site anywhere covered by state law, potentially including sites on federal, state, tribal, local, and private property. In addition, the definition of "Native American burial site"—meaning the burial site of any American Indian, Eskimo, Aleut, Native Alaskan, Native Hawaiian, or other individual of ancient native origin or a territory or possession of the United States and the descendants of such individuals[25]—implied that the bill as a whole went beyond the applicability of ARPA, which included only federal and tribal lands, to including both private property within the United States proper and lands within U.S. territories and possessions. The bill authorized a civil penalty of up to $10,000 for violations and stipulated that any items removed in violation of the legislation would become the property of the United States.[26]

Implementation of Bennett's bill relied heavily on state burial laws. At about the same time Bennett was introducing his bill, H. Marcus Price III was completing research on state and federal laws concerning the disposition of aboriginal human remains. Price's review of state legislation revealed that as of August 1989, only twenty-seven states had enacted legislation specifically protective of aboriginal human remains. Only eleven states required the reburial of newly discovered Native American skeletal remains and associated artifacts, and only one (Nebraska) required the reburial of Native American skeletal remains and associated artifacts from existing scientific or educational collections. Bennett also recognized that state burial laws themselves were not sufficient to effectively address the issue. He pointed out that although several states had recently passed laws to protect Native American burial grounds—including Kentucky, Kansas, and Florida—these laws were still insufficient to protect Native American burial sites where grave robbers avoid prosecution by fleeing to other states, as happened in the Slack Farm situation.[27] Bennett's bill was read twice and referred to the House Committee on Interior and Insular Affairs.

The Udall and McCain Bills

One week after Bennett introduced H.R. 1381, Representative Morris Udall from Arizona introduced H.R. 1646, the Native American Grave and Burial Protection Act. Like Bennett, Udall also had a long-standing interest in historic preservation issues, including, ironically, sponsoring ARPA, the provisions of which were now causing some confusion as they applied to the disposition of Native American human remains and funerary objects. In introducing the new bill, Udall referred to Douglas Preston's recent article in *Harpers* magazine, as well as the bills already introduced by Byron Dorgan (H.R. 5411) and Bennett. "The legislation I am introducing today should not be viewed as a final step in the legislative process but as a starting point to get the debate started. I know that there are a lot of people who feel strongly about these matters and come down on different sides on how to resolve the issues," Udall said. "Hopefully we can work with all concerned parties to accommodate the various interests and still show respect to the Native American cultures and religions by restoring some dignity to their dead."[28]

Udall's bill was significant in that it brought together three sets of provisions previously dealt with separately—those dealing with collections, new excavations, and trafficking—into one comprehensive bill. The eight-point findings section justified the need to clarify ownership interest in Native American skeletal remains, associated grave goods, and ceremonial objects that were either in the possession of federal agencies and museums that receive federal funds or that were located on federal or tribal lands.[29] "Native American" was defined as any individual who is either a member of an Indian tribe or a Native Hawaiian or Alaska Native.[30] "Skeletal remains" were not defined in the bill, but "grave goods" were defined as any object found in the grave or otherwise directly associated with the skeletal remains of a Native American.[31] "Sacred ceremonial object" was defined as any specific item that is or has been devoted to a Native American or tribal religious ceremony and is essential for the continuing observance of such religious ceremony.[32]

Udall's bill expanded on Bennett's effort to deal with both trafficking and collections held by federal agencies and museums. H.R. 1646 would make the sale, use for profit, or transport across state lines of Native American Indian skeletal remains without the consent of the heirs of the deceased or the governing body of the culturally affiliated Indian tribe subject to up to a $10,000 fine on conviction.[33]

Udall's bill also stipulated that any Native American Indian skeletal remains excavated or discovered after the enactment of the bill would be disposed of according to the wishes of the heirs of the deceased or, if they could not be ascertained, the culturally affiliated Indian tribe.[34] Like Bennett's bill, this provision would have applied to federal, state, tribal, local, and private properties. On the other hand, Udall's bill stipulated that only those grave goods and sacred ceremonial objects found on public or tribal lands would be deemed to be owned by the Indian tribe (1) on whose reservation such item was discovered, (2) that aboriginally occupied the area from which such item was discovered, or (3) that can show a cultural affiliation with such item.[35]

Last, Udall's bill required all federal agencies and other institutions that receive federal funds to list and identify all Native American skeletal remains and sacred ceremonial objects in their collections within two years of enactment of the bill and notify appropriate Indian tribes of the results within three years.[36] Concerned tribes were required to decide if they wanted the human remains and sacred ceremonial objects in federal agency or museum collections returned within four years of enactment of the bill.[37] The federal agency or museum was required to return any Native American skeletal remains or sacred ceremonial objects within two years of a request from an appropriate Indian tribe, unless the items were acquired with the consent of the tribe or Native American owners or were indispensable for the completion of a specific scientific study, the outcome of which would be of major benefit to the United States.[38] Any museum not complying with this section would be ineligible to receive any further federal funds.[39]

The bill was read twice and referred to the House Committee on Interior and Insular Affairs. In a letter to his House colleagues inviting them to cosponsor H.R. 1646, Udall explained that the "bill's goal is to reverse the expression of ultimate disrespect which we as a nation have shown Native peoples, namely our sanctioning of robbing Indian graves."[40]

The Native American Rights Fund (NARF) distributed copies of H.R. 1646 and recommended tribes send letters and resolutions supporting the bill to the House Interior Committee.[41] NARF also warned that the SAA strongly opposed H.R. 1646 and had retained Loretta Neumann, a former House Interior Committee staffer, to lobby against the legislation. When a reporter called Neumann about the letter, she didn't know whether or not to be flattered. "Didn't know I would strike such fear in the minds of the opposition!"[42]

In late April, Karen Funk, a legislative analyst with a prominent Washington, DC, law and lobbying firm with many tribal clients, received an urgent call from one of Udall's staff. The SAA had scheduled a meeting with Udall to talk about H.R. 1646, and the staffer thought that those advocating tribal interests in the matter should likewise meet with the Congressman as soon as possible. Funk, who had previously worked on repatriation issues at the NCAI and continued to do so at the law firm, along with NARF attorney Henry Sockbeson, met with Udall the next day. "Our intention was to bolster Mr. Udall's resolve in the face of expected SAA objections," Funk recalls.[43] They need not have worried. After briefly talking about the bill, that Indian graves had and continued to be dug up with the human remains ending up in museums and elsewhere and treated as specimens, Udall placed his legislative efforts into a personal context. "I just returned from visiting my parents' graves in Arizona," Udall told Funk and Sockbeson. "I certainly wouldn't want them treated like that." Udall met with representatives of the SAA and the American Association of Museums the next day. Consistent with his view that H.R. 1646 was a starting point for discussions, Udall agreed to delay action on the bill until the two groups had a chance to develop recommendations and possible alternative legislative language.[44]

On April 24, 1989, Senator John McCain from Arizona joined Udall in the repatriation debate when he announced that he planned to introduce his own repatriation bill "for discussion purposes only."[45] "John and Mo [Udall] had a very, very strong bond," recalled McCain staffer Eric Eberhard. "There was a real friendship between the two of them and I think it only grew over the years." McCain's effort was also stimulated by visits from representatives of the Hopi Tribe, who asked him to do what he could to stop grave robbing.[46] With the number of bills beginning to grow, the SAA established a special task force on repatriation and reburial on May 1, 1989.[47]

On May 17, 1989, McCain introduced S. 1021, the Native American Grave and Burial Protection Act, to provide for the protection of Indian graves and burial grounds. McCain's bill was markedly similar to Udall's H.R. 1646. Both bills precluded the sale, use for profit, or transport from one state to another of Native American Indian skeletal remains without the consent of the heirs of the deceased or the governing body of the Indian tribe from which the objects originated, subject to a maximum $10,000 fine on conviction. McCain's bill expanded Udall's proposed restrictions to include grave goods and sacred ceremonial objects.[48]

Both Udall's and McCain's bills also stipulated that any Native American Indian skeletal remains excavated or discovered after the enactment of the bill would be disposed of according to the wishes of the heirs of the deceased. However, McCain's bill also included grave goods and sacred ceremonial objects within this requirement.[49] McCain's bill elaborated on the criteria for determining the disposition of Native American skeletal remains and grave goods for which the heirs could not be ascertained and any sacred ceremonial objects found on federal or tribal lands. Such items would be considered to be owned by the Indian tribe (1) that has jurisdiction over the reservation on which such items were discovered; (2) that aboriginally occupied the area from which such item was discovered; (3) in the case of remains and grave goods, of which the Native American was a member; (4) in the case of grave goods or sacred ceremonial objects, from which these items originated; or (5) that can show a cultural affiliation with such item.[50]

Like Udall's bill, McCain's legislation required all federal agencies and other institutions that receive federal funds to list and identify all Native American skeletal remains and sacred ceremonial objects in their collections within two years of enactment of the bill and notify appropriate Indian tribes of the results within three years. Concerned tribes were required to decide if they wanted the human remains and sacred ceremonial objects in federal agency or museum collections returned within four years of enactment of the bill. The federal agency or museum was required to return any Native American skeletal remains or sacred ceremonial objects within two years of a request from an appropriate Indian tribe, unless the items were acquired with the consent of the Indian tribe or Native American owners or were indispensable for the completion of a specific scientific study, the outcome of which would be of major benefit to the United States. Any museum not complying with this section would be ineligible to receive any further federal funds. McCain's bill included grave goods within this requirement.[51] The notice provided to Indian tribes by the third year was also to be sent to the secretary of the Interior for publication in the *Federal Register*.[52] Items not returned to the Indian tribe by reason of a scientific study were to be returned within ninety days of completion of the study.[53] McCain's bill was read twice and referred to the Senate Committee on Indian Affairs.

On June 1, 1989, Keith Kintigh from the SAA circulated a draft substitute for Udall's H.R. 1646. "As I have discussed with you," he wrote to members of the SAA Task Force on Repatriation and Reburial, "it is my feeling that sooner or later something related to reburial is going to pass and it is in our best interests to be able to push a bill that might be perceived to 'solve' the reburial problem."[54]

Fowler II

Throughout the summer, Senator Fowler's staff worked with the representatives of the various constituencies to prepare a revised version of S. 2919 from the 100th Congress. A revised draft of the section dealing with the disposition of human remains and associated grave goods was circulated in June.[55] According to Tom King, the revised draft section was the product of negotiations among Senator Fowler's staff, the National Conference of State Historic Preservation officers, the SAA, and Karen Funk. King, who was still employed by the ACHP, served as a sort of *sub rosa* mediator. According to King, the revised section was agreed on by all those who participated in the negotiations.[56]

On August 5, 1989, Senator Fowler introduced his revised bill, S. 1579. The National Historic Preservation Policy Act of 1989 included proposed amendments to the National Historic Preservation Act, ARPA, and the Abandoned Shipwreck Act.[57] Section 120 of the revised bill proposed a new section to be added to ARPA regarding the disposition of human remains and associated grave goods.[58] The definition of human remains included in the earlier bill was removed for the newer version. "Grave goods" meant any object that was found in the grave and appearing to have been deliberately placed in association with the human remains.[59]

The disposition of human remains and associated grave goods were now to be guided by three principles instead of the four outlined in the earlier version. First, human remains and associated grave goods were only to be disturbed if they were threatened with imminent destruction, were necessary for a criminal investigation, or were essential for bona fide archeological research. Fowler's earlier version had limited exhumation of human remains and grave-associated artifacts to situations in which they were in danger of destruction, explicitly forbidding excavations done purely for research or training purposes.

Second, excavation or removal of human remains and associated grave goods was to be done in accordance with appropriate archeological methods of recovery and documentation developed in consultation with descendants of the deceased and archeological and preservation authorities. "Descendant" was defined to mean a living person or group evidenced by biological, archeological, anthropological, folkloric, historical, or other research to be descended from a historic or prehistoric group of people.[60] This replaced the principle in the earlier bill that human remains and grave-associated artifacts that had to be exhumed could be subjected to nondestructive analysis before being reinterred according to state or local law or the wishes of the biological, cultural, or tribal groups associated with the deceased.

Third, the disposition of excavated human remains and associated grave goods should be in a manner that balances respect for the dead, the interests of the descendants, and the interests of research. The items should be subjected to timely analyses to address legitimate scientific research questions, except when the living descendants of the deceased person or an authorized commission determine otherwise. Such commissions would be required to give balanced consideration to respect for the dead, interests of the landowners, interests of those having cultural affiliation with the deceased, and the potential importance of the objects to present and future research. "Cultural affiliation" meant a relationship between a modern group of people and a historic or prehistoric group based on cultural similarities and reflecting the cultural derivation of the modern group from the historic or prehistoric group, whether or not biological relationships could be demonstrated.[61] This general principle combined two much more explicit statements from the earlier bill. First, human remains and grave-associated artifacts with a demonstrated extreme significance in current or likely research should not be reinterred until their research significance was exhausted, and they could be subjected to destructive analysis. Second, human remains and grave-associated artifacts with a demonstrated cultural or religious significance of such magnitude that their analysis would impede the free exercise of religion by their biological or cultural descendants would be reinterred, with only such analysis as would not be inconsistent with their wishes.

The ACHP was directed to adopt standard policies and procedures consistent with the three principles that were to be followed by all federal agencies, states, Indian tribes, or local historic preservation programs receiving assistance under ARPA or the National Historic Preservation Act.

According to King, the proposed language tracked very closely with two statements that Indian tribes and Native American organizations had recently endorsed. The first was the ACHP's September 27, 1988, policy statement regarding the treatment of human remains and grave goods. The second was the so-called Vermillion Accord on Human Remains that was adopted by the World Archaeological Congress at its first Inter-Congress in South Dakota in August 1989. The accord stipulated that disposition of the dead should be negotiated on the basis of mutual respect for the legitimate concerns of communities for the proper dispositions of their ancestors, as well as the legitimate concerns of science and education.[62] The provisions of S. 1579 were consistent with these previous agreements.[63] "It was reasonable to assume that it would be widely accepted," King concluded.[64] Fowler's bill was read twice and referred to the Senate Committee on Energy and Natural Resources.

Bennett II

On October 5, 1989, Representatives Bennett, Sam Gejdenson from Connecticut, and George Brown from California introduced H.R. 3412, a bill that was nearly identical to Fowler's most recent effort.[65] Bennett's bill was read twice and referred to the House Committee on Interior and Insular Affairs. Jeremy Sabloff, president of the SAA, took the opportunity to write Bennett a letter indicating the SAA's support of H.R. 3412. In his response, Bennett highlighted the differences between H.R. 3412 and his "small bill," H.R. 1381.[66] Bennett was concerned that H.R. 3412 mainly impacted remains on public lands. "I remain committed to doing something for remains on private lands." Bennett asked Sabloff to consider working with him to pass a version of H.R. 1381. "Your concerns revolve around allowing professional archaeologists to excavate some burial sites," he wrote. "While I think my bill allows for that by allowing State laws to circumvent it, and while I would really prefer no more remains being brought up, I am willing to consider an alternative from you."

The flurry of bills introduced in late 1988 and early 1989 continued the negotiation of the terms and processes Melcher initiated in 1986. Melcher's bills had opened discussion on the disposition of Native American human skeletal remains and artifacts of a sacred nature in all museums. Inouye's introduction of the National Museum of the American Indian Act focused particular attention on collections in the Smithsonian. Now, Fowler's and Bennett's bills broadened the discussion to include the disposition of recently discovered Native American human remains and grave-associated artifacts. By the end of 1989, there were three separate approaches being negotiated. The Udall and Fowler bills represent early attempts to synthesize these three approaches.

The various bills also continued the evolution of terminology and procedures initiated by Melcher. "Skeletal remains" was briefly defined in Fowler's S. 2912, but the definition was subsequently deleted in the later version and remained undefined in the other bills as well. The definitions of "funerary object," "grave good," or "grave-associated artifact" remained more or less consistent with that of the earlier bills. Udall's and McCain's definitions of "sacred ceremonial object" were expanded slightly over Melcher's version to include not only items currently devoted to a Native American religious ceremony but those previously devoted to such ceremony as well.

Udall's and McCain's bills applied to federal agencies and institutions receiving federal funds, as well as to the Smithsonian. Unlike several of the bills to establish the National Museum of the American Indian, Udall's and McCain's bills set deadlines for preparations of lists of human remains, notification of the appropriate tribes, tribal claims, and ultimate return of the remains, funerary objects, and sacred ceremonial objects. Under the Udall and McCain procedures, federal agencies and museums could retain items acquired with appropriate consent or those that were necessary for completion of a study of major benefit to the nation. Udall and McCain authorized withholding federal funds from museums that failed to comply. Fowler's bill sought a somewhat more ambiguous balancing of respect for the dead, interests of the landowner, interests of those having cultural affiliation with the deceased, and the potential importance of the human remains and grave goods to present and future scientific research. None of the five bills embraced Melcher's earlier focus on establishment of an independent board to assist in the resolution of disputes involving Indian tribes and Native Hawaiian organizations.

The bills introduced by Fowler, Bennett, Udall, and McCain included provisions covering the excavation or removal of certain items following enactment of the relevant statute. Fowler called for development of a set of principles that would apply to the disposition of all human remains and grave-associated artifacts. Bennett sought to resolve such issues through specific reference to state burial laws, with items removed in violation becoming property of the United States. Both Udall and McCain established their own, slightly different criteria for determining the disposition of excavated items to the appropriate Indian tribe or Native Hawaiian organization. Udall's version authorized disposition of such items to the Indian tribe (1) on whose reservation the item was discovered, (2) that aboriginally occupied the area of the discovery, or (3) that could show cultural affiliation. McCain's bill modified this priority listing to authorize disposition to the Indian tribe (1) on whose reservation the item was discovered, (2) that aboriginally occupied the area of the discovery, (3) of which the Native American was a member, (4) from which the item originated, or (5) that could show cultural affiliation with the item. The bills introduced by Fowler, Bennett, Udall, and McCain applied to federal, state, tribal, local, and private property in any state, whereas Bennett's version also included U.S. territories or possessions. Last, Udall's and McCain's bills introduced a process to deal with illegal trafficking of Native American skeletal remains and, in McCain's bill, grave goods and sacred ceremonial objects as well.

Much of the congressional activity during 1989 seems to have been driven at least in part by the increasing amount of press coverage being devoted to the issue. Clara Spotted Elk's op-ed piece in the *New York Times*, Douglas Preston's article in *Harpers*, and the *National Geographic* story on Slack Farm brought the issue to the public's attention and precipitated congressional effort. Patricia Zell, majority counsel to the Senate Select Committee on Indian Affairs, confirmed the importance of such reporting on Congress's deliberations.

> There had been articles in magazines and newspapers. There was a very significant shift from ignorance to awareness in public opinion that formed how the Congress reacted to these matters. Had the museums and scientific institutions come in and made a strong case for their rights to retain remains for scientific inquiry without any limitations, and without any repatriation, without that growing public awareness, and the kind of mail that started coming in, members of Congress might have been inclined to side with the museums and scientific institutions. But the political dynamics of public awareness really changed that and made a very receptive ground for the Native American community to be heard in the Congress.[67]

CHAPTER FOUR

The Way of the Coyote

Although consensus on the Indian museum proposal was not achieved before the expiration of the 100th Congress,[1] negotiations between the Smithsonian and the Heye Foundation of New York continued.[2] Representative Byron Dorgan, apparently frustrated with the retreat on repatriation in other bills, reintroduced a slightly modified version of his Indian Remains Reburial Act on February 27, 1989. Like the earlier version,[3] H.R. 1124 directed the secretary of the Smithsonian to determine the tribal origin of some Indian and Native Hawaiian skeletal remains in the Smithsonian collections. Unlike the earlier version, H.R. 1124 pushed applicability of the inventory provisions back one hundred years to include all skeletal remains originating after AD 1500.[4] Dorgan recognized that using 1500 as the boundary between the historic and prehistoric periods was merely a convention, but he intended the bill to address the estimated 600 skeletal remains dating to the historic period for which tribal affiliation would be more readily identifiable. He did not intend the arbitrary date to preclude the Smithsonian and Indian tribes from reaching agreements on reburial of human remains originating from earlier periods.[5] Dorgan's frustration with the Smithsonian's recalcitrance on repatriation was clear in his introductory remarks. "The Smithsonian contends that these remains are of considerable scientific value," Dorgan explained. "The fact remains that these Native American skeletal remains are being denied proper burial. They've already had 100 years to study most of them. Enough is enough."[6]

It May Take One Hundred Years

On March 9, the House Committee on Interior and Insular Affairs held an oversight hearing to gather testimony on a tentative agreement between the Heye Foundation, trustees of the Museum of the American Indian, and the Smithsonian. Representative Ben Nighthorse Campbell from Colorado chaired the hearing, and his introductory remarks focused on recent visits by representatives of the Southern Ute and Ute Mountain Ute tribes of Colorado to the Museum of the American Indian in New York. "They tell me they were amazed and saddened at the same time," said Campbell. "They saw . . . religious items that belonged to their ancestors, things that no one had seen in a long time. But the sad part," continued Campbell, "was that these precious items were stored in boxes for no one to appreciate at all."[7]

The hearing's first witness was Secretary of the Smithsonian Robert Adams, who did not address the disposition of the Smithsonian skeletal remains in his statement. However, in response to questioning from Campbell, Adams indicated that the repatriation issue was largely extraneous to the Heye Foundation collection because it contained only about a dozen human remains.[8] Adams conceded that the disposition of Native American human remains held by the National Museum of Natural History had not been fully resolved, but the Smithsonian was prepared to return any material that could be identified by a clear and unambiguous line with a living Indian descendant. "But I would stress from the point of view of the Smithsonian," cautioned Adams, "that its collections are valuable scientific material for the study of the past, and we will not willingly and with abandon turn those materials over to people who may not in fact be descendants of the people whose remains we have."[9] Adams did not mention the Cheyenne pipe still lying in a cabinet in the National Museum of Natural History despite the pending claim by the grandson of its owner.

On March 16, Julie Johnson Kidd, chairperson of the board of trustees of the American Indian Museum, signed the memorandum of understanding securing appropriate facilities for the American Indian Museum's collections while fulfilling the purposes of the Heye Trust. The memorandum did not address the disposition of Native American skeletal remains in either the Museum of the American Indian or the Smithsonian collections. Adams signed the memorandum for the Smithsonian on May 8 (see figure 4.1).[10]

Figure 4.1 Smithsonian Secretary Robert McCormick Adams signs a Memorandum of Understanding transferring the collection of the Museum of the American Indian, Heye Foundation, to the Smithsonian Institution at a ceremony on May 8, 1989. Looking on, from left to right: Suzan Harjo, member of the MAI board of trustees; Roland Force, MAI director; Senator Daniel K. Inouye (D-HI), sponsor of S. 978; Dick Baker, member of the Lakota Sioux Red Feather Society; and Congressman Ben Nighthorse Campbell (D-CO), sponsor of H.R. 2668. SIA #89-8343.11. Used with permission of the Smithsonian Institution Archives.

Senate action on the agreement came quickly. On May 11, Senator Daniel Inouye introduced S. 978 to establish a National American Indian Museum within the Smithsonian, the provisions of which were closely based on the May 8 agreement.[11] In addition, Section 9 required the board of regents of the Smithsonian, in consultation with the board of trustees of the National Museum of the American Indian, to identify the geographic and tribal origins of the 14,523 Indian and 4,061 Eskimo, Aleut, and Koniag skeletal remains in the Smithsonian collection.[12] Within three years of the bill's enactment, the board of regents, in consultation with Indian religious leaders, was to make recommendations regarding the final disposition of the remains.[13]

The following day, a joint hearing on S. 978 was held before the Select Committee on Indian Affairs and the Committee on Rules and Administration. In all, seventeen people made statements before the joint committees, representing the Museum of the American Indian, city and state of New York, and the Smithsonian, as well as several Native American organizations and five senators. Most expressed their appreciation to Senator Inouye and his staff for their efforts in reaching the agreement to convey the collections of the Museum of the American Indian to the Smithsonian. Interestingly, only one addressed the provisions in Section 9 of the bill dealing with the disposition of the skeletal remains. "The issue of repatriation of our dead is the most painful issue of all," explained Chief Oren Lyons of the Onondaga Nation of New York. "This memorial to our people can only be that if our people are put to rest in a sacred way."[14] Lyons went on to outline ongoing efforts by the Onondaga Nation to repatriate sacred masks and wampum from both the Museum of the American Indian and the Smithsonian. He recommended that the problems of repatriation of Native American cultural treasures and patrimony be clearly established before any of the collections were transferred to the Smithsonian.

Senator Inouye thanked Lyons for his testimony. "I have been assured—and I will tell you that I am satisfied—that at the present time sincere efforts are being made by the Smithsonian to repatriate and return the skeletal remains for proper reburial in their place of origin." Regarding the sacred masks and wampum, Inouye continued, it "may take 100 years, but if I am around I will try to expedite it for you."[15]

On June 15, Representative Campbell introduced a bill similar to Inouye's in the House. H.R. 2668 expanded on Inouye's original bill by including associated funerary objects within the board of regents' mandate to identify geographic and tribal origin. In addition, the bill authorized an appropriation of $1 million in FY 1990 to pay for the study of the human remains and associated funerary objects, and $300,000 in FY 1990 and FY 1991 to pay for the disposition of the human remains. The secretary of the Interior was also authorized to award grants to tribes totaling $300,000 in FY 1990.

Shortly after the Senate hearing, a teleconference brought together leaders of the three major national Native American organizations—the Association for American Indian Affairs (AAIA), the National Congress of American Indians (NCAI), and the Native American Rights Fund (NARF). Representatives of all three groups were very supportive of the establishment of the National Museum of the American Indian. However, Jerry Flute of the AAIA was adamant that stronger repatriation provisions must be included in the bill. He advocated that the Indian community must take a unified position and be willing to kill the whole bill if stronger repatriation provisions were not included. "I remember an initial hesitation on the part of [some] who did not want to see the museum bill killed," recalls Jack Trope, an attorney with the AAIA who participated in the teleconference. "They thought the repatriation provisions would be the kiss of death."[16] Finally, after some discussion, it was decided to go back to Congress as a unified group to advocate inclusion of stronger repatriation provisions in the National Museum of the American Indian (NMAI) Act. "Congress was very enthusiastic about the NMAI bill, and may have been surprised that the tribes were willing to risk passage of that bill to get a strong repatriation provision included."[17]

Where's My Knife?

Congress clearly heard the concerns of the tribal organizations and responded quickly. On July 20, subcommittees of the House Committee on Public Works and Transportation, the Committee on House Administration, and the Committee on Interior and Insular Affairs conducted a joint hearing on H.R. 2668. Unlike the May 12 Senate hearing, when it was barely discussed, repatriation was a central concern of many of the House hearing witnesses. Representative Eni Faleomavaega from American Samoa was one of the first to speak. He identified Native Americans as the most ill-treated groups now living in the United States. "Regrettably, this has been so for over 200 years, and between the unilateral abrogation of treaties, removal from sacred lands by means of force, marches in violation of religious rights and collection of the skeletal remains for 'scientific study,' the record of the treatment our government has accorded these people is despicable. The good news," continued Faleomavaega, "is that recently our government has started treating the descendants of the original inhabitants of this land with more respect."[18]

Senator Inouye appeared as a witness at the House hearing and pointed out that H.R. 2668 was not a perfect bill. "There are loose ends. I would say we are near consensus," he continued, "but there is still a matter such as the repatriation of skeletal remains of Native Americans, which is not fully resolved yet."[19] Inouye explained that the repatriation of Native American skeletal remains was an issue about which there was much controversy and a considerable variety of viewpoints. Indian nations and villages had almost universally expressed concern about the return of their ancestors, despite their diverse cultures and different ethnic backgrounds. Physical and cultural anthropologists saw an intrinsic value in scientific research on human remains. Museum professionals feared that repatriation, carried to the extreme, might empty their shelves of the world. "In my last meeting with Secretary Adams," Inouye said, "he outlined a proposal that may go a long way toward identifying a middle ground where minds can meet on this issue."[20]

Representative Dorgan generally supported H.R. 2668, but he focused his comments on the part of the bill that required the Smithsonian to study the skeletal remains in their possession. "That's fine," he offered, "but we need to do much, much more. We need to return those skeletal for proper burial."[21] Dorgan concluded that Congress needed to stimulate the return of skeletal remains through both H.R. 2668 and other legislation. "The fact is these Native American skeletal remains are being denied proper burial," he concluded.[22]

Walter Echo-Hawk, staff attorney with NARF, testified on behalf of two tribal clients, the Village of Larsen Bay on Kodiak Island, Alaska, and the Pawnee Indian Tribe of Oklahoma. The 180 inhabitants of the Village of Larsen Bay were attempting to repatriate the remains of 800 individuals and over 1,000 associated burial offerings that were exhumed in the 1930s by Alex Hrdlička. According to Echo-Hawk, the Larsen Bay residents were the direct descendants of Alaska Native people who continuously inhabited Kodiak Island from time immemorial. Furthermore, the skeletal remains and associated burial offerings were removed by Hrdlička without the consent or permission of any individual villager (assuming an individual could legally convey such authority) or of the village governing body. The village council had been negotiating with the Smithsonian since 1986 for permission to rebury the remains in accordance with village sensibilities and religious traditions.[23] The Pawnee Tribe was also attempting to repatriate the remains of seventy-seven individuals. Nine were already identified as Pawnee on Smithsonian computer printouts. The remaining sixty-eight were recovered from various sites in the tribe's aboriginal homelands in Kansas and Nebraska. Echo-Hawk complained that the Pawnee Tribe's repeated written repatriation requests to the Smithsonian since August 1988 had received little serious attention.[24] Both the Village of Larsen Bay and the Pawnee Tribe had retained NARF to prepare for potential litigation against the Smithsonian.

Echo-Hawk began his testimony by expressing NARF's full support of the proposed National Museum of the American Indian. However, he expressed serious reservations about Section 9 of H.R. 2668, "which addresses the growing moral crisis and paramount problem that faces the Smithsonian Institution today involving the deplorable fact that the Smithsonian is America's largest Indian graveyard, and have been withholding many of these dead people from reburial. There are many Trails of Tears," continued Echo-Hawk, "and one of those trails leads directly to the doors of the Smithsonian Institution."[25] Echo-Hawk felt that Section 9 of the H.R. 2668 fell far short of addressing the problem, and he recommended five specific changes.

First, Echo-Hawk objected that the bill only required the Smithsonian to conduct a study and make recommendations on how best to implement a policy of returning or repatriating Native American skeletal remains and associated grave offerings. He pointed out that the common law holds that all dead bodies are entitled to a decent burial and that the wishes of the nearest next of kin control the disposition of the dead. This principle of common decency was already in force in all fifty states, except as it applies to Native American graves. Echo-Hawk cited recent legislation in Nebraska and Kansas requiring the reburial of dead Indian bodies and associated burial goods.[26] He also singled out recent repatriations by Stanford University, the University of Minnesota, and the North Dakota State Historical Society.[27] Last, he pointed out that four other bills already introduced in the 101st Congress went beyond the recommendations required in H.R. 2668 to require federal agencies and museums to grant Native victims of the massive expropriation of Native graves equal protection. He urged Congress to make sure that the national museum be among the first, not the last, to provide responsible leadership on repatriation.[28]

Second, Echo-Hawk pointed out that some portions of the bill seemed, perhaps inadvertently, to omit consideration of associated burial goods.[29] He stressed that society has never tolerated the involuntary separation of the rosary, suit of clothes, or wedding ring that might be buried with our loved ones. An Indian tribe's legal interest in materials that were intentionally interred with their ancestors had recently been affirmed in the case of *Charrier v. Bell.*[30] The court ordered an independent archeologist to turn over all items he had removed from a Native American burial site both before and after the land was transferred from private ownership to the state. "For many injured tribes," Echo-Hawk concluded, "it would be spiritually unthinkable and intolerable to rebury one of the decedents at issue without their sacred belongings."[31]

Third, Echo-Hawk objected to providing the Smithsonian with three years to complete the required study. He pointed out that improper withholding of a dead body—even for a matter of hours—was considered such a serious violation of fundamental common-law rights and so socially repugnant that courts typically award damages.[32] The Smithsonian, he argued, should have been on notice of tribal concerns regarding disposition of Native dead following the 1978 completion of the follow-up report required under the American Indian Religious Freedom Act (AIRFA). He also mentioned that the AIRFA report had been completed by the entire federal government in only one year. Echo-Hawk recommended that if the study currently advocated in H.R. 2668 were to be followed, then the required report should be done in one year.[33]

Fourth, Echo-Hawk felt that requiring the Smithsonian Board of Regents to conduct the proposed study represented a prima facie conflict of interest. Smithsonian scientists had already gone on record opposing reburial requests "in the name of science." He proposed that any such study be conducted by an impartial third party so that the results would not be tainted with admitted bias and prejudgment from the beginning.[34]

Last, Echo-Hawk urged that the bill's language be clarified to ensure that it did not preclude access to the courts, abridge existing legal rights, or delay any repatriation requests.[35]

"The present bill," he summarized,

> gives an excellent opportunity and an extremely appropriate occasion for Congress and the Smithsonian to officially reject popular notions that "the only good Indian is a dead Indian," that Native graves are fair game for trophy hunters, that dead Indian bodies are valuable only as "specimens," and that Indian burial offerings belong to "finders as keepers." The legal fiction that has arisen in the minds of many that deceased human beings are "property," when they can be identified as Native Americans, that can be bought and sold in the marketplace as "chattels" must be dispelled as alien to long-standing principles of American common law. Hopefully, the process of bringing about these needed social changes will begin today with the instant bill.[36]

Representative Campbell responded to Echo-Hawk's testimony with a personal experience. His grandfather had once told him that his most frightening experience was when he visited a museum in the Midwest and saw on display the mummified remains of a man he had known as a youngster. "But I guess that is a special kind of viewpoint that Indian people have that maybe nobody else had, those kinds of tragic things."[37]

Representative Faleomavaega expressed his agreement with Echo-Hawk's testimony and hoped that "the provisions of section nine will be made in such a way that we will put more teeth in it and certainly with the cooperation of the Smithsonian Institution, that the 19,000 skeleton remains of these human beings be treated in a more sensitive and more humane way."[38]

Jerry Flute, acting executive director of the AAIA, was the next witness. He was accompanied by staff attorney Jack Trope. Flute reported that AAIA meetings with over one hundred American Indian traditional and spiritual leaders had shown unanimous agreement that the spirits of Native American skeletal remains would not rest until they were properly reburied.[39] "Where the Smithsonian takes a position that there are few, and maybe a small group of people raising this issue," concluded Flute, "we feel that they are totally out of touch as to what Indian people are actually feeling and how they view the issue of skeletal remains."[40] Flute went on to recount the nineteenth-century research of phrenologist Samuel Morton. Based on what was then the largest collection of Indian skulls in the United States, Morton concluded that because some Native skulls were slightly smaller than some Caucasian skulls, the American Indian would never advance intellectually beyond being a savage. Flute characterized Morton's study and those like it as fanning the flames for the theft of Indian lands, desecration of Indian graves, and attempts to kill Indian language and religion. "We feel that many of the anthropologists who support the Smithsonian's position continue to maintain that type of attitude, the attitude of Samuel Morton."[41]

Flute advocated several changes to H.R. 2668. One was to require the Smithsonian to return or repatriate all Indian skeletal remains and associated grave offerings now in its collection on request by Indian tribes or lineal descendants.[42] He requested that the Smithsonian provide a list of currently identified skeletal remains, associated grave offerings, and sacred ceremonial objects to those Indian tribes with which they were likely to belong or on whose aboriginal lands they were found.[43] Flute recommended that the Smithsonian be required to provide semi-annual updates of the required lists.[44] He also recommended that scientific studies of Native American skeletal remains would be permitted only with the express consent of lineal descendants or the appropriate Indian tribe.[45] Last, Flute suggested that it be made explicit that no legal rights of lineal descendants or Indian tribes would be adversely affected.[46]

Trope added that any scientific studies of skeletal remains should occur only with the consent of those Indian tribes most connected with the particular remains. He also recommended that all currently available documentation of these remains should be provided to all Indian tribes specifically identified as connected to the remains, as well as those from whose current area of residence or aboriginal territory they were recovered.[47]

Campbell asked both Flute and Trope how they would address the return of skeletal remains of unknown provenance. Flute described a recent reburial of unidentified human remains in South Dakota that was directed by a joint decision by a number of spiritual leaders. "We feel that the opportunity ought to be given to the tribes where there is no identification made."[48]

Campbell probed how best to facilitate communication between the Smithsonian and Indian tribes regarding unidentifiable remains. Trope suggested that the list sent to each tribe include all skeletal remains that were discovered within both its current and aboriginal territories. "It would then be up to that tribe to determine whether or not the connection that they felt with those remains was substantial enough to request repatriation."[49]

"I know there are tribal conflicts within tribes on virtually every other subject," continued Campbell, "and I can perceive a tribal conflict on dealing with remains. I think it is a kind of big, unanswered area that we have to deal with before we *carte blanche* say we will give them all back."[50]

"I think we understand that," Trope responded. "But that is an implementation issue, and I think if we were simply fighting over implementation issues, we would be much further along in this process than we are now."[51]

Flute then provided the committee with suggested revisions to Section 9, many of which were apparently based on the March 21, 1989, version of Udall's H.R. 1646.[52] In Flute's proposed revision, the board of regents was directed to identify the geographic and tribal origins of sacred ceremonial objects, as well at the skeletal remains and associated funerary objects. A new section would require the Smithsonian to provide the governing body of each Indian tribe notice of any Indian skeletal remains, grave goods, or sacred objects that were (1) definitely associated with that tribe; (2) not definitely identifiable as being associated but which, given the totality of circumstances surrounding the acquisition of the item, were more likely than not associated; and (3) found in an area currently under the jurisdiction or aboriginally occupied by that Indian tribe. All currently available information would be sent to the relevant Indian tribes within six months, with additional information every six months until the study was completed after three years. Another new section would require the Smithsonian to repatriate any of the skeletal remains, associated grave offerings, or sacred ceremonial objects identified on the lists within six months of receiving a request from a lineal descendant or Indian tribe, unless such items were indispensable for the completion of a specific scientific study, the outcome of which would be of major benefit to the United States, and either the lineal descendant or Indian tribe expressly consented.

Dr. Mike Doss with the National Indian Education Association and member of the Crow Nation recognized that the Museum of the American Indian was currently in the process of repatriating the few skeletal remains still in its possession. He recommended that additional inquiries be made as to the disposition of any remains previously held by the institution. In 1956, most of the Heye Foundation's substantial collection of Native American human remains was transferred to the New York University College of Dentistry.[53] "Very importantly," he continued, "we want the collections of both the Smithsonian and the Museum of the American Indian to be analyzed in terms of how items were acquired. The Smithsonian could be a leader in this area, but we do not believe it will undertake this type of soul-searching activity absent a mandate from Congress."[54] Doss believed that H.R. 2668, although somewhat better than its Senate counterpart, S. 978, "does not go far enough in ensuring that tribal wishes regarding the treatment of their dead now in storage at the Smithsonian will be honored."[55]

The final panel member was Susan Shown Harjo, executive director of the National Congress of the American Indian. Harjo expressed her full and enthusiastic support for the establishment of the National Museum of the American Indian. She reminded fellow Cheyenne Campbell that things need to be done in a good way, with a good mind. "We have precious little of that in this legislation."[56] Harjo was particularly concerned that the "collections which exist in the basement, in the storehouses of the Smithsonian Institution in glutinous proportion are the modern evidence of the racist policy of manifest destiny that has more than defamed our people."[57] She explained that many Indian people felt they were personally at risk when entering the Smithsonian. "The more we hear about its inside working, the more fearful we are—not of things that go bump in the night—but things like the existence of the 'beetle room.'"[58] She explained that flesh-eating beetles were used to clean skeletons before they were stored. "The establishment of the National Museum of the American Indian is the stuff of dreams," concluded Harjo, "but the existence of a beetle room and box upon box of skeletal remains of our people is the stuff of nightmares."[59]

Campbell raised concerns about the upcoming 500th anniversary of "when Indians discovered Columbus. My real concern with this bill is that if it gets so focused just on the skeletal remains, as it is beginning to be, America may come out and make a statement that is not a supportive statement. I would hope that the Institution really is an institution of healing and not divisiveness."[60]

Faleomavaega thanked the panel for their testimony. He singled out Echo-Hawk's comments about the persistence of anthropologists in the Native American community. "Mr. Chairman, the next anthropologist I catch in Samoa," joked Faleomavaega, "I'm going to shoot him. I would invoke the spirits of these 19,000 human beings that they should all visit every official of the Smithsonian Institution, pay them a visit, bother them until they say: 'we'd better get rid of these skeletons, or something is going to happen to us.'"[61]

Continuing in the spirit of Faleomavaega's levity, Campbell introduced the next panel. "As my colleague might notice, this panel of six is made up of anthropologists. I think it is only fair to tell them that weapons are not allowed." "Where's my knife?" Faleomavaega mugged.[62]

Secretary of the Smithsonian Adams was the next to testify. Campbell asked him to reflect on the previous testimony regarding what promised to be the most controversial section of the bill. Adams responded that he had arrived late and had not heard all of the testimony nor seen the proposed amendment of Section 9. He acknowledged that although some harsh things may have been said, he was encouraged that there was not as wide a division between the positions of some of the speakers. He was primarily struck by Harjo's belief that most of the Smithsonian collections would not be returned to Indian tribes. Adams stated that the Smithsonian's current policy allowed return of skeletal remains to living descendants. "We do not need any legislation. We do not need anything other than our own sense of the existing pattern of rights and responsibilities to return materials from our collections to those individuals, to those living descendants."[63] Adams went on to indicate that the Smithsonian seemed to be moving toward negotiating the return of skeletal remains to descendant tribal groups. He considered the disposition of those remains for which no identification can be made to be the most serious, possibility requiring "years and years of research before we reach the point where we know who to deal with on collections of those kinds."[64] In his written testimony, Adams also recommended that Section 9(a)(1)(B) be modified to avoid mandating a specific outcome and to permit exploration of a variety of options regarding the treatment and disposition of the Smithsonian skeletal collections.[65]

Faleomavaega responded to Adams's testimony by asking if he would consider putting the souls that could not be identified to rest in the ground. "No, sir," responded Adams. "I regret to say, although I know it is a very unpopular position for me to do so, but I would not. I am not prepared to see them forever lost when there is no one who has been able to claim a right for those particular individuals," he continued. "We would resist this course of action very strongly."[66]

"I can understand that for inanimate objects," interjected Faleomavaega, "but I'm talking about human beings."

"This is the national collection," answered Adams. "I have the responsibility as custodian of the national collection to not disburse them except for legitimate cause."

"So you say that a spear is just much the same thing as skeletal remains of a human being?"

"It is not the same thing, but I am saying the national collections include many, many things."

"Given the history, the animosity, the racism," Faleomavaega interrupted, "I mean, all that we have admitted to this day and age of what we have done against the Native Americans, wouldn't you think that there is some sense of sympathy on the part of the Smithsonian Institution to understand that these are human beings?"

"I think there is a great deal of sympathy within the Smithsonian Institution for the position that is being taken. We know that this is an issue of great concern to the great numbers of Native Americans, perhaps to the great majority. We also are well aware that the advancing tide of research in this area has good promise in it in the years immediately ahead to take us further, by a factor of ten times or more, than we have managed to go in the last century. I have to be conscious of the scientific loss that would be occasioned by the course of action you are describing."

Representative John Rhodes from Arizona asked Adams to describe the kinds of "research bonanzas" he expected to achieve from the skeletal remains.[67]

Adams anticipated that one day DNA recovered from skeletal remains would allow for the identification of patterns of movement and relationship between aboriginal populations going back millennia. He also explained how it might soon be possible to trace the beginning of agriculture through analysis of diet as reflected in the composition of skeletal material. Detailed studies of major pathologies would yield information on health problems that still present a problem for Indian populations, such as rheumatism and arthritis.[68]

Campbell thanked Adams for his testimony. "Well, Secretary Adams, I guess we are going to put you on the spot today. I certainly didn't mean to do that so furiously." Campbell then extended his personal thanks for Adams's special interest in trying to resolve several issues involving disposition of some artifacts. "I don't want you to think that we are totally negative in our attitude toward what the Smithsonian is doing."[69]

The next witness was Mark Leone, treasurer of the Society for American Archaeology (SAA) and a faculty member at the University of Maryland. Leone indicated that although the SAA had some problems with Section 9 of H.R. 2668, it wholeheartedly supported the idea of the National Museum of the American Indian. Leone contrasted two important views, the first that much of the knowledge of North America prior to European arrival was the product of the actions of archeologists and anthropologists and the second that the Smithsonian and other museums contain human remains that were stolen, and that these collections were sometimes used to propagate and underpin racist statements. "Now that is the dilemma," concluded Leone. "What do we do in the face of that with the collections that are mentioned in section nine of the bill?"[70] Leone recommended mentioning the importance of the scientific study of human remains in the bill. He also pointed out two provisions in H.R. 2668 that went beyond that language in Inouye's S. 978. One was the inclusion of "associated grave offerings" in the study provisions. The second was the language that appeared to extend the grants program beyond the Smithsonian to include tribal agreements with museums and federal agencies.[71] "We are all aware that anytime one requests studies, one always has to be sensitive to the fact that that is just a way of delaying. It is a S.O.P. [standard operating procedure], saying 'Well, we will solve it some other way because it is too difficult to solve now.'"[72] However, he pointed out that the Smithsonian collections were very large and recommended more time and that additional resources would need to be devoted to the study of the skeletal collections. Last, Leone recommended that the scientific community be consulted in the course of determining the ultimate disposition of the skeletal remains and associated grave goods. He promised to work toward making archeologists more sensitive to the issues surrounding skeletal remains. He also advocated ongoing consultation between archeologists, museum people, and Indian people so that the troublesome matters could be debated.[73]

Richard Stamps, an associated professor of anthropology at Oakland University in Michigan was next to address the committee. Stamps pointed out that archeologists are responsible to multiple constituencies, including the individuals preserved in the archeological record, their modern-day descendants, and the public at large, both now and future generations. The primary question, according to Stamps, was "who speaks for past generations?"[74]

"That last sentence, of course, is the crux of our discussion," interrupted Campbell. "Some disagree. In the ongoing discussion, it should be scientific rights or proprietary right of Indian remains. I hope we're going to find an answer to that."[75]

"Remembering, those who ignore the past are destined to repeat it," Stamps continued, "I feel that we as anthropologists and you as elected representatives do have an obligation to, as objectively as possible, preserve, study, and tell the story of those who passed before us. Let us not be remembered for what we destroyed but for what we saved as a society."[76]

Faleomavaega responded strongly, focusing on the anthropological investigations of Margaret Mead. He explained that Mead studied the Samoan people for nine months in the mid-1920s and then wrote *Coming of Age in Samoa*, considered a classic of anthropological literature that has sold millions of copies worldwide. He resented what Mead had written about the attitudes of the culture of his people. "It is the most untruthful thing that I have ever read in my life." Faleomavaega objected to anthropologists' and archeologists' portrayal of "truth."[77] He also cautioned against letting the skeletal issue become a real force behind the establishment of the National Museum of the American Indian.[78]

Responding to Stamps's question regarding who speaks for the past, Secretary Adams made a commitment that the central voice speaking for their past would be American Indians themselves.[79]

Lonnie Selam, member of the Yakima Indian Nation Tribal Council, recommended that the study to be conducted by the board of regents include religious, sacred, and cultural artifacts as well as skeletal remains and associated grave offerings. He also recommended that the bill require the Smithsonian to work with religious leaders on the methods of properly handling sacred objects. Selam recognized that the concept of only including study language in H.R. 2668 was a compromise over stronger bills also under consideration, but he stressed the importance of repatriation of skeletal remains. "Our people believe that until properly interred, the spirit of the deceased is free to linger and grieve. We believe in a direct connection between the spirits of the dead and their living descendants and our people grieve with the spirits of those who are forced to linger and are being held away from their sacred lands. These remains must be properly buried and their spirits allowed to rest."[80]

Selam then singled out Representative Morris Udall for praise. "It is not coincidental that the Congress has exhibited its most enlightened attitude in the history of this country's treatment of Indian people during the time when Mo[rris] has chaired this committee. Mr. Udall's crowning achievements would be to successfully enlighten the Supreme Court on Indian law. But, this seems unlikely, as he is a superb legislator, but not a miracle worker."[81] Selam was referring to the string of Supreme Court decisions that were adverse to Indian interests, particularly the recent *Lyng* opinion.[82]

"Alternatively," continued Selam, "we can only hope that he remains healthy and continues to chair this committee for many years to come."[83] Udall was suffering from Parkinson's disease and had been hospitalized with pneumonia.

Agreement at the Coyote Cafe

Following the July 20 hearing, Campbell initiated discussions between Secretary Adams and representatives of the Indian community to address the issue of repatriation. A dinner meeting was set for August 17 in Santa Fe, and in preparation Adams had several phone conversations with Richard West, an attorney with an Albuquerque Indian law firm and enrolled member of the Cheyenne and Arapaho Tribe of Oklahoma. Adams decided that West should not attend the Santa Fe dinner "in order to keep himself somewhat detached from any kind of protagonist's status in connection with its outcome."[84] Adams thought that all sides were groping for some effective way to avoid endless confrontations and possible litigation that could poison the atmosphere for the new museum. "Flying out to New Mexico," Suzan Harjo later recalled, "I really looked through the material that I had received from the Smithsonian."[85] One of the documents was a copy of the bill of lading for Cheyenne and Arapaho crania collected after the infamous massacre at Sand Creek, Colorado, now in the Smithsonian collection. Harjo was fuming by the time she landed in Albuquerque. She called Adams. "Do you realize that you preside over an institution that has the heads of my dead relatives from Sand Creek?"[86]

"Good Lord," Adams responded. "No, I didn't know that."

"We're through talking," Harjo told him and went on to explain that up until that point she had been holding back, trying to negotiate a solution with the Smithsonian regarding the Native American human remains in its collection. She was now prepared to recommend that Indian tribes file suit against the Smithsonian for the return of their ancestors. "That was all

I could do," she recalled, "except say goodbye."[87] Adams said he would call right back. Harjo immediately called Echo-Hawk and Campbell to tell them she had just blown it and was recommending court action.

Adams called back within a few minutes. "We had been in very specific talks for years and had narrowed things down to the categories and terminology," Harjo recalled. "We just hadn't agreed to agree. And that was it. He agreed."[88]

The agreement provided for a review committee including Indian representatives to oversee the inventory process and further provided that where the evidence established that Indian human remains and associated funerary objects in the possession of the Smithsonian are those of a particular individual or an individual culturally identified with a particular tribe, the items would be returned to descendants of the deceased or to the tribe with which the deceased was culturally identified on request.[89]

Adams and Harjo agreed to give an exclusive story of the agreement to the *New York Times*. After the interviews, Adams, Harjo, Echo-Hawk, and Campbell went for dinner at the Coyote Café in Santa Fe. "My ancestors from Sand Creek made this possible," recalled Harjo, "and they're laughing like hell because the coyote is the trickster. We were at loggerheads for so many years and then all of a sudden a coyote comes and fixes it."[90] The *New York Times* story was "put to bed" before they opened the menus.[91] The story was quickly picked up by other newspapers.

The *New York Times* described the agreement as finding a middle ground between the positions of the American Anthropological Association—which allowed for the return of items only to close relatives—and Stanford University and the University of Minnesota, which were returning entire collections to local tribes.[92] The Smithsonian agreement would return, on request, any remains and artifacts that could be linked with "reasonable certainty" to present-day tribes.[93] "We were at a point of no return on this issue," Harjo was quoted. "It's a grown up Smithsonian and it's a victory for America to solve quite a disgraceful situation where Indians are an archaeological resource of the U.S., our relatives are U.S. property—not quite humans. This kind of policy is a way out of the nightmare."[94] Adams acknowledged that some concession was inevitable. "When this came to the court of public opinion," he said, "we were going to lose."[95] According to Adams, Harjo was very uneasy about references to "negotiations" and a prospective "agreement," although she was very pleased with the article as a whole.[96]

Interpretation of the agreement's implications varied among the negotiating parties. Secretary Adams was quoted in the *New York Times* as saying that most of the human remains in the Smithsonian collection would not be affected.[97] At a press conference, he speculated that between 5 and 10 percent of the Smithsonian skeletal collection might be subject to repatriation under the new agreement, though the percentage might increase as new scientific methods improved the available information.[98] Privately, Adams thought that he and Harjo were in accord that a more realistic objective was to "reduce our differences," to find a modus vivendi that would permit the new museum to go forward without the reburial issue as a major diversion, while leaving fundamental questions of science versus cultural/religion unsettled, perhaps permanently.[99] Congressman Campbell estimated that one-fourth of the Smithsonian's collection might be subject to reburial.[100] In an opinion article that ran in several newspapers across the country, Harjo announced that the Smithsonian had agreed to return all Indian skeletal remains that could be identified with specific tribes or living kin.[101]

The Santa Fe agreement was incorporated into an amendment in the nature of a substitute offered by Representative William Clay from Missouri and adopted by the Subcommittee on Libraries and Memorials when it marked up H.R. 2668 on September 12. The Clay amendment was adopted by voice vote by the subcommittee. The bill as amended was ordered reported favorably to the Committee on House Administration by voice vote of the subcommittee.[102] The markup of H.R. 2668 caught the SAA by surprise, and they quickly submitted a series of recommended revisions.[103] Two additional findings were suggested to recognize the contributions derived from the anthropological study of human remains and funerary objects and the important role that museums play in preserving the heritage of Indian groups. Two new definitions were recommended. "Tribal origin" was defined to mean the Indian tribe of which the deceased individual was a member and whose members interred the funerary objects in question. "Culturally affiliated" was defined to mean that an individual is recognized as a member of a named cultural group as evidenced by shared language, customs, and religion. A new section was recommended requiring that prior to their return, all human remains and associated funerary objects would be fully documented, though such documentation could not result in damage or destruction to the remains or objects or substantially delay their return. The SAA recommend that three of the six committee members should be nominated by the scholarly community. Finally, expansion of the grants section were recommended to provide funds to Indian tribes to develop cooperative agreements with the Smithsonian Institution, federal agencies, and museums, and to museums to prepare inventories of their collections.

The next day, Loretta Neumann (a lobbyist for the SAA) received a testy call from Kim Craven, one of Campbell's staffers.[104] According to Neumann, Craven was critical of the recommendations and did not understand why the SAA was so concerned because the bill only dealt with the Smithsonian Institution. Craven kept referring to the deal that had been made between Adams and the tribal representatives. The conversation ended with polite but cold thank-yous.

Two days later, a House Interior Committee staffer called the SAA.[105] Pablita Abeyta explained that she had shown the SAA comments to Walter Echo-Hawk and Suzan Harjo. Echo-Hawk reportedly viewed the additional findings sections as unnecessary and threatened to include examples of the negative ways collections had been acquired if the new sections were added. He considered the new definitions of "tribal origin" and "culturally affiliated" too restrictive and characterized the documentation requirement as undercutting efforts to expedite the return of human remains and associated funerary objects to the tribes. According to Abeyta, Echo-Hawk felt that the composition of the committee was the result of complicated discussions between tribal representatives and the Smithsonian and considered the recommended expansion of the grant section as inconsistent with the scope of the bill. Abeyta added that it was too late in the game to change that language and felt the House would not support the SAA recommendations.

Neumann had another testy conversation on September 28, this time with Harjo, who characterized the SAA comments as arrogant and designed to undermine the deal cut between the Smithsonian and the tribal representatives. "It was, to say the least, not a pleasant conversation!"[106]

Neumann tried again with Peter Rutledge, a staffer on the House Public Works and Administration Committee, which also had jurisdiction over the Smithsonian. Rutledge told her that no changes to the repatriation provisions of H.R. 2668 would be made without the approval of House Interior and Insular Affairs staff. "Given the reaction we got from Frank Ducheneaux on the Interior Committee staff, I won't hold my breath for that to happen!"[107]

On October 3, the Senate approved S. 978 by voice vote and sent it to the House for consideration.[108] However, the fate of the Senate bill remained in doubt as the House staff continued to amend H.R. 2668 to include provisions of the Santa Fe agreement. Vin Steponaitis, an archeologist at the University of North Carolina and member of the SAA Task Force on Repatriation, reported that the university's lobbyist met with an aide to North Carolina Senator Terry Sanford. He reported that the SAA had not been consulted by the Senate Indian Affairs Committee staff and that the Smithsonian's congressional liaison had deliberately withheld information from Neumann. Sanford's aide was reportedly disturbed by this information. When Steponaitis asked the lobbyist why he was spending time with the Senate staff when the S. 978 had already passed the Senate, he explained that he wanted to "build the case for more favorable treatment in case the House bill falters (which he admits is unlikely)" as well as "laying the groundwork for opposition to the McCain [general repatriation] bill, when and if it comes down the pike."[109]

Instead of taking up the Senate bill, the House first refined its own bill. The November 9 version of H.R. 2668 included three new sections specifying the procedures to be used in completing the inventory and identification of Native American human remains and associated funerary objects in the Smithsonian collections.[110] Section 11 was identified as embodying the agreement reached in August between representatives of the Smithsonian and the Indian community.[111] The secretary of the Smithsonian was to complete an inventory of all Native American human remains and funerary objects in the Smithsonian collections with the goal of identifying their tribal origin.[112] On determining by the preponderance of the evidence the tribal origin of any such human remains and funerary objects, the secretary was to notify any affected Indian tribe, and, on request, expeditiously return the human remains and associated funerary objects to the descendants or culturally affiliated Indian tribes.[113] The House committee report noted that the human remains and funerary objects "acquired by the Smithsonian over the years and under various circumstances, have been held in trust by the Institution and curated for scientific purposes."[114] This was a very significant statement because it clarified that although control or title to the Native American human remains and funerary objects was held by the Smithsonian, the institution also had (and continued to have) accounting and management responsibilities of a trustee under both specific statutes and treaties as well as defined in traditional equitable terms. Under general property law, the beneficiary of the trusteeship is the individual or group descendants of the deceased. The committee report also noted that although the formal repatriation process was defined in terms of repatriations to federally recognized Indian tribes, this was not meant to preclude the Smithsonian from returning human remains and funerary objects to nonfederally recognized Indian groups or other Native entities.[115] The report further noted that funerary objects that could only be associated with mass graves or entire cemeteries, and not with the burial of an individual person, would not be subject to repatriation.[116] A five-person special committee was authorized to monitor the inventory and identification process to ensure fair and objective consideration and assessment of all relevant evidence and, on request, review any findings relating to the origin or the return of human remains and funerary objects and facilitate the resolution of any disputes.[117] The secretary of the Interior was authorized to make grants to Indian tribes to develop and implement agreements for the return of human remains and funerary objects.[118] A letter from the Congressional Budget Office, apparently based on estimates provided by the Smithsonian, assumed that the special committee and the grants program "would cease to exist at the end of FY1995 once all the Indian human remains are properly analyzed and returned."[119]

On November 13, a revised version of H.R. 2668 was taken up by the House. A new section extended the inventory and identification requirements in Section 11 to include Native Hawaiian human remains and funerary objects and required the Smithsonian to enter into an agreement with the appropriate Native Hawaiian organization regarding the return of such remains and objects.[120] Two Native Hawaiian organizations—Hui Malama I Na Kupuna O Hawai'i Nei, a nonprofit organization incorporated the previous April, and the Office of Hawaiian Affairs, a state agency—were specifically identified. Representative Daniel Akaka from Hawaii explained to his colleagues that two weeks before, at a meeting organized by Hui Malama I Na Kupuna O Hawai'i Nei, the Native Hawaiian community had reached a consensus to seek the return of all Native Hawaiian human remains from the Smithsonian, regardless of whether descendants step forward to accept the remains.[121] Representative Faleomavaega was "warmed throughout" that repatriation provisions were included in H.R. 2668.[122] "That action alone is something of which we in Congress should all be proud." Representative Glenn Anderson from California was hopeful that the process outlined in H.R. 2668 would provide for the orderly conveyance of many of the Indian remains and funerary objects in the Smithsonian collections to their families.[123] Representative Dorgan explained that his primary interest in H.R. 2668 was to direct the Smithsonian Institution to return identified Indian human remains and associated funerary objects for reinterment by Indian families and tribes.[124] Dorgan felt that the thrust of his bill, H.R. 1124, which he had introduced at the request of the Indian tribes of North Dakota, was incorporated into Section 12 of the new bill. Representative Charles Bennett identified H.R.

2668 as one of several bills, including his own H.R. 1381, the Native American Burial Site Preservation Act, and H.R. 3412, to amend the National Historic Preservation Act, the Historic Sites Act, and the Archaeological Resources Protection Act, representing a new sensitivity to the cultural and beliefs of Native American.[125] The House passed H.R. 2668, then took up the issue of S. 978 by striking all of the Senate language and replacing it with the text from H.R. 2668.[126]

The next day, Senator Inouye asked his colleagues to concur with the House amendments to S. 978, but not before singling out Suzan Harjo and Walter Echo-Hawk for playing key and vital roles in working with Secretary Adams to effect a resolution to the sensitive and significant matter of repatriation. The Senate passed S. 978 by voice vote.

Passage of the new repatriation provisions by the House and Senate clearly raised concerns among the Smithsonian staff regarding the Tall Bull pipe. On November 14, 1989, the day after the House added the amended repatriation provisions to S. 978, Smithsonian curator William Merrill called a member of the Southern Cheyenne Dog Soldier Society in Oklahoma who reported on a recent meeting with representatives of the Southern and Northern Cheyenne Dog Soldiers. The two Cheyenne groups disagreed as to whether the pipe had been Chief Tall Bull's personal property or was communally owned by the Dog Soldiers. However, the Southern Cheyenne did not oppose the Northern Cheyenne claim. Merrill still personally questioned the Northern Cheyenne claim that the pipe was ceremonial. "Their intention to use the pipe ceremonially appears to be a created, rather than traditional, use for it," he concluded, "and should not influence how we respond to their request. If we should accede to their request on these grounds, we potentially will jeopardize the entire North American ethnology collection. Undoubtedly a ceremonial status and use could be created for every object in the collections."[127] On November 16, 1989, the day after the Senate approved the House amendments, Merrill's memorandum was passed on to National Museum of Natural History Director Frank Talbot. "Attached is the most recent report by Bill Merrill re negotiations with the Northern Cheyenne about the Tall Bull pipe. Bill now feels that it would be unwise to return the pipe. There is some sentiment among the Cheyenne that the pipe should be at the NMNH."[128]

The National Museum of the American Indian Act became law on November 28, 1989. Section 11 dealt with the repatriation of Indian human remains and associated funerary objects at the Smithsonian. The secretary of the Smithsonian was required, in consultation with Indian tribes, to inventory human remains and funerary objects. Using the best scientific evidence, the Smithsonian was directed to identify the geographic origin and cultural affiliation of those human remains. One million dollars was authorized for FY 1991 for this task. Section 13 applied the inventory and repatriation provisions of Section 11 to the Native Hawaiian human remains and funerary objects. Section 12 authorized establishment of a five-member committee to monitor compliance. Three of the appointments were to be made from nominations received from Indian tribes, and the secretary of the Smithsonian was directed to select a committee chair. The proceedings of the committee were exempt from provisions of the Freedom of Information Act. In an accompanying signing statement, President George H. W. Bush noted that the act codified U.S. policy for returning American Indian and Native Hawaiian human remains and associated funerary objects and that the inventory, identification, notification, and repatriation processes represented the substantial efforts and goodwill of many people.[129]

The tenacious spirits of Senator Inouye and Representative Campbell brought the diverse personalities of Suzan Harjo and Robert Adams to a middle ground where minds could meet at the same table. Although Harjo and Adams both heralded the National Museum of American Indian Act as a success, it soon became apparent that they read the legislative text to different ends. Harjo went home that Thanksgiving under the impression that the ancestors of tribal people would soon be reburied, and Adams predicted that the repatriation provisions of the new statute would have only limited effects on the Smithsonian collections. That the archeological community deemed repatriation appropriate only when cultural affiliation was scientifically proven to their satisfaction became a recurring theme underscoring the next round of congressional action.

CHAPTER FIVE

Two Practices, No Policy

On November 21, 1989, seven days before President George H. W. Bush signed the National Museum of the American Indian (NMAI) Act into law, Senator Daniel Inouye offered another repatriation bill. In introducing S. 1980, Inouye began by lauding the Smithsonian Institution for taking a courageous step when it agreed to return remains and artifacts in its collection that belong to Native Americans. "Ideally," he continued, "it should be incumbent on the museum community itself, including anthropologists, archaeologists, and museum professionals to set ethical standards that respect the rights of other human beings and groups of people. In practice, however, not all institutions and individuals who engage in the excavation, collection, or trade of Native American artifacts respect the rights of Native Americans."[1] With the situation regarding human remains and associated funerary objects in the Smithsonian collections resolved, at least for the time being, Inouye joined Representative Morris Udall and Senator John McCain in efforts to expand repatriation requirements to the rest of the nation's museums.

Inouye's S. 1980

Portions of S. 1980 were quite similar to Udall's and McCain's earlier efforts. In particular, the new bill required all federal agencies and other institutions that received federal funds to inventory all Native American human remains, funerary objects, and sacred objects in their collections.[2]

Inouye's bill differed from the earlier efforts by extending the definition of "museum," and thus the related inventory requirement, to persons receiving federal funds.[3] The new bill would have required the inventories to be more comprehensive as well, including Native American group or cultural patrimony along with human remains, funerary objects, and sacred objects. "Cultural patrimony" was defined as items having historical, traditional, or cultural importance to the Native American group or culture itself, rather than property owned by any individual, which therefore could not be legally alienated, appropriated, or conveyed by any individual.[4] Federal agencies and museums were required to initiate an inventory process for such items in consultation and cooperation with traditional Indian and Native Hawaiian religious leaders and tribal government officials.[5] Identification of human remains and other objects was to be based on the best available scientific and historical documentation, the same standard included in the NMAI Act. By June 30, 1992 (three months after the inventories were to be completed), federal agencies and museums were required to notify Indian tribes and Native Hawaiian organizations of all human remains, funerary objects, sacred objects, or items of cultural patrimony established by a preponderance of the evidence as originating with that group.[6]

The repatriation standards in Inouye's bill applied differently to federal agencies and museums. Federal agencies were required to expeditiously return human remains and any associated funerary objects to the descendants, culturally affiliated Indian tribe, or appropriate Native Hawaiian organization.[7] Federal agencies were also required to expeditiously return funerary objects, sacred objects, and cultural patrimony associated with a specific burial site to the culturally affiliated Indian tribe, or funerary objects removed from a specific Native Hawaiian burial site to the appropriate Native Hawaiian organization.[8] In contrast to the clear directive provided for federal agencies, the standard for repatriation to be used by museums involved a process for weighing the museum's legal title against the interests of Native American individuals, Indian tribes, and Native Hawaiian organizations. On receipt of a claim, the initial burden of proof fell on the museum with possession or control of the items to prove that it had legal title.[9] If the museum could not satisfy this requirement, the burden of proof shifted to the claimant to show that the human remains were of an ancestor or were culturally affiliated with the Indian tribe or Native Hawaiian organization, or that the funerary objects, sacred objects, or cultural patrimony were once owned or possessed by the Indian tribe or Native Hawaiian organization.[10] Museums were required to expeditiously return human remains or objects if they could not prove legal title and the claimant satisfied its burden of proof.[11] Some in the museum community argued that these burden of proof requirements reversed the normal property law standard in which the burden always rested with the claimant. However, placing the burden of proof on the museum was consistent with a 150-year-old federal statute that applied to the determination of property rights when one party was an Indian and the other party was not.[12] In these situations, the burden of proof was placed on the party with better access to records and proof.[13]

Even though the repatriation provisions of the NMAI Act had yet to go into effect, Inouye's bill was already trying to clarify the Smithsonian's repatriation obligations. S. 1980 would establish a specific date by which the Smithsonian would be required to complete its inventories and notification[14] and would add the obligation to repatriate sacred objects and items of group or cultural patrimony on the request of the culturally affiliated Indian tribe or Native Hawaiian organization.[15] The Smithsonian was specifically excluded from the requirement to repatriate human remains under the new bill,[16] those requirements having already been established under the NMAI Act.

Harkening back to John Melcher's earlier efforts to establish an independent commission to deal with repatriation issues, Inouye's bill directed the secretary of the Interior to establish a committee to monitor and review the implementation of the inventory and identification process.[17] Four of the seven members were to be appointed from nominations submitted by Indian tribes and Native Hawaiian organizations.[18] The secretary of the Interior was directed to designate one member as chairperson.[19] The committee's duties included monitoring the inventory and identification process, reviewing determinations made by federal agencies and museums, arbitrating disputes, consulting with Native Hawaiian organizations,[20] and submitting an annual report to Congress on the progress made and barriers encountered in implementing the bill.[21] The bill also authorized the secretary of the Interior to make grants to Indian tribes, Native Hawaiian organizations, and museums to assist in implementation.[22]

The excavation provisions of S. 1980 differed significantly from Udall's and McCain's attempts. Any Native American human remains, funerary objects, and sacred objects (group or cultural patrimony was inexplicably missing from this requirement) that were excavated pursuant to a federal permit were to be repatriated to any Native American group, or any member of a Native American group, that asserted an interest in the objects. Native American human remains, funerary objects, and sacred objects were not to be considered archeological resources as defined in the Archaeological Resources Protection Act (ARPA), except for those instances related to the imposition of civil or criminal penalties for the unauthorized excavation, removal, damage, or destruction.[23] Native American human remains, funerary objects, and sacred objects could not be disturbed without the express consent of the culturally affiliated Indian tribe or Native Hawaiian organization.[24]

The leadership of the Society for American Archaeology (SAA) was "extremely disturbed" by Inouye's bill, which they considered to go much further than simply extending provisions of the NMAI Act to other federal agencies. Of particular concern were the excavation provisions that would explicitly override all other legal provisions and required tribal consent before Native American human remains or cultural items could be disturbed. The SAA was also concerned that cultural affiliation was not defined. "Strong stuff, to put it mildly," wrote lobbyist Loretta Neumann to the SAA leadership. "As we suspected, the Smithsonian bill was just the beginning of the next wave of efforts to enact sweeping reburial legislation."[25]

In early December, representatives from the Native American Rights Fund, National Congress of American Indians, and Association for American Indian Affairs met to develop a legislative strategy for the second session of the 101st Congress.[26] Discussions focused on Udall's Native American Grave and Burial Protection Act (H.R. 1646); McCain's Native American Grave and Burial Protection Act (S. 1021); Wyche Fowler's bill to amend the National Historic Preservation Act, Historic Sites Act, ARPA, and Abandoned Shipwrecks Act (S. 1579); and Inouye's Native American Repatriation and Cultural Patrimony Act (S. 1980); along with several bills related to the protection of sacred sites and certain follow-up work for the recently enacted NMAI Act. The Native American Coalition anticipated that the Senate Select Committee on Indian Affairs would hold a single hearing on McCain's and Inouye's repatriation bills in the spring, but that hearings on Udall's bill would not be until after June, making it unlikely that the House measure would be passed before the Congress adjourned. The repatriation provisions in Fowler's bill were considered an obstacle, with the coalition deciding to urge the senator delete to those provisions. The coalition was also concerned that the Smithsonian seemed to be applying a very narrow interpretation to the repatriation standard in the NMAI Act, particularly as it applied to a request from the Alaskan village of Larsen Bay. In planning its lobbying efforts for the next year, the coalition identified six categories of people and groups that needed to be contacted or organized, including legislators and their staffs, Indian tribes and organizations, media, potential allies, federal agencies, and "enemies." Potential allies included individual scientists and museum professionals and organizations, like the World Archaeological Congress, which had recently adopted guidance sympathetic to repatriation; museums that had already implemented repatriation policies; church groups; the Jewish and black community; and the third world diplomatic community. The coalition decided that formal negotiation with federal agencies should wait until after congressional hearings given that agencies might use any ongoing talks to argue that legislation wasn't necessary. Identified opponents of repatriation legislation included the Army Medical Museum, National Park Service, and the SAA, the last specifically described as an "anti-Indian group."

In January 1990, the SAA hosted a meeting to discuss the reburial/repatriation issue and share information about the views and activities of various agencies and organizations, including the American Anthropological Association, National Conference of State Historic Preservation Officers, American Association of Museums, National Park Service, and Advisory Council on Historic Preservation. It was agreed that the group would meet periodically as the No-Name Alliance, to focus "not just on reburial, but also on taking positive steps to support efforts by various Native American tribes to preserve their cultural heritage."[27]

A More Draconian Approach

On February 22, 1990, the Subcommittee on Public Lands, National Parks and Forests of the Senate Committee on Energy and Natural Resources held a hearing on two bills introduced by Senator Wyche Fowler from Georgia. The Historic Preservation Administration Act, S. 1578, would establish an independent historic preservation agency and a national center for preservation technology. S. 1579, the National Historic Preservation Policy Act, would amend the National Historic Preservation Act, Historic Sites Act, ARPA, and Abandoned Shipwreck Act. Section 120 of S. 1579 would add a section to ARPA regarding the disposition of the human remains and associated grave goods that balances respect for the dead, interests of descendants, and interests of research.[28]

The majority of the witnesses at the February 22 hearing were concerned with the organizational aspects of the two bills and did not comment on Section 120. One who did was Jerry Rogers, National Park Service associate director for Cultural Resources, who spoke on behalf of the Department of the Interior. Rogers's appearance before the committee represented the Department of the Interior's first direct testimony regarding repatriation legislation. He explained in his testimony that the Department of the Interior strongly opposed the sweeping organizational changes proposed by the two bills.[29] Regarding Section 120, Rogers indicated that the Department of the Interior was already taking the recently enacted repatriation provisions of the NMAI Act as policy guidance and was setting about revising Interior policy and guidelines accordingly.[30] He closed his testimony by focusing on the disposition of human remains and funerary objects. "We acknowledge that on the question of human remains archaeological research values and human values do have to be balanced. That is absolutely true. But in our view, the human values get a little bit of extra measure in that balance. We are not just dealing with any ordinary source of scientific information."[31]

Another witness was William Lovis, chairman of the SAA's government affairs committee. Lovis identified three major issues facing archeological preservation—looting and vandalism to sites, the illicit antiquities trade, and the protection of sites on private land—and thought that the contributions of S. 1578 and S. 1579 to the solution of these problems outweighed any current minor issues the SAA had with the specifics of the bills.[32] He did not discuss the provisions regarding the treatment of human remains in his oral testimony. However, his written testimony identified the proposed provisions as a consensus position and a major contribution of the bill. "Unlike other legislation pending in Congress on this matter," Lovis wrote, "S. 1579 recognizes that there are important gains that can be made in recognizing both the contributions of long-term scientific study and the interests and concerns of Native American people. The perspective on this issue established by S. 1579 can serve as a model for other bills addressing reburial and repatriation."[33]

The SAA also submitted a detailed analysis of the bill to the committee. The organization preferred that any new reburial legislation wait until the reburial/repatriation provisions of the NMAI Act had a chance to be tested. The SAA found the current proposal a reasonable and fair way to balance the rights of descendants and the concerns of affected Native Americans with the interests of science and the contributions that could be gained from scientific research. The SAA also recommended that the definitions of funerary object and burial site be revised to conform to the definitions already enacted in the NMAI Act.[34]

Karen Funk spoke on behalf of the National Indian Education Association and limited her comments to those provisions of S. 1579 that were of particular importance to Indian and Alaska Native people.[35] She supported S. 1579 with one significant change, that section 120 be deleted. She acknowledged that Section 120 represented a good-faith effort to deal with this difficult issue. However, she continued, there was no consensus among Indian tribes on this approach. In particular, Funk indicated that she had been contacted by the Native American Rights Fund, who wanted it made clear to the committee that they did not agree to the language of Section 120. "Tribes have been working for over a year on independent bills," she concluded. "We would prefer to work through that route."

The following day, Tom King, the self-described sub rosa mediator of the group that had originally developed the reburial provisions of S. 1579, drafted a memo titled "The Inside Story of Section 120 of S. 1579 and Why Karen Funk Is Backing Away from It."[36] King explained that at the time of the original negotiations, all of the participants had agreed on the reburial provisions. However, the Supreme Court's 1988 decision in the G-O Road case had upset the balance—the court ruled that logging and construction of a road through an identified Native American cemetery did not violate the Equal Protection Clause of the Constitution.[37] Some members of Congress were now interested in increasing protection to Native American sacred sites. "It was predictable that if [pan-Indian activists, most notably the Native American Rights Fund] found someone who would support a more draconian approach," King concluded, "they would necessarily have to back away from support of Section 120. That is exactly what has happened."

The National Park Service

The National Park Service's involvement in repatriation derived from its dual role as a land managing agency and as the representative of the secretary of the Interior on certain cultural issues. The service was responsible for the remains of several thousand Native American individuals recovered over the years from more than 300 National Parks, Monuments, and Historic Sites, and it continually faced the prospect of new discoveries in conjunction with natural erosion and development activities. The National Park Service had been delegated some of the secretary of the Interior's department-wide and government-wide responsibilities under several cultural resource statutes, particularly the National Historic Preservation Act and the ARPA. Associate Director Jerry Rogers and his Washington-based staff fulfilled both of these responsibilities by providing technical assistance to park unit managers and formulating policy that applied not only to the National Park Service but to other federal and state agencies as well.

Rogers had been concerned about the potential impact that repatriation might have on the Department of the Interior since at least 1984 when, in a prescient note accompanying a *Time* magazine article on reburial,[38] he wrote to National Park Service Assistant Director for Archeology Bennie Keel, "our friends in SAA had better crank up their public relations machine, or they may lose a big political issue in about 5 years."[39]

In early 1985, Keel responded to several letters requesting clarification of the department's policy on the reburial of Native American human remains. The department's guidelines, dated July 23, 1982, were designed to establish a consistent approach for its bureaus and offices to follow in determining the proper treatment of archeological and historical human remains.[40] The 1982 guidelines made clear that preservation of human remains in situ was generally preferable to removal. Where disturbance could not be avoided, department officials were directed to identify direct kin or a specific living group with an affinity to the human remains to consult regarding the most appropriate treatment for the interment. Costs accruing as a result of consultation, treatment, or curation of human remains were to be borne by the responsible bureau. Keel included a copy of the 1982 guidelines with each response and wrote a cover letter clarifying certain issues that might be applicable to the particular inquiry. He explained that under provisions of ARPA, each federal bureau remained responsible for all archeological resources, including human remains, recovered from lands under its jurisdiction, even if those items were in the possession of a private consultant or were are curated in a nonfederal museum. Reburial of human remains recovered from federal lands could only occur if the remains were no longer of archeological interest, such as isolated or fragmentary finds without firm archeological context, and had been studied to the level appropriate to their ability to provide information that was important to history and prehistory.[41] In another response, Keel explained that federal title and restrictions on reburial may also extend to human remains recovered from state or private lands as part of projects paid for with federal funds.[42]

Response to Keel's interpretation of the federal role in the reburial process was quick and clearly organized. During the spring of 1985, Secretary of the Interior Donald Hodel received letters taking issue with Keel's interpretation from American Indians Against Desecration, the International Indian Treaty Council, the National Congress of American Indians, the Texas Indian Commission, and the Native American Rights Fund. When asked by a reporter how best to resolve the differences between scientists and the Indian community, Keel recommended more rational discussion and less emotion. "What makes it difficult in dealing with this," Keel said, "are the half-truths, innuendoes and disparaging remarks that are made."[43]

Rogers's performance standards for fiscal year 1990 included a requirement to review and revise the department's policy concerning human remains and associated funerary artifacts. He directed his staff to research the legal constraints on repatriation. He also planned three meetings with selected participants, one in Washington and two elsewhere in the country. He was particularly concerned about the attitude of the archeological community. "Get message out to archeologists to <u>kool</u> it," noted NPS Assistant Director Rowland Bowers at a meeting with Rogers, "don't get polarized."[44]

As word of the new Smithsonian policy spread in the fall of 1989, similar discussions were also occurring outside of Washington. A draft press release prepared for National Park Service (NPS) Southwest Regional Director John Cook drew a scathing response from some of his staff. The draft quoted Cook as saying that repatriation had not been an issue for the NPS in the Southwest Region because

> Indian skeletal remains have for years been quietly re-interred by National Park Service archeologists and staff. We have never stockpiled skeletal remains and in fact have very little in storage. Whenever possible, we have placed skeletal materials back in the area of removal, not because reinterment was policy driven but because it was the right thing to do. On the issue of reburial, I'm pleased to report the Southwest is ahead of the curve.[45]

When the draft was circulated for comment, NPS archeologist Walter Wait took issue not only with some of the supporting facts but with the primary contention that the NPS was reinterring human remains on a daily basis. He described the draft as inaccurate and poorly structured and suggested that its release would only harm the region's credibility.[46]

The final press release, dated September 27, 1989, retreated from Cook's earlier statements.[47] The region's policy now focused on ensuring that skeletal materials in the care of the NPS are treated in a respectful and sensitive manner. Cook indicated that several upcoming national meetings would provide an opportunity to discuss the handling, storage, and disposition of human remains. A handwritten note from one Southwest Region staffer accompanying the draft press release stated, "We had a big flap over this. Cook is really POed."[48]

Other NPS staff grew concerned about the disposition of the Smithsonian collections. One was Robert Heyder, superintendent of Mesa Verde National Park in southwestern Colorado. In a November 1, 1989, memorandum to Rocky Mountain Regional Director Lorraine Mintzmeyer, Heyder recommended exploring the possibility of having certain collections that had originated at the park returned from the Smithsonian.[49] Of particular concern to Heyder were the human remains and associated funerary objects collected by Dr. Jesse Fewkes between 1907 and 1921. "Given the apparently uncertain future of the human remains and grave goods presently at the Smithsonian, we would strongly recommend the return of the Mesa Verde material at this time."

Mintzmeyer referred Heyder's memorandum to NPS Director John Ridenour on November 21, 1989.[50] "Conversations with the Division of Anthropology (in Washington) emphasize there is Service-wide concern for the potential loss of information," Mintzmeyer wrote, "especially from the myriad of unstudied collections housed in the National Museum." She also recognized the issue as extremely sensitive and thought that a service-wide approach should be developed to insure consistency in dealing with the National Museum and to minimize the associated tumult. "We require direction from you," she stated. Ridenour referred the issue to Jerry Rogers, who passed it on to his division chiefs and requested a meeting to discuss the issue.[51]

In December 1989, John E. Echohawk, executive director of the Native American Rights Fund, wrote to the organization's supporters. He thanked them for their assistance in what he characterized as a landmark victory for the return of Indian bodies and associated burial goods from the Smithsonian Institution. "But encouraging as the Smithsonian victory is," he continued, "the fight is far from over because the National Park Service, which holds thousands of Indian remains, clings stubbornly to the ethnocentric and insulting notion that the bodies and associated burial goods of Native Americans, as opposed to other Americans are 'archeological resources'—rather than human beings with kin who desperately want to rebury them with respect and dignity." Echohawk accused the NPS of not even knowing how many human remains were in its collections and of exhibiting human remains at its museums. "In stark contrast to the progress we're making with some museums and universities, the

Park Service arrogantly continues to behave as if the bodies and funerary offerings of our ancestors are federal property."[52] In a December 22, 1989, letter, Walter Echo-Hawk formally requested information on how many dead Indian bodies were under the custody or control of the NPS.

At a January 25, 1990, meeting of the NPS regional directors in San Antonio, Rogers spoke about his preoccupation with the service's relationship with Native Americans. Tribal concerns regarding culturally appropriate treatment of human remains and funerary objects was a particular worry. He specifically mentioned recent publications from the Native American Rights Fund and announced he was presently sorting through and analyzing their charges and collecting information to respond factually and thoroughly. He predicted revisions of the Departmental Guidelines for the Disposition of Archeological and Historical Human Remains would be distributed for comment by March 1990. He asked to know as soon as possible of any exhibits of human remains and any plans that were being made to change them. "We must avoid taking any steps that might be interpreted as circumventing provisions of existing legislation," Rogers concluded, and, in an apparent reference to the recent letters from Heyder and Mintzmeyer, added, "particularly the National American Indian Museum Act, even if we believe Park Service materials in the Smithsonian might be affected by repatriation requests."[53]

Despite Roger's admonition, some National Park Service officials continued to consider the possible implications of impending repatriation legislation. Some Native American human remains quietly disappeared from museum shelves.[54]

The National Dialogue on Museum/ Native American Relations

The No-Name Alliance met in Washington, DC, on February 27, 1990.[55] The alliance had learned of the imminent release of the final report of the National Dialogue on Museum/Native American Relations and was concerned about the effect it might have on the ongoing negotiations regarding the reburial of Native American human remains (see figure 5.1).

In fact, the Panel for a National Dialogue on Museum/Native American Relations completed its final report the next day. The idea for the panel dated back to the July 29, 1988, hearing of the Senate Select Committee on Indian Affairs on Melcher's S. 187, when Michael J. Fox of the Heard Museum in Phoenix, Arizona, suggested an immediate and intense

Figure 5.1 Notes (using the mind-map technique) from the February 27, 1990, meeting of the No-Name Alliance. American Anthropological Association Records, Series 4, Subseries 1, Box 164, Folder 1 of 2, "AAA Reburial Commission, Nancy O. Lurie, Chair, 1989–1991," National Anthropological Archives, Smithsonian Institution.

year-long dialogue between museums and Indian tribes on the identification, use, care, and ownership of Native American materials. On December 12, 1988, the Heard Museum hosted representatives of various Arizona tribes, museums, and universities at a day-long meeting to plan the dialogue.[56] The panel was convened for the first time on April 1, 1989, at the Heard Museum, and subsequently met three times.[57] The panel consisted of fourteen representatives of museums, universities, Indian tribes, and regional and national Native American organizations from around the country, although three representatives were unable to attend some or all of the meetings. Paul Bender, dean and professor of law at Arizona State University, served as the panel facilitator. At the meeting on April 1, 1989, Bender opined that it was a golden opportunity when those who know the most are given the opportunity to affect public policy. "We hope to see more than a dialogue," he offered, "we would like to see a solution."[58] Participants tried a number of techniques to facilitate dialogue, including discussion of a list of key issues, formulation of a proposed statement of good practice for museums, and use of a case study. In addition to the fourteen participants, six congressional staffers attended one or more of the meetings. "That was where an awful lot of change happened," concluded Marie Howard, who represented Congressman Udall at the dialogue meetings.[59] "The three major groups—the Indian tribal representatives, the archeologists, and the museum people—came in wanting nothing to do with each other. Then the participants sat in a circle and discussed different issues for hours on end. The positions began to soften." Patricia Zell, representing the Senate Select Committee on Indian Affairs, was initially surprised to see the respect, deference, and collegiality exhibited among the participants. One afternoon, however, the group adjourned for boxed lunches on the Heard Museum grounds. "I happened to sit with a group of scientists who did not know that I was from the Senate Committee on Indian Affairs, so they were talking quite freely. I saw that behind the superficial decorum," she continued "there were still very deeply seated attitudes about these issues."[60]

The pace of negotiations slowed in late 1989 as the Native American representatives quietly brokered a separate repatriation agreement with the Smithsonian over the NMAI Act (see Chapter 4). "They were surprised by that," recalled Suzan Harjo of the reaction of museum and archeology panelists to the Santa Fe agreement, "and were sort of knocked off their thrones a bit."[61] The drafting group finally met at the Heard Museum on February 9, 1990. According to some, all of the participants orally agreed on the application of internationally understood human rights principles to the repatriation of Native American human remains. This turned out not to be the case. "We Indian participants were saddened, but not surprised, that three of the non-Indian scientists subsequently went back on their word."[62] At one point, Lynne Goldstein, Michael Moratto, and Douglas Ubelaker considered walking out of the drafting session, but eventually they stayed and committed their own sense of frustration in a separate memorandum.[63] Goldstein asked that the SAA's name be removed from the report.[64]

The panel's final report contained six specific recommendations. Three were unanimously supported by the panel members: (1) the disposition and treatment of Native American human remains, funerary objects, religious objects, and object of national or cultural patrimony should be governed by respect for the human rights of Native peoples and for the values of scientific research and public education; (2) all human remains must at all times be treated with respect; and (3) the repatriation standards recommended in the report should be judicially enforceable. Nine of the eleven attending panelists recommended that the wishes of the culturally affiliated Native American group be followed regarding the disposition of human remains and other materials. Eight of the attending panelists recommended that the disposition of culturally unidentifiable human remains be determined in cooperation with and with the permission of Native nations. The same eight considered federal legislation necessary to implement the panel's recommendations. Goldstein, Moratto, and Ubelaker explained that their footnotes in the final report "reflect our attempts to argue for equality."[65]

On March 1, 1990, several members of the panel presented their final report to the chair and vice chair of the Senate Select Committee on Indian Affairs at a press conference in Washington, DC. Paul Bender heralded the final report as a "great compromise."[66] "Clearly, this legislation is inevitable," announced McCain, adding that he planned to hold hearings and markup on repatriation legislation as soon as possible.[67] Privately, Inouye indicated that expanding the provisions of the Smithsonian compromise and the panel's recommendations to private institutions would not be easy. "The Indians have waited a long time for this," he concluded, "they can wait another year."[68] After the press conference, Loretta Neumann, representing the SAA, spoke with panel members Paul Bender, Michael Fox, and Peter Welch to explain that the archeological community could not support the extreme position outlined in the report. Bender and Welch responded that the practical effect would not be as bad as was feared because "Indians are reasonable to work with and they care about science too, etc. etc." Neumann argued that this was an issue not of personalities but of law. "People on both sides need more assurance that decisions would be made that truly reflect a balanced approach."[69]

Dan Monroe, vice president of the American Association of Museums, later characterized the dialogue findings as achieving a modicum of progress toward guiding repatriation principles, but they were not the breakthrough for some hoped for. An unintended consequence of the dialogue was the shocking realization by some in the museum community that the Indians were right.[70] "To me and to, at first, a comparatively small number of museum professionals," Monroe recalled, it was becoming progressively clear "that the ethical position museums had sought to defend was very questionable with respect, especially, to Native American human remains."[71]

The SAA leadership of considered the panel report a somewhat mitigated disaster. "If Goldstein, Moratto, and Ubelaker had actually walked out, the remaining panel members would have presented the report as a unanimous report, and it would have been even more of a disaster."[72]

McCain's S. 1980

Members of the No-Name Alliance requested a meeting with Senator Inouye[73] and circulated a draft set of general principles derived from the policy statements of its constituent organizations.[74] On May 2, Inouye met with representatives of the SAA, the American Association of Museums, the National Conference of State Historic Preservation Officers, and the American Anthropological Association, along with Lurline McGregor, Steve Heeley, and Patricia Zell of the Senate Select Committee on Indian Affairs staff. Inouye explained that S. 1980 was modeled on the repatriation provisions of the NMAI Act. He assumed it would be acceptable to everyone. Representatives of the various organizations objected to the definitions of cultural patrimony and Indian tribe, the burden of proof, committee makeup, and the cost and complexity of the inventories. Inouye bridled at first. He didn't think the bill would affect very much and would be limited to remains less than 150 years. When Pru Rice pointed out that under the current bill 5,000-year-old unaffiliated remains could be subject to return, Inouye scoffed, saying that he couldn't imagine anyone claiming something 5,000 years old. When Inouye stressed that some places are sacred and should not be dug up, Neumann responded that the SAA would agree with that. Inouye seemed surprised. Neumann noted that the SAA really wasn't that far apart from what Inouye was saying.[75]

Though the meeting with Inouye ended on an upbeat note, Neumann was extremely disheartened when she read the revised version of S. 1980. In the new draft, the name was changed to the Native American Graves Protection and Repatriation Act with Senator McCain now identified as the sponsor. Patricia Zell ascribes the shift in authorship to the availability of staff time. "Senator McCain's staff saw an opportunity, something that could use more attention, and they picked up the ball."[76] "The direction we got as staff from both Inouye and McCain was these are not partisan issues," recalls McCain staffer Eric Eberhard.[77] "This is nonpartisan work, and they expected the two staffs to work together on everything."

One of the new features of McCain's draft was an extended set of findings outlining the reasons for consideration of federal legislation to deal with the issues of Native American grave protection and repatriation.[78] Similar findings had originally appeared in Udall's H.R. 1646 but had not been incorporated into the earlier version of S. 1980.

Like Inouye's earlier version, the McCain draft did not include a definition of human remains, and the definitions of funerary object[79] and cultural patrimony[80] were largely unchanged. However, the definition of sacred object was significantly changed. Its earlier definition required that such items currently be imbued with sacred character or have ceremonial or ritual importance in the practice of a Native American religion.[81] McCain's redraft deleted the sacred character requirement and rephrased the remaining requirements so that evidence of either present or past use of such items in religious ceremony was sufficient.[82]

The McCain draft redefined "Indian tribe" to mean any tribe, band, nation, or other organized group or community of Indians, including any Alaska Native village, that is recognized as eligible for the special programs and services provided by the United States to Indians because of their status as Indians.[83] The revised definition represented a close paraphrase of the definition of Indian tribe in the Indian Self-Determination and Education Assistance Act. In addition, the new definition explicitly included Native American groups recognized by the state in which they are located. The term "Native Hawaiian organization" was also amended to require such groups also to have expertise in Native Hawaiian affairs and explicitly included the Office of Hawaiian Affairs and Hui Malama I Na Kupuna O Hawai'i Nei.[84] A new term—"Native American group"—

was added to include both Indian tribes and Native Hawaiian organizations.[85]

The term "cultural affiliation," which had been used in the text of the original version of S. 1980 without further explanation, was defined in McCain's redraft to mean a direct relationship between a present-day Native American group and an identifiable historic or prehistoric Indian tribe or Native Hawaiian group that indicated a continuity of group identity from the earlier to the present-day group.[86]

The excavation section, previously included as the final section in Inouye's November 21, 1989, bill, was moved forward and placed immediately after the definition section and retitled "ownership."[87] The first part of the Inouye's original bill specified that any Native American human remains, funerary objects, or sacred objects excavated pursuant to a federal permit must be repatriated to a Native American group or member that asserts an interest in the items.[88] This was divided into two parts and expanded in McCain's draft. The first part stipulated that Native American human remains, funerary objects, sacred objects, or cultural patrimony excavated or discovered after the date of enactment of the act must be disposed of according to the wishes of (1) the heirs, or (2) the Indian tribe of which the objects originated or an appropriate Native Hawaiian organization.[89] This part appears to have applied to excavations or discoveries on private and state lands as well as those on federal and tribal lands. The second part applied only to Native American human remains, funerary objects, sacred objects, and cultural patrimony found on federal or tribal lands.[90] "Federal lands" was defined as any lands controlled or owned by the federal government.[91] Tribal lands include all lands within the exterior boundaries of an Indian reservation for which legal title is held by the United States in trust; all dependent Indian communities, including lands conveyed to Alaska Native corporations; and all lands administered for the benefit of Native Hawaiians pursuant to the Hawaiian Homes Commission Act of 1920.[92] In McCain's redraft, any Native American human remains or funerary object for whom the heirs could not be ascertained and any sacred object or objects of cultural patrimony were to be considered owned by a Native American group based on (1) the group's jurisdiction over the reservation land on which the item was discovered; (2) the group's aboriginal occupation of the area from which the item was discovered; (3) origination of the funerary object, sacred object, or cultural patrimony from the group; or (4) the group's cultural affiliation with the item.[93] The secretary of the Interior was now directed to consult with the review committee instead of with Native American governmental and religious leaders in developing regulations for the repatriation of items excavated under the authority of federal law or permit.[94]

Another new subsection was inserted making it unlawful to sell, use for profit, or transport from one state to another for sale or profit human remains or funerary objects without the express written consent of the heirs[95] or sacred objects, cultural patrimony, or funerary objects for which the heirs could not be ascertained without proof of legal title.[96] Any person who knowingly violated or counseled, procured, solicited, or employed another person to violate the ownership provisions could be fined up to $10,000 and imprisoned for up to one year. A second violation could earn the offender a $100,000 fine and five years in jail.[97] A new part also made it clear that Native American groups could relinquish title to Native American human remains, funerary objects, sacred objects, and cultural patrimony found at any time on federal or tribal land, or on state or private land after the date of enactment of the act.[98]

McCain made several important changes to the inventory requirements of S. 1980. The purpose of the inventory was changed from determining the tribal origin of objects to determining their cultural affiliation,[99] though such determinations were still to be based on the best available scientific and historical documentation.[100] The time period allowed to compile the inventory was lengthened from slightly over two years to five years.[101] A new provision allowed a federal agency or museum that had made a good faith effort but was unable to complete its inventory to appeal to the secretary of the Interior for an extension of the deadline.[102] Notification of the affected Native American group was now required within six months of inventory completion, instead of three months in the original bill.[103] The notice was required to list each item that more likely than not either originated from or was culturally affiliated with the Native American group.[104] The museum or federal agency was also to send a copy of such notices to the secretary of the Interior, who was required to publish them in the *Federal Register*.[105]

Use of "Native American group" to refer collectively to Indian tribes and Native Hawaiian organizations resulted in a reduction in the number of repatriation sections. The federal requirements remained largely unchanged, except that they were now required to consult with the requesting Native American group to determine the place and manner of delivery of items to be repatriated.[106] In addition, federal agencies were now also required to prove by a preponderance of the evidence that they had legal title to remains or objects in their possession or control.[107] McCain's proposed substitute amendment would have also allowed federal agencies or museums to retain possession of human remains, funerary objects, sacred objects, or objects of cultural patrimony that are indispensable for the completion of a specific scientific study, the outcome of which would be of major benefit to the United States.[108] Such items were to be returned to the appropriate Native American group no later than ninety days after the study was completed.[109] Any museum that failed to comply with the inventory and repatriation section of the bill would not be eligible to receive any federal grants until it had complied.[110]

In addition to the duties already specified in the earlier version, McCain's proposed substitute also charged the review committee with compiling an inventory of unidentifiable human remains in the possession or control of each federal agency and museum, recommending specific actions for developing a process for their disposition, and implementing a process for the disposition of these remains.[111] A preliminary report on the inventory of unidentifiable human remains was to be submitted to Native American groups and Congress within three years of the committee's establishment, with a final report to be submitted to Congress and the president within six years.[112]

The SAA quickly began drafting its comments on the McCain version of S. 1980, suggesting that it went beyond the intent as described by Senator Inouye at their May 2 meeting.[113] Of particular concern was the provision directing the review committee to compile an inventory of unidentifiable human remains and recommend specific actions for developing and implementing a process for their disposition.[114] "We cannot live with this subsection. By including implementation of the return of unaffiliated remains, this creates an enormous task that has not been adequately considered. If this must be dealt with, let's do it later, and get on with the business of dealing with the affiliated remains about which there is so much immediate concern."

In a May 11, 1990, letter, the Friends Committee on National Legislation urged Congress to consider the various bills thus far introduced to deal with repatriation issues. "While there are those in our contemporary society who feel no hesitation in employing human remains for the purposes of scientific research," the letter read, "this is clearly not common to all Americans. This being the case, we believe that respect for a diversity of cultures mandates that when the will of the individual in question is not known, this decision should be left to the affiliated culture or religious group." The letter was signed by representatives of the American Baptist Churches, American Ethical Union, Baptist Joint Committee on Public

Affairs, Church of the Bretheren, Church Women United, Evangelical Lutheran Church in America, Friends Committee on National Legislation, Episcopal Church, Jesuit Social Ministries, Mennonite Central Committee, Presbyterian Church, Unitarian Universalist Association of Congregations, United Church of Christ, and the United Methodist Church.[115]

Senate Hearing

On May 14, 1990, the Senate Select Committee on Indian Affairs heard testimony on the two bills that were under consideration by the Senate. In attendance were committee Chair Inouye, sponsor of the original version of S. 1980, the Native American Repatriation and Cultural Patrimony Act; committee Vice Chair McCain, sponsor of S. 1021, the Native American Grave and Burial Protection Act and proposed sponsor of an amended version of S. 1980, to be called the Native American Graves Protection and Repatriation Act (NAGPRA); and Senator Kent Conrad.

McCain opened the hearing by acknowledging that repatriation was charged with high emotions in both the Native American community and the museum community. He identified two milestones of the past year in efforts to bring both sides closer to agreement. The first was the recently completed National Dialogue on Museum/Native American Relations. The second was President Bush signing into law the NMAI Act, which included provisions requiring the Smithsonian Institution to repatriate Native American human remains and funerary objects currently in its collections. McCain explained that he was very interested in hearing from the witnesses regarding his proposed substitute amendment to S. 1980, NAGPRA.[116]

The witness list for the hearing consisted of six panels representing the Department of the Interior, the National Dialogue on Museum/Native American Relations, the Native American community, and the museum community.

Jerry Rogers again represented the Department of the Interior. Much had happened in the three months since Rogers had appeared before the Senate Subcommittee on Public Lands, National Parks, and Forests regarding Fowler's bills, S. 1578 and S. 1579. On February 28, 1990, the same day the final report of the Panel for a National Dialogue on Museum/Native American Relations was completed, Rogers responded to Walter Echo-Hawk's request for information regarding the number of Native American human remains under the custody or control of the National Park Service.[117] An attachment detailed the remains of 3,539 individuals at 59 different NPS facilities. Rogers met with Echo-Hawk and other Native American leaders on March 1, 1990.[118] Finally, on March 7, 1990, Rogers reported to the director of the NPS that the goal of reviewing and revising the department's policy concerning human remains and associated funerary artifacts had become unrealistic.[119] He explained that there had been a sudden and unforeseeable shift in the political framework within which the work was to be accomplished, due in part to Inouye's introduction of S. 1980. Until recently, Rogers explained, American Indian leaders appeared to be happy with the standard established by the NMAI Act, and the NPS had been moving toward a policy revision in accordance with that law. Many American Indian leaders now felt the NMAI standard was no longer enough. "It would be irresponsible for me to forge ahead with drafting and circulating a policy statement in these circumstances. It is going to be necessary to begin our formal consultation with Native Americans not with a draft of a new policy, but with a set of principles, perhaps even questions, from which we can evolve a draft policy."

In a telephone conversation the same day with Senior Anthropologist Muriel Crespi in the Anthropology Division, Rogers indicated that he was "ready to rebury as [a] matter of course."[120] Rogers proposed treating all human remains equally, dealing with Native American remains in the same way as the remains from other groups. He directed the Departmental Consulting Archeologist Frank McManamon to prepare a series of questions to solicit public comment on the Department's guidelines. Rogers explained that he was glad he had gotten involved in the issue and that it had been a learning experience for him. Crespi's notes of the conversation end: "a switch."

At a March 20, 1990, press conference, Secretary of the Interior Manuel Lujan Jr. announced that he was directing the NPS to develop a new policy statement and revise the existing departmental guideline to ensure a more sensitive treatment of archeological human remains and associated objects. "While recognizing the potential scientific value of such remains, the new policy and guideline will also affirm the right of Tribes and other Native American groups to determine the treatment afforded to remains and funerary objects that clearly are related to these Tribes or groups."[121] The secretary's press aide elaborated: "It's the secretary's personal conviction that this is the right thing to do in this situation."[122] Walter Echo-Hawk called the new policy "a nice gesture" but stressed that federal laws defining human remains found on federal land as archeological resources must be changed.[123]

Rogers was reluctant to testify at the May 14, 1990, Senate hearing if the administration's position was against S. 1980.[124] He ultimately did testify, explaining to the committee that the administration had yet to complete its review of McCain's proposed substitute amendment for S. 1980. He hoped that an interagency review would be completed by early summer.[125] Rogers also explained to the committee that the NPS was currently revising the departmental guidelines and predicted that consultations with Native Americans would require the balance of the year before the service would be prepared to draft a policy on this issue.[126] Later in the hearing, McCain took issue with Rogers's call for more consultation. "It seems to me that to go out and consult again all over Indian country on an issue on which there is clear consensus is a waste of time, and further outrages will be perpetuated."[127]

Under questioning by Inouye, Rogers explained that there was no single government-wide policy relating to the repatriation of human remains. Although each federal agency makes its own policy depending on applicable statutes, he acknowledged that in some cases there have been two general practices. He illustrated the first practice with an example from Custer Battlefield National Monument. Fragments of human bodies were recovered, most from the bodies of soldiers who had been killed in the fight and had been hastily buried a few days later. These fragments were studied to gain possible information and were then buried with honors at the monument. Rogers acknowledged that the same practice was not followed when dealing with Native American human remains.[128] "The white soldier gets buried with honors," Inouye later commented. "God knows what happens to the Indian collection. We now have an opportunity to undo this."[129] When McCain asked if a single government-wide policy on repatriation was needed, Rogers agreed, but suggested that the proposed revision to the Department of the Interior's guidelines might also be adopted by other federal agencies.[130] He stressed that the department's revised policy would make it clearer that "this is a human rights issue."[131] "I believe that a resolution that treats all human remains the same regardless of ethnic derivation should be one that is satisfactory to all parties."[132]

When questioned by McCain about the National Dialogue on Museum/Native American Relations, Rogers identified the disposition of culturally unidentifiable human remains as the one big question yet to be resolved. He postulated that a reasonable accommodation would be reached once it was agreed that all segments of the population should be treated the same. "We should deal with people as people, living or dead."[133]

Senator Conrad followed up with a question about what tribes intended to do with repatriated human remains. He asked, "It is my understanding that the tribes' position is that they would like to have the remains returned to them for proper burial. Is that your understanding of the tribes' position?"[134] Rogers responded by stressing that there was broad spectrum of possible outcomes. Many tribes want human remains reburied in a manner that would allow continued deterioration. Others do not want materials returned at all. Still others are willing to have materials returned to a tribal museum under curatorial circumstances. "I think that once we have gotten past the very basic point of treating everyone the same, we will be able to come to some very reasonable accommodations on many of these points."[135]

"We should not deal with one segment of our population differently than we deal with another segment of the population, living or dead," Rogers concluded.[136]

The second panel consisted of two members of the National Dialogue on Museum/Native American Relations: Paul Bender and Willard Boyd. Bender, an attorney and trustee of the Heard Museum, had served as facilitator of the dialogue panel. In his testimony, he recalled that if one had asked the members of the panel whether they could reach agreement on most of the issues, the answer would have been no. The panel members perceived that they had vastly differing views. However, it turned out that there was an amazing amount of agreement.[137] Bender considered the principle of tribal determination of the disposition of culturally affiliated materials to be the central substantive recommendation of the National Dialogue on Museum/Native American Relations. This recommendation derived from the recognition of repatriation as a civil rights issue. "It is a civil rights issue because museums only have this material as a result of human rights violations."[138]

Bender went on to focus on three primary aspects of McCain's proposed substitute amendment for S. 1980. He recommended that the present language be modified to emphasize the range of options existing between the logical extremes of reburial and leaving the items in museum collections.[139] Second, he took issue with the provision of the bill allowing a museum or federal agency to retain a cultural item if it could prove "legal title" to the item, on the grounds that this undefined term in effect might remit determinations of ownership to inconsistent state property laws.[140] Last, Bender was troubled by the new provision that would allow museums and federal agencies to retain items necessary for the completion of a scientific study considered of major benefit to the United States.[141]

The second member of the National Dialogue on Museum/Native American Relations to testify was Willard Boyd, president of the Field Museum of Natural History. Boyd fully subscribed to portions of the dialogue report relating to the role and responsibilities of museums and the exchange of information between museums and Native American groups. He also agreed to the need for an impartial process to resolve disagreements. However, he objected to what he called an ex post facto change of the substantive law applicable at the time Native American remains and cultural objects came into the possession of museums and the law applicable to museum fiduciary duties respecting the stewardship of collections.[142] "I believe that all legal standards should be applicable," he continued, "including the Native American customary law and also the important standards that apply to museum stewardship such as fiduciary duties and the like."[143]

Boyd had not had time to review the proposed substitute amendment for S. 1980. However, he thought that any legislation should contain a three-step process to encourage mutually agreeable solutions, provide an impartial administrative tribunal to resolve differences, and institute judicial review of the administrative tribunal's decisions to provide finality and satisfy constitutional requirements.[144] He cautioned against legislation regarding the appropriate burden of proof, fearing it would again result in ex post facto alterations of preexisting substantive rights.[145] He also felt that the term "cultural patrimony" was overly broad.[146] Finally, Boyd recommended a case-by-case approach to repatriation over what he called a "doomsday date" approach to keep costs as low as possible.[147]

A letter from panel participants Lynne Goldstein and Michael Moratto was also included in the hearing report. "In the recent revision of S. 1980," they wrote,

> we note that several statements, phrases, and conclusions from the Report of the Panel of the National Dialogue on Museum/Native American Relations have been added as part of the Bill. As participants in this Dialogue, we are concerned that these items—particularly those concerning unaffiliated human remains—have been added without fully understanding the context of the Panel's deliberations.[148]

Goldstein and Moratto asked that the section of S. 1980 dealing with unaffiliated remains be removed.

Two panels included witnesses representing various Native American organizations. Most were supportive of the proposed substitute amendment. McCain specifically questioned several witnesses regarding the appropriateness of particular definitions. Referring to the definition of Native Hawaiian organization, McCain explained that Inouye had encouraged the Native Hawaiian community to get together to decide who should be the lead organization to receive remains and that under a compromise he named both the Office of Hawaiian Affairs (OHA) and Hui Malama I Na Kupuna O Hawai'i Nei. McCain asked Lydia Mai'oho, chair of the OHA Native Hawaiian Preservation Task Force, if that compromise was satisfactory. "That's agreeable," Clarence Ching, one of the OHA trustees quickly interjected. "Congress should follow the lead of the State of Hawaii in designating one lead organization. Having two organizations that are sometimes in competition may be troublesome and create more problems."[149] Representatives of Hui Malama I Na Kupuna O Hawai'i Nei did not appear before the committee. In written testimony dated two weeks after the hearing, the organization's president, Edward Kanahele, emphasized the need for a broad interpretation of the definition of Native Hawaiian organization "since we have no recognized sovereign government or entity separate from the State of Hawai'i."[150]

McCain also mentioned that some were concerned about the definition of sacred object. "Sacredness is always defined by the practitioners and the religious leaders," responded Suzan Harjo, president and executive director of the Morning Star Institute. "It is self-definition. There is no religion that would have anything identified for it as to its sacred nature outside itself."[151] Kanahele's written testimony indicated that conferees at a recent seminar on Native Hawaiian burials had rejected the notion of defining traditional religious leaders.[152]

Edward Lone Fight, chairman of the Three Affiliated Tribes in North Dakota and speaking on behalf of the National Congress of American Indians, objected to use of the term "inventory" in Section 5 of the proposed substitute amendment on the grounds that it could be misconstrued as study. "We do not want any further study [of the bones]."[153] Kanahele argued that no osteological analysis should be conducted as part of the inventory of any prehistoric remains removed from the Hawaiian Islands.[154] Lone Fight also objected to allowing museums and federal agencies five years to complete their inventories, with the possibility of additional deadline extensions, proposing instead a two-year deadline with a maximum ninety-day extension.[155] Written comments from Echo-Hawk questioned the inclusion of federal agencies under the repatriation provisions outlined in Section 5(c) because they were already covered under Section 5(b).[156] He also recommended the term "legal title" be clarified in Section 5(c) to ensure that such title could not be established solely on the basis of the Antiquities Act or ARPA.[157]

Cecil Antone, director of the Physical Resources Department for the Gila River Indian Community, recommended that Section 6(a) be changed to stipulate that review committee members be selected by the Senate Select Committee on Indian Affairs and not the secretary of the Interior.[158] Lone Fight suggested that the committee should include no archeologists or anthropologists, only Indian people associated with the reinterment issue.[159] Harjo recommended that the review committee section be rethought "especially in light of what has happened with the appointments and the interpretation of the repatriation section of the new museum law over at the Smithsonian, where Indian people are now faced with a stacked deck."[160] Harjo recognized the importance of the inventories required by the proposed amendment in both achieving the goals of repatriation and educating the public. "If some appropriations are required for it," concluded Harjo, "so be it, but it shouldn't be at the level that would overburden the act and overwhelm us to the point of a veto threat on the appropriation point. This is not the 'National Museums Relief Act.'"[161]

Jerry Flute, assistant director of the Association of American Indian Affairs, was accompanied by Dr. Emery Johnson, assistant surgeon general (retired) with the U.S. Public Health Service. In response to a question from McCain, Flute concurred with Jerry Rogers's earlier suggestion that additional consultation would be needed prior to revising the Department of the Interior's repatriation policy. "To answer your question directly, senator, I think there ought to be more consultations. There need to be field hearings and there need to be field meetings in locations where elderly, traditional people, spiritual leaders can come and express their thoughts. Many tribal governments are not speaking on behalf of the traditional people," Flute concluded, "nor are they reflecting the views of the traditions of these people."[162]

Johnson introduced himself as a physician interested in the prevention, diagnosis, and treatment of disease in Indian people.[163] Flute had asked him to conduct a literature search at the National Library of Medicine. Johnson's review resulted in three primary points. First, he was unable to identify any recent studies of Native American human remains that had any potential to impact the health of Indian people. Second, he pointed out that tribal control and scientific research are not mutually exclusive, citing significant studies conducted by the Indian Health Service after it established the policy that no research would take place without the approval of both the individual involved and the local tribal government. "My final point is simply this," Johnson concluded. "I can't imagine the kind of benefit we might get from research on human remains that can compensate for the negative impact that this long-standing violation of human rights has had on the mental health of our American Indian and Alaskan Native communities."

McCain again raised the issue of timing. "I don't believe there's any need for another year," Johnson responded. "We've been talking about this for how many years now?"

"That's exactly my point," McCain interjected. He considered continued consultation on an issue on which there was clear consensus a waste of time. "I have never met a single [Native American] who said to me, 'Let's keep doing what we are doing on Native American remains.'"[164]

In summary, Echo-Hawk described McCain's proposed substitute amendment as combining the very best of S. 1980 with the very best of S. 1021. He felt that it took into account both the well-thought-out recommendations of the National Dialogue and the precedent that Congress established in 1989 with passage of the NMAI Act.[165] Echo-Hawk thought that the proposed substitute amendment—which he described as the most important civil rights legislation and human rights legislation for Native people since passage of the American Indian Religious Freedom Act in 1978—would accomplish three basic things: (1) grant needed legal protection for Indian graves; (2) allow Indians and Native people to bury their dead under specified repatriation guidelines and procedures; and (3) restore stolen and improperly acquired property to the rightful Native owner on request. "These are basic human rights, Mr. Chairman, and property rights which most Americans commonly take for granted. Sadly, this has never been the case for Native people."[166]

In subsequent questioning by Inouye, Echo-Hawk objected to Boyd's characterization of the proposed substitute amendment as an ex post facto law that would redefine the property rights of museums and federal agencies. Echo-Hawk felt that there was no legal basis to such claims because human remains are not property under the eyes of the common law, and funerary objects, which can be property, belong either to the person that furnished the grave to begin with or that person's descendants. "Therefore, if you return it to them, you are not interfering with anybody else's property right."[167] The same was true with regard to cultural patrimony that was very narrowly defined to that rare category of Native property that is inalienable by definition.

The next panel consisted of representatives of several national museums and scientific organizations. Tom Livesay, director of the Museum of New Mexico, spoke on behalf of the American Association of Museums.[168] While arguing that museums have traditionally exercised social leadership by preserving Native American culture and helping change social attitudes toward Native Americans, Livesay acknowledged that many museums have undeniably failed to recognize emerging social values and professional standards with respect to Native American human remains. The written statement submitted by the American Association of Museums underscored this point. "Museums recognize that its duties to the public are not advanced by sacrificing respect for the human rights of Native people."[169]

Livesay stressed that the relationship between some museums and Indian tribes have grown and improved over the years. For example, in 1987 the Museum of New Mexico began a close examination of the need to retain Native American human remains in its collections. A new proactive policy placed responsibility within the museum to consult with Indian tribes regarding possible repatriation. As a result of ongoing consultation, the Pueblo of Zuni informed the museum in November 1989 that it wished the museum to continue as caretaker for human remains recovered from Zuni tribal lands.[170] Livesay urged that this type of relationship must be duplicated by museums in every part of the nation.

Regarding the proposed substitute amendment, Livesay reported that the museum community continues to be concerned over the definitions of sacred object, cultural patrimony, and legal title, as well as the expense of the proposed inventory and identification process. He suggested that the definition of sacred object be revised to focus exclusively on their use at the present time for religious or ceremonial purposes instead of including both present and past use as in the proposed definition.[171] Livesay suggested that the definition of cultural patrimony—particularly the suggestion that such items could not be alienated by any individual—would alter existing substantive property rights arising under state law and constitute a taking under the Fifth Amendment to the Constitution.[172] Livesay further objected to use of the term "legal title" in the proposed bill. He interpreted it to require a museum to prove it possesses legal title superior to all other potential claimants, instead of just to that of the Indian tribe making the particular claim.[173] He was also concerned about how overlapping and possibly conflicting tribal, state, and federal property laws would complicate such decisions.[174] Livesay identified three primary issues that must be considered in determining legal title and the associated rights to control and/or possess particular objects: (1) the type of object in question, (2) the relevant transactions and/or events that led to the object's current disposition, and (3) whether there are any relevant real property rights that may affect title. "All three of these issues become interrelated in any given analysis."[175] Last, Livesay thought that the requirement in Section 5 that museums identify all remains and objects to the fullest extent possible based on the best available scientific and historical data constituted an overwhelming burden, requiring massive amounts of time and money. "Even if these resources were available," he continued, "there is serious doubt as to whether there are presently enough physical anthropologists and other qualified scientists necessary to complete such a project within five years."[176]

Following his testimony, Inouye asked Livesay about the Museum of New Mexico's policy regarding the disposition of non–Native American human remains. "Mr. Chairman, our policy covers all ethnic groups."[177] He went on to describe ongoing discussions with the families of thirty-one Confederate soldiers recently discovered at the site of the battle of Glorietta Pass, northeast of Santa Fe.[178]

Philip Thompson, director of the Museum of Northern Arizona, was the next witness. He pointed out that although society values both the preservation of museum collections and the rights of Native Americans, "the superior right is that of intrinsic human remains."[179]

"We do not hold the grandparents of Anglos for study in significant numbers. Why should we do that to others?" he asked. "There is no answer."

"Why should we display the intimate physical remains of Native Americans," he continued, "when we do not do so with others? There is no answer."

"Why do we trivialize the religion, history, and origin belief of Native Americans when we do not do so with others? There is no answer."

"Why do we treat Native Americans differently at all from other Americans? There is no answer."

Thompson went on to outline four areas of discussion where both museums and Native American people have rights that must be accommodated. The first concerned the disposition of human remains. Thompson believed that all Native American remains should be returned to Indian tribes, with the condition that museums be provided a specific period of time to complete studies of remains not culturally associated with a specific Indian tribe.[180] On the issue of sacred and ceremonial objects, Thompson felt that the tribe that produced and used the item in religious practice has a dominant right to control the item. "I would not feel qualified to make decisions on what is or is not sacred," he continued. "That should be a Native American decision, and museums should honor that right, not argue it."[181] Thompson's third issue concerned the concept of cultural patrimony, which he felt should legitimately be in tribal control, though he was concerned that the term not be defined so broadly as to be impossible to implement. Last, he felt that when a museum has both the human remains and the associated funerary objects, the objects should be reinterred with the remains at a secure location. So-called unassociated funerary objects, where the museum does not possess the remains with which they were originally found, should stay with the museum in its role as keepers of a multicultural patrimony for all citizens.

When asked by McCain to estimate how much it would cost to complete the inventory, Thompson cited Dr. Ray Thompson from the Arizona State Museum's estimate of between $500 and $600 per individual. "It would have minimal impact, senator, assuming that funding was there for the inventory. Procedurally," he continued, "it would not be materially different than what we are already doing."[182]

Keith Kintigh, a professor of anthropology at Arizona State University, spoke on behalf of the SAA, with the additional support of the Archaeological Institute of America and the Society of Professional Archaeologists.[183] He recognized many strengths in the proposed substitute amendment. Kintigh strongly supported the inventory, identification, and notification provisions, which would provide Native American groups with the information necessary to prepare repatriation requests as well as a tremendous knowledge about their heritage. However, he also recognized that these activities would be costly and urged Congress to appropriate the necessary funds. Kintigh also supported using the concept of cultural affiliation to ensure that human remains and objects are returned to the appropriate group. "Anthropologists were painfully aware that repatriation may result in the loss of information about the past. However, we recognize that where a modern group has a reasonably clear cultural affiliation with human remains or objects, that group's desire to control its own material heritage should take precedence over the broader scientific and public interest."[184] Finally, Kintigh supported the ownership and sale provisions of the proposed substitute amendment. "Elimination of the market for these items by prohibiting their sale or purchase would do far more to protect Native American human remains than all other provisions of this bill and all other antiquities legislation combined."[185]

The last museum witness was Elizabeth Tatar, chairperson of the Anthropology Department at the Bishop Museum in Honolulu. She described the ongoing repatriation efforts at the museum, including repatriation of 375 Hawaiian burials with another 250 currently in the process of being released. She pointed out that of the approximately 2,590 Hawaiian human remains in the Bishop Museum collections, 1,230 belong to the Department of Defense and the National Park Service.[186] Senator Mc-Cain was particularly interested in how much the Bishop Museum's repatriation efforts had cost. According to a detailed cost estimate submitted after the hearing,[187] minimum costs, including preparation of a list of the remains, summary of past research information, analysis by a physical anthropologist, and preparation for shipping, ranged from $70 to $220 per individual. Additional services, such as metrical, morphological, and pathological examination; DNA extraction and analysis; comprehensive ethnographic and historical research; preparation of burial materials—including *tapa* and *lauhala* woven caskets—could add another $1,000 per individual.

Lydia Mai'oho, chairperson of the Native Hawaiian Historic Preservation Task Force and curator of the Hawaiian Royal Mausoleum, was particularly concerned about two collections of human remains in the possession of the Bishop Museum.[188] The first were the remains of two Hawaiian chiefs—Lilio and his great-grandson Lonoikamakahiki, famous ruling chiefs of the fifteenth and sixteenth centuries. On death, the two chiefs' bodies were believed to have been encased in separate basketry containers, called *ka'ai*, and placed in mausoleums on the Island of Hawaii. In 1828–1829, Regent and Premier Ka'ahumanu ordered their removal and Christian burial in a secluded cave, along with the remains of thirty other named chiefs. In 1858, all of the remains were transferred to the Royal Tomb on the grounds of Ioloni Palace on the Island of Oahu. The dampness of the Royal Tomb resulted in some deterioration of the basketry containers, precipitating Prince Kuhio to have them removed to the Bishop Museum in 1918.[189]

Mai'oho was also concerned about approximately 1,500 individuals recovered from the Mokapu Peninsula on the windward side of Oahu. Excavated at various times between 1915 and 1989, most of the remains were found in sand dune formations along the northeast end of the peninsula. The peninsula had been under the control of the U.S. Marine Corps since 1940.[190] The remains were stored at the Bishop Museum.

Following passage of the NMAI Act on November 28, 1989, Inouye and McCain began working to expand repatriation provisions to all the nation's museums and federal agencies. Inouye's initial version of S. 1980 was refined by McCain after issuance of the final report of the National Dialogue on Museum/Native American Relations on February 28, 1990. Both versions of S. 1980 applied to four specific categories of items. Human remains were still undefined. The term "funerary objects," which had been defined in a somewhat rudimentary fashion in earlier bills, was defined in much more precisely in both versions of S. 1980. A new category of cultural patrimony was introduced by Inouye and retained by McCain. The concept of sacred object remained the most controversial as it had since Melcher's earliest efforts. The Inouye definition required that such items currently be imbued with sacred character or have ceremonial or ritual importance in the practice of a Native American religion. McCain's redraft deleted the sacred character requirement and rephrased the remaining requirements so that evidence of either present or past use of such items in religious ceremony was sufficient.

The discovery and excavation of items after enactment was specifically addressed in both bills. Unlike Charles Bennett's earlier efforts, which relied on state law to permit excavations, both versions of S. 1980 provided an explicit set of criteria for the "ownership" of human remains, funerary objects, sacred objects, or objects of cultural patrimony. These criteria were bifurcated according to the land status of the discovery site. On private and state lands, items were to be disposed of according to the wishes of the heirs or governing body of the Indian tribe or Native Hawaiian organization of which the items originated. On federal and tribal lands, ownership was extended to include Native American groups with jurisdiction over the reservation on which the items were discovered, which aboriginally occupied the area of the discovery, or which were culturally affiliated with the items. Discovered or excavated items would not be considered archeological resources, nor could they be disturbed without the consent of the culturally affiliated Native American group.

A new section in McCain's version made it a criminal offense to sell, use for profit, or transport for sale or profit from a state to another state or from the United States to another country human remains or funerary objects without written consent or legal title.

In the wake of the Senate hearing, on June 19 the Smithsonian Institution convened a high-level group to begin formulating an institution-wide repatriation policy. Included were Secretary Robert Adams and Assistant Secretary Dean Anderson and the directors of the National Museum of Natural History, National Museum of American History, and National Museum of the American Indian. In a memorandum to the participants, assistant general counsel Lauryn Guttenplan Grant summarized the Smithsonian's current repatriation policy and practice.[191] Several of her comments were directed at the so-called McCain amendment to S. 1980. She highlighted the definitions of sacred object and object of cultural patrimony contained in the draft, concluding that both were overly broad. Grant recommended that the Smithsonian group consider developing a repatriation policy that has the support of the Indian community and work with American Association of Museums (AAM) to persuade the museum community to adhere to it for their own collections, to render federal legislation unnecessary.

> If, as some argue, it is too late for museums to come up with their own solutions, and federal legislation is inevitable, what should that legislation look like? Perhaps a working group should attempt to develop an alternative piece of legislation that we can live with in the event we fail to persuade Congress that legislation is unnecessary. Other interested parties like the AAM, SAA, and the natural history museums might have ideas and/or be willing to develop alternative legislation.

The next day, Secretary Adams and other Smithsonian officials met with representatives of the AAM, several large museums, and Indian leaders at the Smithsonian Castle in Washington. The announced purpose of the meeting was to begin to sensitively examine and review issues related to the repatriation of funerary, sacred, and other objects in the collections of museums nationwide.[192] Although Walter Echo-Hawk speculated that the meeting might eventually lead to constructive talks with the AAM and the Smithsonian,[193] the coalition had also heard the Smithsonian was threatening to recommend that the president veto any repatriation bill that might pass Congress unless the Smithsonian was exempt.[194] After the meeting, Echo-Hawk reported there was little discussion of legislative issues. "Interestingly," he added, "I did learn that the SI is or may become the 'lead agency' in responding to our bills for the Administration, which could be bad news."[195]

Unbeknownst to Echo-Hawk, the Smithsonian had already moved to assert its control of the federal position on repatriation. In early June, the

Office of Management and Budget authorized circulation of a draft letter for comment objecting to new repatriation legislation in the strongest of terms.[196] "We have a number of concerns," wrote Secretary Adams in the sixteen-page draft, "some of which are legal in nature, others of which are practical, and still others that appear to require further analysis by the Department of Justice. Thus," he concluded, "we must object to the proposal." The draft, intended for Senator Inouye, was apparently never sent.

CHAPTER SIX

A Defining Moment

On July 10, 1990, Representative Morris Udall (see figure 6.1) introduced a new bill as a compromise among the various bills already under consideration by the House.[1] The first section of H.R. 5237 provided the short title for the new bill—the Native American Graves Protection and Repatriation Act[2]—testament to the close connection between Udall's bill and the draft revision of S. 1980 of the same name being circulated by Senator John McCain.[3]

Udall's new bill applied to all federal agencies, defined to include any department, agency, or instrumentality of the United States (including the Smithsonian Institution),[4] as well as to all museums, defined to include any person, state, or local government agency (including any institution of higher education) that receives federal funds and has possession of or control over Native American human remains, funerary objects, sacred objects, or objects of inalienable communal property.[5] Congress clearly has the authority to require the disposition of property belonging to federal agencies,[6] and it also has broad authority to place conditions on the receipt of federal funds as long as such conditions are not used to induce an otherwise unconstitutional result.[7]

H.R. 5237 identified four categories of protected items, including Native American human remains, funerary objects, sacred objects, and objects of inalienable communal property. The new bill changed the way the term "Native American" was used, from a noun meaning any individual who is either a member of an Indian tribe or a Native Hawaiian or Alaska Native, which was used in earlier bills,[8] to an adjective meaning of

Figure 6.1 Representative Morris K. Udall (D-AZ), chairman of the Interior and Insular Affairs Committee, in his office, March 15, 1985. MS 325, Box 738, Folder 1, Udall Papers; Courtesy of University of Arizona Libraries, Special Collections.

or relating to a tribe, people, or culture that is indigenous to the United States.[9] Human remains were not defined. Udall introduced a new, simpler definition of funerary object, meaning an object that, as part of a death rite or ceremony of a culture, was intentionally placed with individual human remains, either at the time of burial or later.[10] The definition of sacred object was also simplified to include any item whose primary purpose when possessed by Native Americans was devoted to a traditional Native American religious ceremony or ritual and which may have a religious significance or function in the continued observance or renewal of such ceremony or ritual.[11] "Inalienable communal property" was defined as an item having historical, traditional, or cultural importance central to the Native American group or culture itself, which is associated with such group or culture, rather than property owned by an individual Native American, and which therefore could not be alienated, appropriated, or conveyed by any individual Native American regardless of whether the individual is a member of the Indian tribe or Native Hawaiian organization.[12]

The new bill authorized claims by lineal descendants, Indian tribes, and Native Hawaiian organizations. "Lineal descendant"—which replaced the term "heirs" used in McCain's version of S. 1980—was not defined in Udall's bill. "Indian tribes" were defined by explicit reference to the meaning given the term in Section 4 of the Indian Self-Determination and Education Assistance Act.[13] "Native Hawaiian organization" meant any organization that serves and represents the interests of Native Hawaiians, has as a primary purpose the provision of services to Native Hawaiians, and has expertise in Native Hawaiian affairs. The Office of Hawaiian Affairs and Hui Malama I Na Kupuna O Hawai'i Nei were explicitly identified as Native Hawaiian organizations.[14] As with McCain's version of S. 1980, Udall's bill used the term "Native American group" to identify both Indian tribes and Native Hawaiian organizations.[15]

Section 3—titled "ownership" as in McCain's version of S. 1980—outlined provisions for determining the ownership or right of control of any human remains, funerary objects, sacred objects, or objects of inalienable communal property found on federal or tribal land after the date of enactment. Federal land was defined to include any land, other than tribal lands, that were controlled or owned by the United States.[16] Udall's definition of "tribal lands" refined that introduced by McCain in his version of S. 1980 and included all lands within the exterior boundaries of any Indian reservation; all dependent Indian communities; any lands conveyed, or subject to an interim conveyance to, Alaska Native corporations pursuant to the Alaska Native Claims Settlement Act; and any lands administered for the benefit of Native Hawaiians pursuant to the Hawaiian Homes Commission Act of 1920 and Section 4 of Public Law 86-3.[17]

Subsection 3(a) established criteria for determining the ownership, control, or right of possession of any Native American human remains, funerary objects, sacred objects, or objects of inalienable communal property excavated or discovered on federal or tribal lands after the date of enactment. Udall's bill stipulated that ownership of all such items would be with, in priority order: (1) the lineal descendants, (2) the Indian tribe or Native Hawaiian organization on whose land the item was found, (3) the Indian tribe or Native Hawaiian organization that has the closest cultural affiliation with the item, or (4) the Indian tribe or Native Hawaiian organization that aboriginally occupied the area where the item was found.[18] Starting with McCain's definition of cultural affiliation from S. 1980,[19]

Udall provided a detailed explanation of the term as a reasonable relationship, established by a preponderance of the evidence, between a requesting Indian tribe or Native Hawaiian organization and the Native American from which the items derived, regardless of age or antiquity, which can be evidenced by geographical, kinship, biological, archeological, anthropological, linguistic, folkloric, oral traditional, historical, or other relevant information or expert opinion.[20] Udall further stipulated that in the absence of clear and convincing evidence to the contrary, there shall be a presumption of cultural affiliation for items obtained, discovered, excavated, or removed from an Indian tribe or Native Hawaiian organizations tribal lands or aboriginal territory.

Subsection 3(a) reflected an important change in the priority given to each criterion. When the similar criteria were initially introduced by Udall in H.R. 1646, priority had been assigned to the (1) heirs of the deceased, (2) Indian tribe on whose reservation the item was discovered, (3) Indian tribe that aboriginally occupied the area from which the item was discovered, or (4) Indian tribe that could show cultural affiliation with the item.[21] A similar priority order was included in McCain's S. 1021[22] and S. 1980.[23] H.R. 5237 shifted the emphasis from previous bills giving cultural affiliation priority vis-à-vis aboriginal occupation.

But what of situations where the ownership criteria might not apply? Subsection 3(b) provided a mechanism to resolve these situations by directing the secretary of the Interior to promulgate regulations regarding the disposition of such items, in consultation with the review committee and Native American groups.[24]

Subsection 3(c) provided new criteria to cover those situations where Native American human remains, funerary objects, sacred objects, or objects of inalienable communal property needed to be excavated or removed. Such items could only be excavated or removed from federal or tribal lands with the consent of the appropriate Native American group (if any) and following issuance of a permit issued under Section 4 of the Archaeological Resource Protection Act. Ownership and right of control of the disposition of such items would follow provisions of Subsection 3(a) and (b).[25]

Subsection 3(d) established procedures for situations in which such items were discovered on federal or tribal lands. Any person who knew or had reason to know that he had discovered an item covered by the act was required to notify the head of the federal entity with primary jurisdiction over the land in question and any appropriate Native American group. If the item was discovered during an activity such as construction, mining, logging, and agriculture, that activity would have to stop in the area of the discovery, and a reasonable effort would have to be made to protect the item. The activity could resume after a reasonable amount of time. The head of the federal entity with primary jurisdiction over the discovery area could delegate his or her responsibilities under this subsection to the secretary of the Interior.[26]

Subsection 3(e) clarified that nothing in Section 3 would prevent the governing body of any Indian tribe or Native Hawaiian organization from giving up their rights to any human remains, funerary objects, or sacred objects.[27] Objects of inalienable communal property were not included in this provision, although cultural patrimony had been included in a similar provision in the May 1990 version of S. 1980.[28]

Section 4 provided criminal penalties for illegal trafficking.[29] These provisions prohibited the sale, purchase, use for profit, or transport for sale or profit of any Native American human remains, funerary objects, sacred objects, or objects of inalienable communal property obtained in violation of the act. Fines were to be calculated in accordance with Title 18 of the U.S. Code, with imprisonment of up to one year for a first offense and up to five years for subsequent offenses.

The fifth section required any federal agency or museum that had possession or control over human remains, funerary objects, sacred objects, or objects of inalienable communal property to inventory the items, listing their geographic and cultural identity.[30] An inventory, consisting of a simple itemized list,[31] would summarize the results of consultation with tribal government and Native Hawaiian organizational officials and traditional religious leaders[32] and the best available scientific and historical documentation.[33] "Documentation" meant a review of existing records, inventories or catalogs, relevant studies, or other pertinent data for the limited purposes of determining the geographic origin, cultural affiliation, and basic facts surrounding acquisition and accession of the Native American human remains, funerary objects, sacred objects, and objects of inalienable communal property. The bill explicitly precluded interpretation of the term "documentation" or of the act itself to be an authorization for the initiation of new scientific studies of human remains, funerary objects, sacred objects, or objects of inalienable communal property, or other means of acquiring or preserving additional scientific information of such items.[34] Federal agencies and museums were to complete inventories no later than five years after the enactment of the statute.[35] Federal agencies and museums that made a good-faith effort to carry out the inventory requirements but had been unable to complete the process could appeal to the secretary of the Interior for an extension of the time requirement.[36] Within six months of completing the inventory, federal agencies and museums were to notify the affected Indian tribes and Native Hawaiian organizations.[37] The notice was to identify each Native American human remain, funerary objects, sacred object, and object of cultural patrimony and the circumstances surrounding their acquisition, and distinguish between those items that were clearly identifiable as to tribal origin and those that were not clearly identifiable as being culturally affiliated but which, given the totality of the circumstances surrounding their acquisition, were reasonably believed to be culturally affiliated with an Indian tribe or Native Hawaiian organization.[38] A copy of the notice was to be sent to the secretary of the Interior, who was required to publish it in the *Federal Register*.[39]

The sixth section provided for the return of human remains, funerary objects, sacred objects, or objects of inalienable communal property identified in the inventory process. Human remains and associated funerary objects were to be expeditiously returned on the request of a known lineal descendant or culturally affiliated Indian tribe or Native Hawaiian organization.[40] Likewise, funerary objects removed from a specific burial site as well as sacred objects and objects of inalienable communal property were to be expeditiously returned on the request of a known lineal descendant or culturally affiliated Indian tribe or Native Hawaiian organization.[41]

A burial site was defined as any natural or prepared physical location, whether located originally below, on, or above the surface of the Earth, into which as part of a death rite or ceremony of a culture individual human remains were deposited.[42] The return of human remains, funerary objects, sacred objects, or objects of inalienable communal property was to be accomplished in consultation with the requesting lineal descendant, Indian tribe, or Native Hawaiian organization to determine the place and manner of delivery.[43] Provisions of the National Museum of the American Indian Act would have been effectively amended by an explicit requirement that the Smithsonian Institution comply with the subsections on repatriation of nonassociated funerary objects, sacred objects, and objects of inalienable communal property and consultation regarding return of human remains, funerary objects, sacred objects, and objects of inalienable communal property.[44] All items were to be expeditiously returned on the request of a lineal descendent or culturally affiliated Indian tribe or Native Hawaiian organization, unless the item was indispensable for the completion of a specific scientific study, the outcome of which would be of major benefit to the United States.[45] Such items were to be returned no later than ninety days after the scientific study was completed.

Subsection 6(c) established the burden of proof for evaluating repatriation claims. On receipt of a request for return from a lineal descendant, Indian tribe, or Native Hawaiian organization, the burden of proof was initially on the federal agency or museum to prove by a preponderance of the evidence that it had right of possession to the item.[46] "Right of possession" was defined as possession obtained with the voluntary consent of an individual or group that had authority of alienation.[47] If the federal agency or museum could not prove it had right of possession to the item, the burden shifted to the lineal descendant, Indian tribe, or Native Hawaiian organization to prove by a preponderance of the evidence that the individual whose remains or funerary objects were being requested was an ancestor or was either culturally affiliated with or previously owned or possessed by the Indian tribe or Native Hawaiian organization.[48] To assist the lineal descendant, Indian tribe, or Native Hawaiian organization in meeting its burden of proof, the Federal agency or museum was required to share what information it possessed regarding the items.[49]

Any museum that failed to comply with the repatriation provisions would be ineligible for federal grants or other assistance during the period of noncompliance.[50]

Section 7 provided for establishment of a committee to monitor and review the inventory and return sections of the act.[51] The committee was to be comprised of seven members appointed by the secretary of the Interior, four from nominations received from Indian tribes, Native Hawaiian organizations, and traditional religious leaders.[52] Federal officials or employees could not be appointed. Members would serve without pay but would be reimbursed the daily rate of a federal employee (level GS-18) for time actually engaged in committee business.[53]

The committee was charged with eight specific tasks:

1. monitoring the inventory and identification process to ensure a fair, objective consideration of all available relevant information and evidence;[54]
2. reviewing findings related to the identity, cultural affiliation, or return of human remains, funerary objects, sacred objects, or objects of inalienable communal property;[55]
3. arbitrating disputes among lineal descendants, Indian tribes, and Native Hawaiian organizations;[56]

4. compiling an inventory of unidentifiable human remains and recommending specific actions for developing a process for the disposition of them;[57]
5. consulting with Indian tribes and Native Hawaiian organizations;[58]
6. consulting with the secretary of the Interior in the development of regulations;[59]
7. submitting an annual report to Congress on progress made and barriers encountered in implementing its responsibilities;[60] and
8. performing other related functions as assigned by the secretary.[61]

The inventory of culturally unidentifiable human remains and accompanying recommendations regarding their disposition were to be completed within six years of the date of enactment, in consultation with Indian tribes and Native Hawaiian organizations.[62] The secretary of the Interior was responsible for designating the committee chair, establishing committee rules and regulations, providing reasonable staff support necessary for the deliberations of the committee,[63] and ensuring that the committee had full access to Native American items and associated scientific and historic documents under review.[64]

Section 8 provided for grants to Indian tribes, Native Hawaiian organizations, and museums to assist in the inventory and return of human remains, funerary objects, sacred objects, and inalienable communal property.[65]

The ninth section established savings provisions. Nothing in the act could be construed to limit the authority of any federal agency or museum to return or repatriate Native American human remains, funerary objects, sacred objects, or objects of inalienable communal property to Indian tribes, Native Hawaiian organizations, or individuals, or enter into agreements with the consent of the culturally affiliated Indian tribe or Native Hawaiian organization as to the disposition of control such items.[66] Furthermore, nothing in the act could be construed to delay actions on repatriation requests that were pending on the date of enactment.[67] Nothing in the act could be construed to deny or otherwise affect access to any court.[68] Nothing in the act could be construed to limit any procedural or substantive right that might otherwise be secured to individuals or Indian tribes or Native Hawaiian organizations.[69]

The tenth section provided for the secretary of the Interior to promulgate regulations to carry out the act, in consultation with the review committee, Indian tribes, and Native Hawaiian organizations.[70]

Section 11 authorized the appropriation of such funds as might be necessary to carry out the act.[71]

Figure 6.2 Richard Thompson, Somebody's Great Great Grandpappy. *National Parks* (July/August 1990). Used with permission of National Parks and Richard Thompson.

The July Hearing

On July 17, 1990, the House Committee on Interior and Insular Affairs held a hearing on the protection of Native American graves and the repatriation of human remains and sacred objects. The purpose of the hearing was to receive testimony on three bills: Charles Bennett's H.R. 1381, the Native American Burial Site Preservation Act; Udall's H.R. 1646, the Native American Grave Burial Protection Act; and Udall's H.R. 5237, the Native American Graves Protection and Repatriation Act. Bennett's bill came into the hearing with twenty cosponsors.[72] Twenty-three representatives had cosponsored H.R. 1646, including Bennett.[73] H.R. 5237 had no cosponsors at the time of the hearing.

Representative Eni F. H. Faleomavaega, from American Samoa, brought the committee to order. "For too long," he explained, "Native Americans have been denied access to many museums when seeking information about their ancestors and tribal objects housed therein."

"For too long," he continued, "museums fear that if repatriation were to proceed, their collections would be pillaged, lost forever, along with other vital historical and scientific knowledge."

"For too long, both sides have been mistrustful of each other. It is time that all concerned parties should come together and work out fair resolutions to these issues."[74]

Faleomavaega then introduced Representative Ben Nighthorse Campbell from Colorado. "I think for too long," Campbell said, picking up the cadence set by Faleomavaega,

> the treatment of deceased American Indians found in unmarked graves has been really in sharp contrast with those of non-Indian people being found in marked graves. . . . It has caused a great deal of trauma and grief for American Indians when they know they have a right to those remains and they cannot get them back because we don't have an established procedure for retaining them, where there has been some resistance on the part of museums, archeologists, and a number of other people that think they should be studied at length.[75]

Faleomavaega next introduced Representative Charles Bennett from Florida. "Most civilizations believe in burying their dead and allowing them to remain in the ground unmolested. Many of us have 'rest in peace' inscribed on the graves of their loved ones. Unfortunately," Bennett continued, "as a nation we have failed to accord the same respect to the graves of Native Americans, our chief predecessors."[76] Faleomavaega invited Bennett to sit with the committee.

Prior to introducing the other witnesses, Faleomavaega explained that the Department of the Interior had been invited to testify but had declined.[77] Four panels of witnesses had agreed to provide testimony.

The first panel consisted of Henry Sockbeson, senior staff attorney with the Native American Rights Fund (NARF); A. Gay Kingman, executive director of the National Congress of American Indians; Michael S. Haney, chairman of the repatriation committee of the United Indian Nations of Oklahoma; and Patrick Lefthand, councilman for the Confederated Salish and Kootenai Tribes of the Flathead Nation.

Sockbeson opened by supporting H.R. 5237, which he described as reflecting what already applies in the common law—that dead bodies could not be owned by any individual, or museum, or federal agency. He explained that under the common law that next of kin retain a "right of disposition" to the dead. In the absence of kin, the state would have the right to determine where and when the remains should be disinterred. "I think most people would recognize that dead bodies should not be disturbed. This view," he concluded, "is not universally shared, and it is particularly not applied in the context of Native American remains."[78]

Sockbeson estimated that between 100,000 and 2 million Native people had been dug up from their graves in the United States and are now in museum and federal agency collections. Because no hard data were available to evaluate these estimates, the NARF had recently requested information from most federal land managing agencies. The six agencies that had reported thus far claimed over 14,000 Native American bodies.[79]

In closing, Sockbeson provided the committee with a word of caution regarding what he considered recalcitrance on the part of some museums. "I would ask that the committee, when it considers these conflicting approaches to this legislation, really look to what the museums are attempting to accomplish here. They are simply attempting to maintain control over these collections."[80]

Gay Kingman thanked Bennett for his efforts and supported the three bills that had been introduced. She explained that the National Congress of American Indians was working closely with the NARF and the Association on American Indian Affairs in analyzing the bills.[81] She presented the committee with twenty-two resolutions from various Indian tribes and Native American organizations supporting the legislation.[82]

Michael Haney, representing the United Indian Nations of Oklahoma, introduced himself as an enrolled member of the Seminole Nation of Oklahoma and a member of the Alligator Clan. According to Haney, the Alligator Clan was responsible for the preparation and burial of deceased tribal members. He explained how clan members protect themselves while engaged in their duties, including extensive training and use of special medicines. Haney considered his work with the dead very dangerous, equating it to digging into uranium ore. "That's why we're always a little alarmed when the archeologists go in what we consider unprotected and start digging in these sacred burial grounds."[83]

Haney went on to describe his travels to assist other Indians in protecting Native American gravesites. In Nashville, Tennessee, he stood in front of bulldozers and earthmovers to stop the destruction of approximately forty-six burial mounds. In Illinois, he spoke to the state assembly to try to stop the display of 237 Native American human remains at the Dickson Mounds Museum in Lewiston. Haney urged the committee to pass federal repatriation legislation that might facilitate passage of similar state laws to help resolve these issues.[84]

Patrick Lefthand introduced himself as a medicine man among the Kootenai people of the United States and Canada. He explained that he was the keeper of the jump dance, one of three major songs that together comprise a ceremony going back over 14,000 years. "We have lost several of these kinds of songs for our traditions," continued Lefthand, "because our people have been dug up by what you call scientists." He urged the committee to pass repatriation legislation to ensure that these ancestors are put back in their final resting place so the songs can travel further and guide the younger generations.[85]

Following the first panel, Bennett raised the issue of Native American remains that are not associated with a living Indian tribe, such as the Timuquan or Ocali people of Florida. "Their remains and their ways of being buried should also be respected and taken care of in any legislation we pass."[86]

"The chair happens to agree very much with the gentleman's statement," responded Faleomavaega, "and not just the modern descendants but even the ancient descendants or, for that matter, any human being given its resting place."[87]

"I would like to comment briefly," Haney responded, "that one of the most common arguments by the scientists was that they have no modern-day descendants." He explained that he had been at the Slack Farm site, near Uniontown, Kentucky, the destruction of which had inspired Bennett to introduce H.R. 1381. According to Haney, the archeologists at Slack Farm had said that the Kaw Paw residents of the site had no modern-day descendants. "The Kaw Paw Indians reside in Miami, Oklahoma, and you could have put that whole town of Uniontown in their bingo hall."[88]

Following the first panel, Faleomavaega took the opportunity to introduce Senator Daniel Akaka from Hawaii. Akaka, who was of Native Hawaiian ancestry, had previously been a member of the House, where he was one of the cosponsors of H.R. 1381. Akaka was the first Native Hawaiian to serve in the Senate.[89]

Akaka spoke briefly in favor of H.R. 5237, which he identified as the next step, after the National Museum of the American Indian Act, to ensure the return of human remains and objects in the possession of federally funded museums and government agencies to their native homeland. He pledged to work in the Senate to ensure the legislation's passage. "We need to restore the dignity that was taken from Native Americans and Native Hawaiians."[90]

Faleomavaega responded by reminding everyone that he had often said he would shoot that next anthropologist he caught coming to American Samoa. He traced many social problems, ill feeling, misunderstandings and confusion to the "so-called scientific community," which he characterized as pontificating on the issues of humankind while being in total ignorance of what has happened in their own communities.[91]

Referring to Bennett and Faleomavaega's earlier discussion, Akaka recommended that H.R. 5237 explicitly address the issue of those Native American human remains that are related to extinct Indian tribes. Perhaps the government could be the caretaker of peoples who are extinct.[92]

The second panel consisted of Keith Kintigh, chair of the task force on reburial and repatriation committee of the Society for American Archaeology (SAA), Raymond H. Thompson, director of the Arizona State Museum and representing the American Association of Museums, and Martin E. Sullivan, director of the Heard Museum in Phoenix, Arizona.

"First," Kintigh began, "I want to make clear that the Society [for American Archaeology] is not here to defend the status quo."[93] He pointed out that when the Dickson Mounds Museum, previously referred to by Haney, had tried to take the human remains off display and was prevented from doing so by the Illinois legislature and the governor, the SAA had written to support closing the exhibit. He recognized that repatriation was the central goal of H.R. 5237. "Anthropologists are painfully aware that repatriation results in the destruction of information about the past. However, we recognize that where a modern group has a reasonably clear affiliation," he continued, "that group's desire to control its own heritage take precedence over scientific and public interests."[94] Kintigh felt that although H.R. 5237 was in need of revision, the bill could become an important vehicle for appropriate repatriation of human remains and objects, enhancement of Native American access to material aspects of their heritage, and protection from looting of Native American cemeteries.[95]

Thompson appeared as a representative of the American Association of Museums (AAM), which comprised more than 2,500 museums and more than 8,000 individual members. The AAM had previously solicited comment from approximately 400 of those museums regarding the proposed legislation and had received many thoughtful responses. Thompson indicated that the museum community accepts the philosophical positions included in the proposed legislation regarding human rights, respect for the dead, freedom of religion, and Indian self-determination. He urged, however, that the bill should also permit a balanced review of the human rights involved, the legitimate desires and needs of the Indian groups, the fiduciary and stewardship responsibilities of museums, and the scientific and educational missions of museums serving the American people.[96]

Before assuming his position as director of the Heard Museum, Martin Sullivan had served as director of the New York State Museum. He was the principal negotiator in the return of twelve wampum belts held by the museum to the Onondaga Nation. The belts were created between

1650 and 1800 as a record of the history, precepts, and structure of the Iroquois Six Nations Confederacy. Four of the belts were originally sold by an Onondaga in 1891, with the understanding that they would be preserved in the Smithsonian Institution. Instead, the buyer sold them to John Thatcher in 1894. The Onondaga Nation filed suit to recover the belts from Thatcher in 1897. In 1898, in recognition that other belts were in danger of being dismantled or lost, the Onondaga named the University of the State of New York as Wampum Keeper, a role previously reserved for a respected tribal member. Eight belts were transferred by the Onondaga to the University of the State of New York, and the state joined the suit to recover the four belts sold in 1891. The case was subsequently dismissed. The title of Wampum Keeper and the eight belts in state control were transferred to the director of the New York State Museum in 1908. Finally, in 1927, Thatcher's widow donated the four belts to the museum.[97] Sullivan recognized that under the proposed provisions in H.R. 5237, the New York State Museum might not be required to repatriate the wampum belts to the Onondaga Nation, because the museum's right of possession had been determined a century before. He also recognized that the primary questions revoled around what they were needed for, who could better care for them, and how the museum and tribe could work together in the future. On October 13, 1989, the two parties signed an agreement—a settlement actually, not an assertion of title one way or another, but recognition that the entire populace of the state of New York had an interest in the belts (see figure 6.3). From this perspective, Sullivan was concerned that although H.R. 5237 adequately described the required technical processes and definitions, "it seems to not reflect an awareness that this is, at root, an ethical issue and one of human rights and self-determination."[98]

Faleomavaega was struck by the differences between the tribal representatives on the first panel and the archeologists and museum professionals on the second. "We've just had two cultural leaders from the Native American community, Mr. Lefthand and Mr. Haney, testify before the committee, and it seems as though they're speaking Chinese and you're speaking English."[99]

Faleomavaega turned to Thompson. "You stated that the bill should reflect some kind of a balanced approach and I don't quite understand what you meant by that. I think that's what the attempts have always been, to give this a balanced approach. Are there some areas that you consider unbalanced?"[100]

"No, Mr. Chairman," Thompson responded. "I think the problem that

Figure 6.3 Repatriation of the Hayehwatha belt from the New York State Museum to the Onondaga Nation, New York, October 21, 1989. From left to right: Chief Irving Powless Jr.; Tadodaho Chief Leon Shenandoah; Dr. Martin Sullivan, director, New York State Museum. Courtesy New York State Museum, Albany, NY.

we perceive is that a balance is permitted but not encouraged in the language of the legislation. The problems that museums have is that we are already burdened with a variety of legal and ethical considerations and we must balance those off with the concerns and needs of the Indian community."[101]

The third panel consisted of James Reid, vice president of the Antique Tribal Art Dealers Association (ATADA), accompanied by Diana Lopez, representing Sotheby's. Reid explained that ATADA represents the interests of tens of thousands of serious collectors of tribal arts and have in common many of the concerns of museums around the world. He indicated that ATADA fully supports reasonable efforts to ensure Native American cultural integrity. However, they could not support the bill before the committee.[102] "That any group has a right to the quiet enjoyment of its religious practice and to communal or personal rights of ownership of objects associated with that practice is well established by law," Reid explained.

That a group has a right to exclusive control of its own cultural history and the objects associated with that history that supersedes the rights of the general public and interested individuals is a concept foreign to the pursuit of knowledge and to commonly accepted rights of property. That Government would subordinate the legitimate interest of the general public to those of various tribal special interests and their concepts of the sacred is to abdicate its responsibility to the general public and may violate the First Amendment injunction against the promotion of one religion over another.[103]

Faleomavaega thanked Reid for this testimony. "The bottom line of your testimony is that you do not support this piece of legislation, right?"[104]

"I think it's a bad bill."

Falaeomavaega asked Reid how much certain tribal arts might be worth.

"Somebody was talking about a war shirt the other day," Reid responded. "A Plains war shirt with scalp locks that was actually worn when people were cutting hair and stealing horses might bring as much as $200,000 on the market today. But that would be a very fine example, a pristine example, a great example."[105]

Lopez then addressed the committee. "I'm a lawyer and speak on this issue from a lawyer's perspective," she began. The issue that really concerns them here "is that something that is ingrained in us as Americans is that you can't take someone's property without due process or just compensation."[106]

"It's your feeling that this proposed legislation will totally set a new precedent," asked Faleomavaega. "According to finder's common law, when you find something that is not anybody's personal property? Your feeling is that that's going to upset the common law?"

"Certainly Article II of the Uniform Commercial Code. It totally contradicts those provisions."[107]

"Are you suggesting," continued Faleomavaega, "that federal law does not hold precedence over the Uniform Commercial Code?"

"No," Lopez responded. "I'm not. But there's a certain practice that this country has in terms of dealing with ownership, whether it's personal property or real property. The provisions of this do contradict, both on the federal level and on the state level, which is the Uniform Commercial Code."

"What federal level is contradicted in the proposed bill?"

"One provides that stealing from the Indians is a federal offense. Now the thrust of this bill — "[108]

Faleomavaega cut her off. "Did you say stealing from the Indians is a federal offense? I think we need to enforce that statute. We've been stealing from the Indians for how many years now? What does the UCC say about the traffic in human dead?"

"That would not be covered by the Uniform Commercial Code," responded Lopez.[109]

"Presuming that the bill becomes law," Reid interjected,

> there should be some distinction made between human remains that are buried and human parts, if you will, that may be part of a medicine object or something of that nature. For example, in our testimony one collector speaks about an antique decorated skull that is in his collection. It's not a piece that was ever buried. It was a ceremonial object, or a sacred object, that belonged to an individual and, in one way or another, came into the general collections. Some objects that are in the trade do have some human parts, and some objects in museums do have human parts that are not buried things — things like scalp locks, things like finger bone necklaces that the Crow Indians put together, things like various aspects of Hawaiian culture, skulls or things like that that may have been heavily freighted with medicine but were never buried that were not sent to repose.[110]

"It was an incredibly defining moment," recalls Marie Howard, who, as committee staff, was sitting behind Faleomavaega facing the witnesses and the audience behind them. As Reid spoke about finger bone necklaces and the amount of money they could command on the market, a look of horror crossed the faces of many in the audience — all except Walter Echo-Hawk, who was sitting in the first row. He "smiled, because he could see what was happening." The ATADA testimony — which Echo-Hawk later described as "uniformly considered to be very arrogant and insulting to Indian interests"[111] — seemed to act as a catalyst. "It very much jelled," Howard continued. "The similarities of what was desired by the three groups for protection, preservation, and respectful handling became much more apparent. From that point it was very apparent to the museums and archeologists that something was going to happen."[112]

Laying aside his role as committee chair for a moment, Faleomavaega expressed his personal feelings. "I pray to the spirits that anybody who possesses these things that are sacred to people will have the worst curse they could ever face in their lives." Several members of the audience applauded.[113]

The last panel consisted of Edward Kanahele, president of Hui Malama I Na Kupuna O Hawai'i Nei, and Charles Maxwell with Hui Alanui O Makena. The two men had traveled to Washington from Hawaii to repatriate the remains of 212 Native Hawaiians from the Smithsonian National Museum of Natural History (see figure 6.4). Kanahele explained the extreme physical deprivation that occurs when ancestral remains are disturbed. "It is to be condemned whenever our ancestors are disturbed. It is to be condemned when they are studied, bones are prodded, crushed, drilled. It is to be condemned when they are moved out of their burial sites. It is to be condemned that we cannot repatriate and get back our bones from institutions or other entities that have them now."[114]

Several of the witnesses, along with additional written comments included on the hearing record, had specific comments on the text of H.R.

Figure 6.4 Native Hawaiian representatives in Washington, DC, to attend the July 17, 1990, House hearing on H.R. 5237. Front row, left to right: Pualani Kanaka'ole-Kanahele, Ulunui Kanaka'ole-Garmon, Pele Hanoa, Ipo Nihipali, Phyllis Cayan. Back row: Edward Halealoha Ayau, Parley Kanaka'ole, Edward Lavon Huihui Kanahele, Charles Uluwehi Maxwell, Ka'ohuoka'ala Seto, Kunani Nihipali, Atwood Makanani, Alapai Hanapi. Photo by Lurline Wailana McGregor. Used with permission.

5237. Martin Sullivan recommended including a findings section, like that in S. 1980, to make clear the human rights principles that Native American groups understand to be at the core of the initiative as well as the values of scientific research and public education that relate to the fiduciary obligations of museums and governments.[115]

Most of the definitions in Section 2 drew little comment, indicating a general agreement that the bill should apply to "museums" and "federal agencies," including the Smithsonian Institution, and should formalize the rights of "Indian tribes" and "Native Hawaiian organizations." The text also provided standing to make a claim to lineal descendants, though this term was not defined. The NARF did recommend that the definition of "Indian tribe" be expanded to include state-recognized Indian groups.[116]

Likewise, most of the definitions of the items covered by the bill were addressed with only minimal comment. Ed Kanahele recommended that the definition of "Native American," used now as an adjective referring to the items covered by the bill, be expanded to include Polynesian remains from New Zealand, Tahiti, the Marquesas, the Society Islands, and Samoa in the possession or control of federal agencies or museums.[117] The AAM recommended that the term "intentionally" be deleted from the definition of "funerary object," on the basis that determining the reason an object was placed with human remains would be extremely difficult to ascertain using only circumstantial information. They also recommended that separate definitions be provided for "associated" and "unassociated" funerary objects, phrases used in the text but not specifically defined.[118]

The NARF, SAA, and ATADA all preferred the phrase "inalienable communal property" over "cultural patrimony" as used in S. 1980.[119]

The definition of sacred object remained controversial. The NARF supported the definition as not overly broad, excluding primarily secular objects, which may have been used only incidentally for religious purposes, and reducing the probability of spurious claims.[120] On the other hand, ATADA recommended that the definition be deleted entirely to avoid disturbing precedential and constitutional implications.[121] In the middle, the AAM urged that the definition be narrowed to include only those objects that are necessary for traditional religious practices by living cultures.[122] The SAA supported the definition in S. 1980 allowing evidence of either past or present use of such items in religious ceremony.[123]

The definition of cultural affiliation also drew considerable comment. The NARF supported the definition as liberal and remedial in nature, clarifying the various types and quantum of evidence needed, by establishing a "reasonable relationship" standard and by including a rebuttable presumption of affiliation based on geographic relationship.[124] The Friends Committee on National Legislation also supported the definition, stating that it struck an appropriate balance by not requiring solid demonstration of a historical relationship while also not establishing unattainably high demands of scientific proof. However, the Friends Committee cautioned that how the definition was interpreted would determine whether the policy intention of the bill become practice.[125] The AAM objected to the "reasonable relationship" standard as establishing a virtually limitless category of affiliated Indian tribes and Native Hawaiian organizations.[126] Both the AAM and the SAA objected to the "presumption of cultural affiliation" based on aboriginal occupation, which they said would provide an almost insurmountable presumption of cultural affiliation to Indian tribes, many of whom have no reasonable relationship.[127]

Both the NARF[128] and the SAA[129] were disappointed that Section 3 of the bill (dealing with excavations and discoveries) had backed away from the courageous stand taken by H.R. 1381 and H.R. 1646 regarding discoveries and excavations on all lands, including privately owned lands. ATADA and Sotheby's supported the limitation.[130]

The SAA voiced several objections to the ownership priority list in Section 3(a). They recommended that Sections 3(a)(2)(A) and 3(a)(2)(B) be reversed, so that priority would be given to culturally affiliated Indian tribes and Native Hawaiian organizations over those on whose tribal land such items were discovered.[131] They also recommended deleting the provision in Section 3(a)(2)(C) allowing claims by Indian tribes and Native Hawaiian organizations that aboriginally occupied the area in which an item was discovered.[132] "If this subsection is kept," they stated in their written testimony, "it must be recognized that there are likely to be many groups that fit this criterion. However, without considerable research it may not be evident which are the relevant groups. While all relevant groups may not make claims, all have a legitimate interest in the outcome and must be involved in the decision-making."[133]

The SAA also recommended the deletion of Section 3(b) regarding the disposition of Native American items for which ownership or control could not be ascertained. If the section were to be retained, they recommended that "disposition" be defined to include curation in a public repository and that scholarly groups be consulted in developing regulations.[134]

The SAA generally supported the provisions in Section 3(c) regarding the excavation or removal of Native American human remains and objects. They were concerned, however, that requiring prior tribal consent would make these provisions unworkable by stalling road construction and housing development, as well as frustrating the process of determining cultural affiliation.[135]

Regarding the section on inadvertent discoveries, the NARF recommended deleting the section allowing activities to resume after a reasonable time.[136] The SAA pointed out that in the great majority of cases, cultural affiliation of discovered items would only be determined after their excavation.[137] Ed Kanahele also found this section problematic, pointing out that many archeologists could not make such a determination without excavation, and he recommended that the person making the discovery be required to notify the coroner or medical examiner.[138]

Comments regarding the trafficking provisions in Section 4 came primarily from NARF and ATADA. The NARF preferred the provisions originally set out in the May 1990 version of S. 1980.[139] The earlier version precluded trafficking without the consent of the heirs or legal title. On the other hand, H.R. 5237 precluded trafficking of human remains, funerary objects, sacred objects, or objects of inalienable communal property obtained in violation of the act. Sockbeson urged that if the H.R. 5237 version were to be retained, it should be revised to clarify that illegally obtained items that were secured prior to the effective date of the bill would not be made legal subsequent to passage of the bill.[140] The ATADA supported the H.R. 5237 version but recommended replacing the phrase "obtained in violation of this Act" with "obtain in violation of Section 3 of this Act."[141]

Comments on Section 5 regarding the inventory of human remains, funerary objects, sacred objects, and objects of inalienable communal property focused on the nature and timing of the required documentation. The AAM considered phrases like "to the extent possible" in Subsection (a) and "best available" in Subsection (b)(1)(C) as establishing a level of specificity impossible to reach without increased funding.[142] Sockbeson supported the provision prohibiting the initiation of any new studies, citing recent experience with the Smithsonian Institution, which he alleged was insisting on additional time to study human remains for the Alaskan native village of Larsen Bay.[143] The SAA was puzzled by the same section, which they thought discouraged study of items to determine cultural affiliation.[144] The NARF objected to provisions in Subsection (c) that would allow museums to apply for an extension of the inventory deadline.[145] Finally, the NARF recommended language to make it clear that the inventory represents a "preliminary identification" and not a "final determination."[146]

Several witnesses took issue with various aspects of Section 6, title "Repatriation." Sullivan argued that the section should be retitled "Disposition" to emphasize the bill's intent of ensuring that the human rights of Native peoples are the paramount principle guiding all fiduciaries and that lineal descendants and culturally affiliated groups would be assured the right to determine the disposition of human remains and other sensitive objects.[147] Sockbeson was concerned that unlike earlier bills, the section seemed to deal with federal agencies and museums together. He supported a distinction between federal agencies — which he believed should have an absolute obligation to repatriate based on a public policy determination that repatriation was morally appropriate — and museums that might have a legal right to retain certain items based on legitimately obtained property rights.[148] Sockbeson also recommended that scientific study provisions in Section 6(b) be revised to require the consent of the lineal descendant or Indian tribe.[149] He supported the language in Section 6(c) that placed the burden of proof on the museum or federal agency when a request for repatriation was made.[150] The AAM felt that this provision established an overwhelming standard of proof for museums that otherwise hold good title.[151] The AAM objected to the provisions that would permit the transfer of items to parties with only a "reasonable relationship," but who do not necessarily have the strongest or closest relationship.[152] The AAM objected to penalties in Section 6(f) for failure to comply, which included making the museum ineligible for federal funds, arguing that the proposed penalties went well beyond the mild encouragement to the point of compulsion cited by several Supreme Court cases.[153] The NARF supported the definition of "right of possession in section 6 (d) as a legally sound codification of American property law on disposition of human remains."[154] Martin Sullivan preferred the concept of "right of possession" over the more elusive and complicated notion of "legal title."[155]

Several witnesses were concerned about the membership and responsibilities of the review committee in Section 7 of the bill. The AAM objected to the composition of the review committee, considering that having four of the seven members appointed from tribal nominations was fundamentally unfair and unconstitutional.[156] The NARF recommended the committee chair should be selected by the committee and not the secretary.[157] Sockbeson considered it a mistake to place arbitration within the review committee's jurisdiction.[158] The AAM felt that the committee should be given the flexibility to craft solutions that would be acceptable to all parties concerned, fearing that the current structure would only serve to alienate museums and Native Americans and frustrate previous efforts to develop better relationships.[159] The SAA strongly suggested "that the difficult and highly contentious provisions concerned with unaffiliated remains be deleted."[160] On the other hand, the Friends Committee on National Legislation urged that the section be broadened to provide that present-day Indian tribes most closely connected to the Native American dead have the authority to speak on their behalf.[161]

Finally, Sockbeson pointed out that the National Museum of the American Indian Act contained a provision permitting Indian tribes to exercise their rights by going to federal court, and he recommended that this bill include similar provisions.[162] The NARF recommended including a section establishing a cause of action.[163]

Any intent that the Smithsonian Institution might have had to serve as the lead government agency on national repatriation legislation had apparently evaporated. A week after the House hearing, recently appointed National Museum of the American Indian (NMAI) Director Richard West made two important calls. The first was to the Senate Select Committee on Indian Affairs.[164] West requested that the Smithsonian be exempt from the provisions of S. 1980. "My reasoning . . . is that the Smithsonian currently is the process of considering on an institution-wide basis policies relating to the matters addressed in S. 1980, and that the [Senate] Committee is likely to get a more thoughtful and comprehensive response from us if we are not driven by the present legislative markup schedule." Senators Inouye and McCain acquiesced to the Smithsonian request with an implicit quid pro quo that the Smithsonian would remove itself from further comment on the S. 1980. West's second call was to the House Committee on Interior and Insular Affairs.[165] "What [House staffer] Frank [Ducheneaux] indicated is that the position he takes will be heavily influenced by what some of the Indian lobbyists say," he wrote in a note to Smithsonian Secretary Robert Adams following the call. "Suzan [Harjo] has agreed to help me with [Walter] Bunky Echo-Hawk. Another of the principal lobbyists is my old client, the Association on American Indian Affairs, which is now headed by . . . a fellow Indian lawyer and very close friend—I'll see what I can do there."

Help!

An eighth repatriation measure appeared in late July in the guise of a draft amendment to one of the fiscal year 1991 appropriation packages. H.R.

4739 had been introduced by Les Aspin, chairman of the House Committee on Armed Services, back in May to fund the Department of Defense for the coming fiscal year.[166] The bill had been referred for consideration and markup to various subcommittees and now, in preparation for the August recess, was being prepared for markup by the whole committee. On July 27, a draft amendment was circulated that dealt with the repatriation of Native American human remains and objects.[167] The definitions of the proposed amendment showed a connection with H.R. 5237, given that the terms "Native American," "funerary object," "sacred object," "inalienable communal property," "Indian tribe," "Native Hawaiian organization," and "cultural affiliation" were nearly identical to those in Udall's bill. The amendment would have required completing an inventory of all Native American human remains, funerary objects, sacred objects, and inalienable communal property under the jurisdiction of the secretary of Defense within two years. All human remains and associated funerary objects not claimed by Indian tribes or Native Hawaiian organizations within three years were to be reburied unless some other disposition was agreed to by a direct lineal descendant or the closest culturally affiliated Indian tribe, group, or Native Hawaiian organization. Representative Bennett was identified as the sponsor of the repatriation provisions.

"HELP!!!!!!!!!" read the cover sheet of Loretta Neumann's July 31 fax to the No-Name Alliance.[168] "Congressman Bennett is trying to strike again." Neumann reported that H.R. 4739 was being marked up that afternoon by the House Committee on Armed Services. She was not sure if Bennett's draft amendment had been formally offered. "If ever there was a need for a full alert," she wrote, "this is it." Later that day she wrote again indicating that Bennett had agreed to withdraw the draft amendment and work with the SAA. "Hooray, our lobbying worked!"[169]

The next day McCain offered a revised version of his May draft of S. 1980 as an amendment in the nature of a substitute. The bill was considered by the Select Committee on Indian Affairs and, by a unanimous vote of the quorum present, reported S. 1980 with the recommendation that the Senate adopt the bill.[170] The same day, the Department of Justice (DOJ) provided the Senate committee with comments on the bill.[171] The DOJ declined to comment on the policy goals and efficacy of the bill, deferring to the federal agencies responsible for administering Native American programs. Instead, the DOJ focused its comment on three specific areas with potential constitutional implications. The department was concerned that the repatriation provisions of the bill might constitute a taking of private property for public use. For example, the department argued, the bill might require a private party who had excavated an archeological site on federal land in accordance with an Antiquities Act permit and subsequently provided for permanent preservation of the excavated objects in a public museum to repatriate what might be considered their private property to another party.[172] The DOJ proposed two alternatives: either limit the bill's repatriation provisions to items acquired after the date of enactment, or include provisions for just compensation as required under the Constitution. The DOJ's second major concern was that the review committee provisions might provide more than advisory powers, which would require conformance with the Appointments Clause of the Constitution. Last, the DOJ was concerned that the clause that ensured the review committee full and free access to any protected objects might unreasonably impair the economic value of private property. The DOJ recommended amending the bill to provide the review committee with "reasonable" access to protected items.

With so many bills under consideration and momentum beginning to build behind S. 1980 and H.R. 5237, some in the museum community were beginning to get nervous, particularly the large natural history museums that held extensive collections of Native American human remains and ethnographic items. On August 3, 1990, the six largest natural history museums in the country expressed their concerns in a letter to Senator Inouye. The museums argued that the proposed bills would deprive millions of Americans the opportunity to learn more Native American heritage, establish an adversarial relationship between museums and Native American groups, and force museums to conduct extensive and extremely costly inventories. They felt the bills would force museums to a Hobson's choice: "yield up substantial parts of their collections and thus run the risk of violating State fiduciary laws, or sacrifice Federal funding." The American Museum of Natural History, Field Museum, Denver Museum of Natural History, Los Angeles County Museum, University Museum of Philadelphia, and the Peabody Museum of Archaeology and Ethnology were listed as opposing the bills.[173]

Neumann's earlier celebration over the apparent demise of Representative Bennett's draft amendment to H.R. 4739 proved premature. On August 15, she wrote that Bennett had decided to ask the House Rules Committee to allow him to offer the proposed amendment when the Department of Defense appropriation bill was considered by the whole House.[174] "It's time to take off the gloves," she wrote. "We need to get his amendment killed." Neumann doubted if any Democrat on the House Armed Services Committee would be willing to challenge Bennett, "who is second ranking on the committee and well liked if not always taken seriously. Perhaps a Republican would be willing to challenge him." Copies of Bennett's draft amendment were circulated. Within two years of enactment, the amendment would have required the secretary of Defense to inventory all human remains, funerary objects, sacred objects, and objects of inalienable communal property within the jurisdiction of the Department of Defense and any items requested by any descendant or geographically or culturally affiliated Indian tribe or Native Hawaiian organization. Any human remains and associated funerary objects not claimed within three years of enactment would be reburied.[175] "I just received a copy of this jewel," wrote one museum director, referring to the draft amendment. "It's deadly!"[176] "I have been told that Bennett wants this because he believes 'in his heart' that every human deserves a decent burial and it should be law," explained the director. "Maybe I should have been a stock broker." A memorandum from Walter Echo-Hawk to a long list of interested parties asked them to write Representative Bennett to support the amendment.[177]

CHAPTER SEVEN

The Biggest Thing
We Have Ever Done

The number of repatriation bills ostensibly under consideration when Congress reconvened after the August 1990 recess had grown from the single ill-fated effort introduced without a cosponsor by Montana Senator John Melcher in the waning days 99th Congress, to seven different measures sponsored by five different senators and representatives and cosponsored by fifty-eight of their colleagues. In the Senate, John McCain's Native American Grave and Burial Protection Act, S. 1021, though still technically under consideration by the Senate Select Committee on Indian Affairs, had been effectively superseded by Daniel Inouye's S. 1980, the Native American Repatriation and Cultural Patrimony Act. In the House of Representatives, two bills under consideration by the Interior and Insular Affairs Committee—Charles Bennett's Native American Burial Site Preservation Act, H.R. 1381, and Morris Udall's Native American Grave and Burial Protection Act, H.R. 1646—had likewise been superseded by H.R. 5237, the Native American Graves Protection and Repatriation Act (NAGPRA), also introduced by Udall. Senator Wyche Fowler's bill (S. 1579) to amend the National Historic Preservation Act, Historic Sites Act, Archaeological Resources Protection Act, and Abandoned Shipwrecks Act, which also included repatriation provisions, had been referred to the Senate Committee on Energy and Natural Resources, and Representative Bennett's companion bill, H.R. 3412, had been referred to the House Committee on Interior and Insular Affairs. With the end of the congressional session in sight, the Senate and House began to narrow their focus in the hope of passing some type of comprehensive repatriation legislation in the 101st Congress.

Some in the Native American community also recognized that the multiple bills under consideration were beginning to stand in the way of any agreement among the Native American, archeological, and museum communities. On August 20, Walter Echo-Hawk took steps on behalf of the Native American Rights Fund (NARF) to reduce the number of repatriation bills in play. "While we greatly appreciate the well intentioned effort of S. 1579," Echo-Hawk wrote to Senator Fowler, "we respectfully recommend that the repatriation language of Section 112 be dropped in favor of, or in deference to, the more comprehensive treatment of these issues in S. 1980 and H.R. 5237 which are now moving through Congress."[1] As congressional focus began to narrow, subgroups of the No-Name Alliance of scientific and museum organizations and certain federal agency representatives began independent efforts to affect the proposed legislation.

Jack Trope recalled that even though there was considerable momentum behind passage of a repatriation bill, there was a "window of opportunity" of which the Native American representatives needed to take advantage. "There were some influential people in the museum and scientific communities that were very much opposed to a bill," he recalled. "We were also aware of the old truism that it is far easier to block a bill, then to pass one. The Society for American Archaeology (SAA) and the American Association of Museumes (AAM) were feeling the pressure and were willing to negotiate. We decided that the best strategy was to negotiate modest changes to build consensus behind the bill to maximize its chances for passage."[2]

SAA Negotiations

The SAA began negotiating separately with Native American representatives in early August. "I talked with Walter Echo-Hawk about working together to change S. 1980," reported the SAA's Keith Kintigh. "He appreciated the initiative and said that if we could agree on ANYTHING, we should do it."[3] Kintigh faxed draft comments to the NARF.[4] Echo-Hawk's skepticism about working out an agreement with the SAA was reflected in his handwritten question on the fax coversheet forwarding the proposal to the Association for American Indian Affairs (AAIA). "Jack, Is there anything here we can agree to?"[5] Trope identified a number of proposals on which the two sides agreed. He and Kintigh talked at length on August 30, with Kintigh reporting that "we both agreed that we would like to have a bill that our organizations could support and that we weren't far away from that."[6] Representatives of the SAA, NARF, and AAIA met in Washington on September 6 to develop a joint set of recommended changes to Inouye's S. 1980.

One of the principal proposals was a set of interrelated changes defining cultural affiliation as "a relationship of shared group identity which can be reasonably traced historically or prehistorically between a present day Indian tribe or Native Hawaiian organization and an identifiable earlier group" and requiring an Indian tribe or Native Hawaiian organization to provide a preponderance of the evidence of cultural affiliation based on geographical, kinship, biological, archaeological, anthropological, linguistic, folkloric, oral traditional, historical, or other relevant information or expert opinion. The agreement stressed that "the process of determining cultural affiliation is as important as defining what it is." The November 28, 1989 version of S. 1980 had not included any definition of cultural affiliation, but the July 10, 1990, version of Udall's H.R. 5237 had, defining the term as "a reasonable relationship, established by a preponderance of the evidence, between a requesting Indian tribe or Native Hawaiian organization and the Native Americans from which the human remains or other material covered by this Act were derived, regardless of age or antiquity."[7] The joint SAA/Indian recommendations clarified that a relationship of "shared group identity" was required and, in a major concession by the Native American representatives, omitted the Udall bill's presumption of cultural affiliation based on the item's recovery from a tribal or aboriginal lands. The related recommendation dealt with situations in which cultural affiliation was not established in the required inventory. The new provision required a museum or federal agency to expeditiously return a cultural item if an Indian tribe or Native Hawaiian organization could show cultural affiliation by a "preponderance of the evidence," a legal term meaning that the claimant must present a more convincing amount of evidence than the museum or federal agency has. A similar requirement in Inouye's November 21, 1989, version of S. 1980 had placed the burden of proof on the claiming Indian tribe or Native Hawaiian organization when the cultural item was in the possession or control of a museum. The new agreement expanded this shifting of the burden of proof to also include cultural items in federal collections.

A second agreement between the SAA and Indian negotiators recommended revising the criteria for disposition of human remains and other items that would be excavated or discovered on federal or tribal lands after the date of enactment. The November 28, 1989, version of S. 1980 stipulated that ownership would be with a claiming Indian tribe or Native Hawaiian organization that aboriginally occupied the area in which the items were discovered if no lineal descendant could be identified, the items were not found on tribal land, and no culturally affiliated Indian tribe or Native Hawaiian organization stated a claim.[8] The parties agreed to recommend revising this section by specifying that the determination of aboriginal occupation be based on a final judgment of the Indian Claims Commission and adding additional criteria requiring disposition to a claiming Indian tribe or Native Hawaiian organization with the strongest "cultural relationship." The joint memorandum cautioned that linkage to the Indian Claims Commission would work for aboriginal claims in the "lower 48 States," but that other language would likely be required to deal equivalently with claims in Alaska and Hawaii.[9] The memorandum also explained that the addition of the "cultural relationship" criteria was designed to reduce the possibility of multiple tribal claimants while also ensuring that the most appropriate tribe or organization could assert a claim.

The final recommendations were sent to the Senate Select Committee on Indian Affairs staff on September 12, 1990.[10] Signing for their respective organizations were Keith Kintigh, SAA; Gay Kingman, National Congress of American Indians (NCAI); Walter Echo-Hawk and Henry Sockbeson, NARF; and Jack Trope, AAIA. Echo-Hawk also faxed a copy to the American Association of Museums (AAM)'s Dan Monroe and Martin Sullivan and to Suzan Harjo with the Morning Star Institute, explaining that the proposed amendments focused primarily on SAA's interests in burials still in the ground and the definition of cultural affiliation. "This is an invitation to AAM and Morning Star to review and hopefully support these amendments."[11] The agreement was also passed on to Marie Howard with the House Interior and Insular Affairs Committee for consideration in revising H.R. 5237.[12]

A number of issues raised during the negotiations could not be resolved.[13] The SAA proposed language to elaborate on the inventory process to allow for the initiation of new scientific studies with the consent of the relevant Indian tribe or Native Hawaiian organization. Kintigh reported that the Indian negotiators "had no philosophical objection to this but argued that any hint of raising the cost of the bill will kill it." Likewise, the Indian negotiators would not agree to an SAA proposal to outlaw the sale of funerary objects. "They agree with us in principle," Kintigh reported, "but have been running around telling everyone that the art dealers were not affected by the act, and to ignore their complaints. They felt that recommending this at this stage might hamper passage of the bill."

While the SAA was negotiating with the Indian representatives regarding S. 1980, a coalition of archeological organizations continued its efforts to stop Bennett's proposed amendments to the National Defense Authorization Act.[14] On September 19, 1990, H.R. 4739 finally passed the House of Representatives. Although the bill included two last-minute amendments offered by Representative Bennett, his repatriation provisions were not among them.[15]

Agency Correspondence

The executive branch agencies were beginning to weigh in. The Department of the Army recognized that many of the provisions of H.R. 5237 overlapped those of the Archaeological Resources Protection Act (ARPA) and recommended that to avoid duplication of existing law and confusion to program managers, additional protection to Native American burial sites should be framed as amendments to ARPA. The army was also concerned that the provisions prohibiting excavation of Native American remains without notice and consent of the affiliated Indian tribes or Native Hawaiian organizations would create an impossible burden for federal land managers that would virtually stop the progress of any project. The army was unable to provide the current number of Native American skeletal remains and funerary objects in its possession or control, nor any general policy regarding those items.[16]

The Department of Justice (DOJ) sent comments to the House on September 17, 1990. The DOJ was concerned that the repatriation provisions of H.R. 5237 might call into play the Takings Clause of the Constitution that precludes taking private property for public use without just compensation. They proposed several alternatives, including exempting private museums, and thus private property, from repatriation; broadening the provisions under which a museum may decline repatriation to exempt all objects in which the museum has a property interest cognizable under federal or state law; or explicitly providing for payment of just compensation to private museums required to repatriate items in which they have a property interest. The DOJ was particularly concerned that the conditioning of federal funding on consent to an uncompensated taking might be an unconstitutional exercise of Congress's spending power. The DOJ recognized that the section of the bill establishing the review committee did not accord it binding legal force, but cautioned that if Congress intended otherwise the bill would need to be amended to conform to the Constitution's Appointments Clause. The DOJ was also concerned that the review committee was ensured full and free access to protected objects, which might be read broadly to authorize the sequestration of such items that would otherwise be part of a major exhibition in a private museum, which might be argued to constitute a taking of private property for public use.[17]

On September 21, 1990, the legislative branch's Congressional Budget Office (CBO) provided cost estimates for implementing S. 1980.[18] The CBO assumed that museums and federal agencies held between 100,000 and 200,000 Native American human remains and 10–15 million other objects that would have to be reviewed. It also assumed, based on the experience of museums that had already repatriated human remains that inventorying these remains and reviewing existing studies and research to determine their origin would cost between $50 and $150 per individual. More extensive studies were considered beyond the requirements of the bill. Reviewing the existing information on other objects in archeological collections was estimated to cost between $10 and $15 million over five years. Based on these assumptions, the CBO estimated the total cost of implementing S. 1980 to be between $20 and $55 million over five years. These costs were considered discretionary. "The more funds made available, the more accurate and comprehensive will be the information."

H.R. 5237 and S. 1980

After considering the various agreements and agency correspondence, Marie Howard circulated a new draft of H.R. 5237 on September 24.[19] A brief cover memo requested comments as soon as possible "as the committee may take this to mark up in the *very* near future." A fax cover sheet from Walter Echo-Hawk forwarding the draft to Dan Monroe, Martin Sullivan, and Suzan Harjo indicated that the revisions were made to make H.R. 5237 resemble S. 1980. Two days later, Senator Inouye introduced another version of S. 1980 with an accompanying report by the Senate Select Committee on Indian Affairs.[20] Though increasingly similar in form and content, there remained important differences between the two bills.

The September 24 draft of Udall's bill included eleven sections, whereas there were now fourteen sections in Inouye's bill, including additional sections on findings and enforcement and the separation of the ownership section in Udall's draft into two sections in Inouye's bill. The findings section in Inouye's bill was a slightly reworked version of the one introduced in McCain's version of S. 1980.[21] The enforcement section in Inouye's bill gave the U.S. district courts jurisdiction over actions alleging a violation of the act.[22]

The definition section in Inouye's new version included nineteen terms, sixteen of which were also included in H.R. 5237. However, there remained several significant differences in how terms were defined in the bills. In terms of jurisdiction, both bills applied to museums and federal agencies, with the same definition of "museum" in both bills. Udall's definition of "federal agency" explicitly included the Smithsonian Institution.[23] Inouye's definition explicitly excluded the Smithsonian.[24] Both bills dealt with the disposition or repatriation of four types of objects: human remains, funerary objects, sacred objects, and objects of cultural patrimony, which H.R. 5237 referred to collectively as cultural items. Neither bill defined human remains, and the definitions of funerary object were nearly identical. Sacred object was also defined in the same manner in both bills, referring to any item whose primary purpose when possessed by Native Americans was devoted to a traditional Native American religious ceremony or ritual and had a religious significance or function in the continued observation or renewal of such ceremony or ritual.[25] Both definitions of cultural patrimony were similar, though Udall's version made it explicit that such an item must have been considered inalienable by the Native American group at the time it was separated from the group.[26] Both bills authorized claims by lineal descendants, Indian tribes, and Native Hawaiian organizations. Neither bill provided a definition of lineal descendant. Indian tribe was now defined in both bills by reference[27] or with explicit text[28] from the Indian Self Determination and Education Assistance Act, although the Inouye version of S. 1980 followed McCain's earlier lead of explicitly including Alaska Native villages.[29] Inouye also narrowed the definition of Native Hawaiian organization in H.R. 5237 to require that such organizations have a membership of which a majority is Native Hawaiian.[30]

Cultural affiliation was defined differently in the two bills. In Inouye's version, the term meant a relationship between a present-day Indian tribe or a Native Hawaiian organization and an unidentifiable historic or prehistoric Indian tribe or Native Hawaiian group that reasonably establishes a continuity of group identity from the earlier to the present-day group.[31] In Udall's version, the term meant a relationship of shared group identity that can be reasonably traced historically or prehistorically between a present-day Indian tribe or Native Hawaiian organization and an identifiable earlier group.[32] It is interesting to note that although the September 12 agreement between the SAA, NCAI, NARF, and AAIA was addressed to the Senate Select Committee on Indian Affairs, it was the House bill that first adopted the compromise definition of cultural affiliation.[33] The new version of S. 1980 continued to use "Native American" as a noun, meaning any individual who is an Indian, Alaska Native, or Native Hawaiian.[34] H.R. 5237 continued to use the term as an adjective meaning of or related to a tribe, people, or culture that is indigenous to the United States.[35]

The excavation and discovery provisions of Inouye's new version of S. 1980 were nearly verbatim from H.R. 5327. Both applied to federal lands and tribal lands, the latter defined to include lands already conveyed to Alaska Native corporations.[36] In both bills, ownership of cultural items that would be excavated or discovered on federal or tribal lands would be, with priority given to the order listed: (1) the lineal descendant; (2) the Indian tribe or Native Hawaiian organization on whose land the items were discovered; (3) the Indian tribe or Native Hawaiian organization with the closest cultural affiliation; and (4) the Indian tribe or Native Hawaiian organization that aboriginally occupied the area in which the items were discovered. Language specifying use of final decisions of the Indian Claims Commission to determine aboriginal occupation, which was recommended in the SAA/NCAI/NARF/AAIA letter, was not included in either bill.[37] S. 1980 specified that activities in the vicinity of inadvertently discovered human remains, funerary objects, sacred objects, or objects of cultural patrimony could resume thirty days after the appropriate federal official had certified receipt that he or she had been notified of the discovery.[38] Udall's bill only stated that the activity could resume after a "reasonable amount of time."[39] Inouye's bill deleted the provision of H.R. 5237 explicitly acknowledging that an Indian tribe or Native Hawaiian organization could relinquish control over Native American human remains or title to or control over any funerary object or sacred object.[40]

Both bills included penalties for trafficking in Native American human remains, funerary objects, sacred objects, and objects of cultural patrimony. Unlike the earlier version of H.R. 5237 that included a single set of provisions that applied to trafficking of all cultural items,[41] the new bills bifurcated the provisions.[42] One subsection made it a crime to traffic in any cultural item obtained in violation of the statute. A second made trafficking in human remains without the right of possession sufficient to merit federal prosecution.

The collections provisions of S. 1980 were likewise nearly identical to those of H.R. 5237. Unlike Udall, however, Inouye exempted the Smithsonian Institution from the new requirements.[43] Inouye's bill also did not include the definition of documentation in H.R. 5237 stipulating that the bill could not be construed to be an authorization for the initiation of new scientific studies or other means of acquiring or preserving additional scientific information from Native American human remains, funerary objects, sacred objects, or objects of communal property. Both the Udall and Inouye bills included temporary exemption from expeditious repatriation if the remains or objects would found to be indispensable for completion of a specific scientific study, the outcome of which would be of major benefit to the United States.[44]

The new version of S. 1980 retained the language from the original version of H.R. 5237 that established membership of the review committee to include four members nominated by Indian tribes,[45] instead of the three specified in the new draft of Udall's bill. Inouye added reviewing and making recommendations regarding requests for inventory extensions to the review committee's responsibilities.[46] The committee's role of arbitrating disputes was changed to facilitating the resolution of disputes in both bills.[47] Both bills added an additional subsection to the savings provisions so that nothing in the statute would limit the application of any state of federal law pertaining to theft of stolen property.[48]

There were rumors that two senators were planning to place holds on S. 1980 until certain issues were resolved, including objections raised by dealers of indigenous artifacts. "We all knew that the bill would have to pass by unanimous consent in the Senate," recalls Senate staffer Eric Eberhard.[49] "That forces you to legislate, in a sense, to the lowest common denominator. What is the most that you can pass without drawing an objection that will kill the bill?" As had happened with the National Museum of the American Indian (NMAI) Act, the House staff seemed to be waiting to see what happened in the Senate before moving ahead with H.R. 5237.[50]

AAM Negotiations

While preparing for markup on H.R. 5237, one of Congressman George Miller's staffers visited Marie Howard. Miller, who represented a district near the University of California at Berkeley, had recently been contacted by university officials who were concerned about the effects H.R. 5237 might have on their museum collections.[51] Congressman Udall, though still chairman of the House Interior and Insular Affairs Committee, had become affected by Parkinson's disease, and Miller, as the next highest ranking Democrat, had assumed a leadership role on the committee. "I realized that politically we weren't going to go anywhere unless we had Miller on board," Howard recalled, "so I stopped the markup for a time. I know several in the Indian community were upset with me for that, but I also knew the reality of life here."[52]

The AAM had long assumed it held the moral high ground in the repatriation debate based on underlying beliefs in the necessity to preserve collections, the priority of the right of scientific inquiry, and preeminent role of museum professionals in interpreting collections.[53] Melcher's introduction of the first repatriation bill in the 99th Congress led the AAM to create general repatriation policy guidelines in the hope that it would allay congressional concerns without the need to enact legislation.[54] As the pace of legislative efforts increased in the 100th Congress, the AAM proposed the yearlong National Dialogue on Museum/Native American Relations, which instead of stemming the legislative tide led some in the museum community to the shocking realization that the Indian community might be right. At a June 1990 meeting organized by the Smithsonian Institution to discuss the prospect of establishing a dialogue between the Smithsonian, the AAM, and Native American communities around the issue of object repatriation and increased accessibility, Dan Monroe characterized the wide diversity of opinion over repatriation within the professional museum community but suggested that it might be possible for a small, proactive group to lead the field at large toward a universal repatriation policy.[55] The basis of compromise amendments to S. 1980 was born over after-session drinks with Monroe, the AAM's Martin Sullivan, Walter Echo-Hawk, and Suzan Harjo.[56] In a September 17 memorandum to selected museums, Monroe provided a three-page list of proposed changes to S. 1980.[57] The AAM considered three of the definitions in the bill to be overly broad. They proposed narrowing the definition of "cultural affiliation" along the lines already agreed to by the SAA/NCAI/NARF/AAIA. They identified the definition of "sacred object" in H.R. 5237 as superior to that in S. 1980. "The important element of this definition is the concept of primary importance to continued religious practice today." The AAM also recommended replacing the term "object of inalienable communal property" with "object of national cultural patrimony." The association proposed that the inventories be defined as a simple itemized list based on existing records. "This change would remove the burden of providing research that meets the standard of 'best available scientific or historical information' and limits the amount of initial inventory information thereby substantially reducing the cost of compliance." The AAM recommended several changes in the repatriation section. One clarified that once the cultural affiliation of human remains and associated funerary objects was established, they would be returned on request for reburial or reconsecration according to the traditional practices of the group, unless the museum could demonstrate that the remains and objects were originally acquired with the full knowledge and consent of the next of kin or the official governing body of the appropriate Indian tribe. Another recommended change was to reverse the priority order of the requirement in S. 1980 under which a museum would first identify the items for which it could not prove right of possession, which lineal descendants and culturally affiliated Indian tribes could then claim. The AAM also objected to right of possession being strictly based on proof that the object was obtained with the voluntary consent of an individual or group with authority of alienation. "Among the factors to be considered in review of ownership claims will be facts and circumstances behind original acquisition of the objects; claims to legal ownership, control, or right of possession; review of whether or not objects ever could have been legally alienated; role of the objects in religious practices or Native tribal or group identity; and artistic or scientific importance of the objects." Last, the AAM objected to the composition of the review committee, characterized as a "stacked deck," and recommended a seven-person committee composed of one anthropologist, one museum director, one archeologist, two tribal elders, one expert in Native American art, and one attorney. They also recommended the committee's mandate include making recommendations on both the disposition of objects and their future care.

On September 27, Monroe, Martin, and AAM President Ellsworth Brown met in Washington, DC, with Echo-Hawk and Harjo. The AAM offered the Native American negotiators an alternative bill that dealt only with human remains and associated funerary objects. "The decision to try this strategy was based on the fact that we had picked up some Congressional support during the prior week and therefore had a stronger negotiating position."[58] However, Monroe was aware of the limits of congressional support. "[California Congressman George] Miller has directly requested that we negotiate with the Natives." Monroe came away from the meeting reasonably optimistic that they would be able to agree to exclude sacred objects and objects of cultural patrimony completely and include a very narrow definition of unassociated funerary object. "In our judgment," he wrote, "if an agreement can be reached with Natives on such a bill, it would represent an optimal outcome to the issue of Repatriation. Stalling to work on legislation in the future would only expose us to renewed discussions of sacred objects and objects of cultural patrimony."

The AAM's hope of negotiating a bill that would not include sacred objects or objects of cultural patrimony quickly evaporated. "It appears that after testing this proposition of the constituents," Monroe wrote on September 28, "this approach proved unacceptable."[59] He next proposed a three-point negotiation strategy to the AAM government affairs office. First, he recommended continuing negotiations to determine if there was any way to ease the legislation's burden on museums. Second, he thought that continued negotiation would prove valuable in demonstrating to the AAM's congressional supporters that it had made a sincere effort to resolve differences with the Native community. Finally, resolving some of the differences with the Native community while still retaining the right to oppose the legislation in its present form would provide the AAM with a strong lobbying position in the future. "In the event that our efforts to forestall passage of the bill this year fail then we may seek last minute improvements to the legislation, including provisions regarding sacred objects and objects of cultural patrimony."

On Sunday, September 30, 1990, Dan Monroe and Ellsworth Brown from AAM began face-to-face negotiations with Walter Echo-Hawk, Jack Trope, and Suzan Harjo in Washington, DC. The meeting started at noon and continued until nearly 1 a.m. At 8 a.m., Monroe and Brown held an emergency meeting with representatives of several museums before returning to meet with the tribal representatives in the afternoon. At 5 p.m., Monroe, Brown, and Harjo met with Senator Inouye to report an agreement "in concept." Negotiations via conference call and fax continued on Tuesday, Wednesday, and Thursday.[60] The marathon negotiations between representatives of the AAM and the Native American organizations finally yielded an agreement on October 4.[61] A final draft was hastily prepared and handed out to members of the House Resources Committee. "With the following proposed amendments to H.R. 5237," the agreement began, "the American Association of Museums can support H.R. 5237." The AAM was concerned about three definitions: those for funerary objects, sacred object, and right of possession. The agreement recommended revising the definition of funerary object to distinguish between those associated with human remains in the control of a museum and unassociated funerary objects for which previously associated human remains were not collected or could not be located. The agreement recommended deleting the final clause of the definition of sacred object regarding the continued observance or renewal of a traditional Native American ceremony or ritual. Last, the agreement recommended deleting the last sentence of the definition of term "right of possession," which stipulated that the original acquisition of human remains with the full knowledge and consent of the next of kin or the official governing body of the appropriate culturally affiliated Indian tribe or Native Hawaiian organization would give right of possession to those human remains.

The AAM agreement also made several recommendations regarding the inventory and repatriation sections of H.R. 5237. It recommended that the inventory section be revised to focus only on human remains and associated funerary objects and an additional section be added requiring production of a briefer summary of unassociated funerary objects, sacred objects, and objects of inalienable communal property. It also recommended striking the requirement that the inventory of human remains and associated funerary objects be based on the best available scientific and historical documentation, and instead asked that the inventory be based simply on information possessed by the institution. The agreement recommended revising the definition of documentation to indicate that such a summary of available information would only be required on the request of an Indian tribe or Native Hawaiian organization and was not a requirement of the inventory itself. The agreement proposed adding a separate section regarding the repatriation of unassociated funerary objects, sacred objects, and objects of cultural patrimony. It recommended a new section authorizing the federal agency or museum to retain control of an item when there would be multiple requests for repatriation and the museum could not clearly determine which requesting party is the most appropriate claimant. It also recommended adding language to indicate that any museum that repatriates an item in good faith would not be liable for claims by an aggrieved party or for claims of breach of fiduciary duty, public trust, or violation of inconsistent state laws. The agreement proposed a new penalty section authorizing the secretary of the Interior to assess a civil penalty on any museum that fails to comply with the act. Finally, the agreement's proposed changes to ensure that the review committee would consult with national museum organizations, and the committee was directed to make recommendations regarding future care of items to be repatriated. With the proposed amendments, the AAM was prepared to support H.R. 5237.

"I am very pleased to report that AAM reached consensus today with Native leaders on Repatriation legislation," Monroe wrote to his respondents on repatriation.[62] "House and Senate staffs are incorporating the

changes into both the House and Senate bills at this time." He acknowledged that there would be some objections from the museum community
to the decision to negotiate with Native leaders, to various provisions in
the legislation, and to the process used to reach consensus. "I can only say
we have made every effort to represent specific concerns while at the same
time representing the museum community as a whole within the context
of the constraints." Monroe also reported that although the compromise
had the support of a substantial number of natural history museums, the
American Museum of Natural History would continue to oppose repatriation legislation and was seeking support from other museums.[63]

The next day, Marie Howard reported the agreement between the
AAM and Native American representatives to interested committee staff.
Of particular note was the agreement to delete language regarding the
continued observance or renewal of a traditional Native American ceremony or ritual from the sacred object definition. "My only concern here is
that [changing the definition] would affect the agreements made with the
Dealers," Howard wrote. "I would recommend keeping the language as
is."[64] Representative Bill Richardson had been working with representatives of the Antique Tribal Art Dealers Association (ATADA) to make several revisions to the bill, including revising the definition of cultural affiliation to include anthropological and archeological criteria; changing the
definition of cultural patrimony to add an "ongoing" cultural or religious
importance requirement and that the object must have been inalienable
at the time of its expatriation; narrowing the definition of museum to exclude private individuals who receive federal funds; clarifying the definition of sacred object to indicate that such items would be necessary for the
practice of tribal religion; shifting the burden of proof from the museums
to the tribal claimants; and revising membership requirements for the review committee to include equal numbers nominated by tribes and muse-
ums/scientific organizations, plus a seventh member nominated with the
agreement of the other six members.[65]

While the AAM was desperately trying to negotiate changes to the bills,
the House finally received executive comment from the Department of
the Interior.[66] In contrast to the agreements reached between the SAA and
AAM and the Native American negotiators, Deputy Assistant Secretary
Scott Sewell wrote Udall that although the department generally supported the goals of H.R. 5237, it would oppose the bill until amended
as suggested.[67] In a position similar to that initially proposed by the AAM
but subsequently abandoned in the negotiation process, Interior recommended that the bill be amended to apply only to Native American hu-

man remains and funerary objects, suggesting the definitions of sacred object and object of cultural patrimony were too broad and unformulated. In the ownership section, the department recommended revising the cultural affiliation criteria to remove reference to "closest" cultural affiliation, as well as the entire section regarding ownership based on aboriginal land, and requested language be included in the committee report providing the secretary of the Interior with broad authority regarding the disposition of unclaimed items, ranging from museum curation to reburial. The department recommended that the section precluding use of the statute as authorization for the initiation of new scientific studies be revised to ensure correct determination of affinity. They also asked that federal agencies be allowed to request extensions of the inventory deadline. They recommended deletion of the section requiring the review committee to compile an inventory of culturally unidentifiable human remains. Finally, they opposed provisions authorizing open-ended and unlimited grants to tribes and museums involved in the repatriation process. The Native American organization representatives provided the House committee staff with their analysis of the letter the next day, concluding that all of Interior's concerns had either already been resolved in the changes negotiated between the SAA, AAM, NARF, NCAI, and AAIA or could be resolved by language in the House committee report.[68]

Markup and Report

Markup of H.R. 5237 was finally held on Wednesday, October 10, with Representatives Udall, Ben Nighthorse Campbell from Colorado, Sam Gejdenson from Connecticut, George Miller from California, John Rhodes from Arizona, and Bill Richardson from New Mexico present. Representative Campbell led the discussion.

The revised bill provided to the committee included several changes recommended by the AAM and Native American organizations, along with several others recommended by the SAA.

The requirement in Section 5 for museums and federal agencies to prepare an item-by-item inventory of all cultural items was significantly revised. The inventory requirements were limited to only human remains and associated funerary objects, and the basis for determining the geographical and cultural affiliation of such items was changed from "best scientific and historical documentation"[69]—the standard used in the repatriation provisions of the National Museum of the American Indian

Act—to information currently in the possessed by the museum or federal agency.[70] To provide information to Indian tribes regarding other items, a new section was added requiring a written summary of collections that may include unassociated funerary objects, sacred objects, and objects of cultural patrimony.[71] Like the inventory, the summary was to be based on available information, but instead of an item-by-item listing it was to be limited to a description of the kinds of objects included, references to geographical location, means and period of acquisition, and cultural affiliation, where readily ascertainable. The summary was to be completed no later than three years after the date of enactment of the act and was to be followed by consultation with tribal officials and traditional religious leaders.[72] Separate definitions of associated and unassociated funerary objects were added to clarify applicability of the inventory and summary requirements.[73] In addition, the definition of sacred object was revised, changing the focus from items whose primary purpose was devoted to a traditional Native American religious ceremony or ritual[74] to objects currently needed by traditional Native American religious leaders for the practice of traditional Native American religions by present-day adherents.[75] The revised definition was intended to cover objects needed for currently practiced ceremonies as well as objects needed to renew ceremonies that had been interrupted because of governmental coercion, adverse society conditions, or the loss of certain objects by means beyond the control of the tribe at the time. "The operative part of the definition," the committee explained, "is that there must be present day adherents."[76]

Section 3, concerning the future ownership of cultural items excavated or discovered on federal or tribal lands, was revised following the joint SAA–tribal recommendations to include the possibility of a tribe having a "stronger cultural relationship" than one based only on the items being recovered from a tribe's aboriginal territory.[77] In addition, representatives of the scientific community were added to the list of parties that must be consulted in developing regulations for the disposition of cultural items that were unclaimed.[78]

The requirements for the Smithsonian to comply with specific repatriation requirements was stricken, and the definition of federal agency was modified to apply to the Smithsonian "except as may be inconsistent with the provisions of P.L. 100-185 [*sic*]."[79] The committee explained that it did not wish to change the agreements reached under the National Museum of the American Indian Act regarding the inventory and repatriation of human remains and funerary objects, but it did intend to expand the Smithsonian's repatriation obligations to include sacred objects and objects of cultural patrimony and, to the extent it did not weaken provisions in the NMAI Act, unassociated funerary objects as well.[80]

The penalty section stipulating that any museum that failed to comply with the repatriation provisions would be ineligible for federal grants or other assistance during the period of noncompliance[81] was stricken and replaced with a new section authorizing the secretary of the Interior to assess a civil penalty on any museum that failed to comply with any of the requirements of the act.[82] Penalty amounts were to take into account: the archeological, historical, or commercial value of the item involved; the economic and noneconomic damages suffered by aggrieved parties; and the number of violations that had occurred.[83] No penalty could be assessed unless the museum was given notice and opportunity for a hearing.[84] Museums aggrieved by a civil penalty assessment were provided the opportunity to file a petition for judicial review with a U.S. district court.[85]

A new subsection was added exempting any museum from liability for claims by an aggrieved party or for claims of breach of fiduciary duty, public trust, or violation of state law if it repatriated items in good faith pursuant to the act.[86] Another new section was added stipulating that the act reflects the unique relationship between the United States and Indian tribes and Native Hawaiian organizations, which should not be construed to establish a precedent with respect to any other individual, organization, or foreign government.[87] The section requiring the secretary of the Interior to issue regulations was revised to stipulate that such regulations would be promulgated within twelve months of enactment.

During markup, Representative Rhodes offered an amendment to the definition of right of possession to clarify that it would not affect the application of relevant state law to the right of ownership of unassociated funerary objects, sacred objects, or objects of cultural patrimony. The committee explained that the language was adopted to address the concerns expressed by the Department of Justice about the possibility of a Fifth Amendment taking of the private property of museums through the application of the terms of the act.[88]

During the discussion, Representative Richardson presented a letter from ATADA.[89] ATADA asked for an amendment to the definition of sacred object to require such items be "essentially irreplaceable" for traditional Native American religious practice. They objected to the provision allowing disposition of cultural items found on federal land to an Indian tribe based on a cultural relationship or discovery on the tribe's aboriginal land. They asked that "human remains" be defined to exclude materials that fall under the general category of trophy items that were never a part of a burial, such as scalps and finger bones used in necklaces. ATADA also asked that an institution only be required to prepare an inventory following receipt of sufficient federal funds appropriated specifically for the purpose of the inventory.

The committee did not include any of ATADA's proposed amendments. Following the markup session, Loretta Neumann, representing SAA and the No-Name Alliance, approached Walter Echo-Hawk. "I assured him that we think that these folks are as slimy as he does."[90]

Representative Miller spoke in support of the markup version of H.R. 5237. "I had a great many reservations about this legislation a couple of weeks ago. I was deeply concerned about what I viewed as almost a never-ending process where we would never really gain certainty either for Native Americans or for museums. I think that much of that has now been rectified," he said. "We do have a process that in fact will work, will protect peoples' rights, and will certainty curtail some of the legal issues that were hanging around with the previous language."[91] The committee adopted an amendment in the nature of a substitute and recommended it to the full House for consideration.

The next day, Kintigh contacted representatives of NARF, AAIA, and AAM suggesting the possibility of issuing a joint letter of support to help advance the compromise version of H.R. 5237.[92] A final letter, sent on October 12, 1990, and signed by representatives of the AAIA, NARF, SAA, and NCAI, characterized the bill as having broad-based support that would create a workable framework that would foster sensitivity and cooperation in achieving the appropriate repatriation of Native American human remains and cultural objects. The organizational representatives thanked Udall and the members and staff of the House Interior and Insular Affairs Committee for working with them. A separate letter was attached from the AAM indicating that the October 10, 1990, version of H.R. 5237 accurately reflected agreements made between the AAM and Native American representatives and offered its support for passage.[93]

Following markup, the House Committee on Interior and Insular Affairs issued its report on H.R. 5237.[94] Although no findings section was included in the bill itself, the committee explained that the purpose of H.R. 5237 was to protect Native American burial sites and the removal of human remains, funerary objects, sacred objects, and objects of cultural patrimony on federal, Indian, and Native Hawaiian lands. The act established a process for federal agencies and museums to inventory such items and work with appropriate Indian tribes and Native Hawaiian organizations to reach agreement on repatriation or other disposition of these remains and objects.[95]

The committee report explained that although the definition of cultural affiliation was intended to ensure that the claimant has a reasonable connection with the materials, the committee was aware that it would extremely difficult for claimants to trace cultural affiliation to an item without some reasonable gaps in the historic or prehistoric record. "In such instances, a finding of cultural affiliation should be based upon an overall evaluation of the totality of the circumstances and evidence pertaining to the connection between the claimant and the material being claimed and should not be precluded solely because of some gaps in the record."[96]

The committee considered one of the purposes of H.R. 5237 to be the protection of Native American burial sites and regulation of the removal of human remains, funerary objects, sacred objects, and objects of cultural patrimony from federal, Indian, and Native Hawaiian lands.[97] "If any of such remains or objects are found on Federal lands and it is known which tribe is closely related to them, that tribe is given the opportunity to reclaim the remains or objects. If the tribe does not want to take possession of the remains or objects, the Secretary of the Interior will determine the disposition of the remains or objects in consultation with Native Americans, scientific and museum groups."[98] The report stressed that the bill would allow for the repatriation of culturally affiliated items as well as any other agreement for disposition or caretaking that may be mutually agreed on by involved parties.[99]

The report stressed that federal agencies and museums should notify Indian tribes and Native Hawaiian organizations as soon as possible after the inventory was completed. The allowance of six months in Section 5(d) was added to assist museums with very limited staffs.[100]

Regarding the new summary section, the report explained that due to the possible high number of unassociated funerary objects, sacred objects, and objects of cultural patrimony, the section was intended to make it easier for the federal agencies, museums, and institutions of higher education to compile and survey the objects in their possession or under their control. It was also intended that there be a shorter time frame for completion of the summary (three years) than for the item-by-item inventory (five years) to permit earlier contact with the appropriate tribe so open discussions could begin.[101]

In commenting on Section 7(b), which refers to scientific studies the outcome of which would be of major benefit to the United States, the committee recognized the importance of these studies and urged the sci-

entific community to enter into mutually agreeable solutions with culturally affiliated tribes in such matters.[102]

All tribes that either received notice or should have received notice
pursuant to the inventory process because of a potential cultural affiliation
(regardless of whether the showing of such affiliation would be based on
museum records or nonmuseum sources) would have standing to request
such information.[103]

The committee recognized that there was general disagreement on the
proper disposition of culturally unidentifiable human remains and looked
forward to the review committee's recommendations in this area.[104]

The savings provisions preserved the right of all parties to enter into
other mutually agreeable arrangements beyond those provided for in the
act. The committee encouraged all sides to negotiate in good faith and
attempt to come to agreements where possible, which would keep certain
items available to all those with legitimate interests.[105]

The committee highlighted one term that was used throughout H.R.
5237 but was not defined separately. "Consultation," the committee recommended, meant "a process involving the open discussion and joint deliberations with respect to potential issues, charges, or actions by all interested parties."[106]

Two days after the report was issued, a letter to members of Congress
further broadened support for H.R. 5237. "Preservation of the right to wor-
ship and engage in religious activities often depends on possession of an
access to ritual artifacts and objects. The NAGPRA secures this important
right for Native Americans. We urge your support for the bill."[107] The let-
ter was signed by representatives of the American Baptist Churches (USA),
American Civil Liberties Union, American Jewish Committee, American
Jewish Congress, Central Conference of American Rabbis, Church Women
United, Episcopal Church, Friends Committee on National Legislation,
Mennonite Central Committee, National Council of Jewish Women,
Presbyterian Church (USA), Union of American Hebrew Congregations,
Unitarian Universalist Association of Congregations, United Church of
Christ, and the United Methodist Church.

S. 1980 was stalled in the Senate because Senator Pete Domenici from
New Mexico had placed a hold on the bill, reportedly to ensure that the
recent agreement between the AAM and Native American representatives
was adequately incorporated.[108] This changed shortly after publication of
the House Committee report on H.R. 5237, with four different versions of
S. 1980 being circulated between October 14 and 22.[109] With momentum
apparently shifting to the Senate version, Walter Echo-Hawk wrote to

House committee staff, suggesting a "fall-back option" if S. 1980 was passed in the Senate before H.R. 5237 passed the House.[110] Echo-Hawk suggested that the House could make technical changes to the Senate bill to more fully incorporate the AAM/Indian agreements, he and provided two memos, one from the AAM and another from NARF, with suggested language. "This option does not solve the Smithsonian issue, which still would have to be resolved between the two Houses—NARF hopes that this issue can be resolved by agreement between the two Houses and not become a sticking point that sinks the legislation. NARF would like to chart a neutral course on this issue at this stage and let the two Houses decide the best course of action on the Smithsonian."

Passage by Congress

On Monday, October 22, Representative Campbell stood before the House of Representatives and asked his colleagues to pass H.R. 5237 into law.[111] "Mr. Speaker," Campbell began, "H.R. 5237 is a bill whose time has come."[112] He explained that it was the result of many hours of negotiation and conformed to agreements between representatives of the museum community, scientific community, and Indian community. Other representatives rose to support the bill, including John Rhodes from Arizona, Cardiss Collins from Illinois, Bill Richardson from New Mexico, Charles Bennett from Florida, and Patsy Mink from Hawaii. H.R. 5237 passed the House by voice vote. "The House bill just passed an hour ago," wrote AAM's Dan Monroe to Marty Sullivan.[113] "We still have a problem with the Senate." According to Monroe, Senator Inouye was going to try to pass S. 1980, which he now considered far out of line with H.R. 5237. "Sen. Inouye is trying to clear the deck in the Senate by promising Senators with concerns that the House bill will prevail [in conference]," but Monroe was concerned whether these promises would be kept. Monroe asked Sullivan, who had recently become director of the Heard Museum in Phoenix, to contact Arizona Senator McCain. The same day, AAM Government Affairs Director Geoffrey Platt wrote to House staffer Marie Howard. "The amendments to S. 1980 that are expected to be offered, and some original language that is retained, represent substantive departure from the agreements made between the AAM and Native American representatives, which are accurately reflected in H.R. 5237."[114]

Following passage of bill by the House, the White House released a statement. "The Administration supports the goals of H.R. 5237," the statement began, "but opposes enactment in its current form. We will work in the Senate to address the following issues."[115] The issues included ensuring that federal agencies would maintain stewardship of culturally unidentifiable human remains and funerary objects; removing aboriginal occupation as a criteria for establishing affinity; allowing additional studies and extensions for federal agencies to complete inventories; deleting the categories of sacred object and object of cultural patrimony; and ensuring the opinions of the review committee would be purely advisory.

Focus now shifted to the Senate. "It was very, very intense," recalls Senate staffer Eric Eberhard.[116]

> We had people on every side coming to us saying "change this," "change that." And at one point I remember saying to the staff: "okay, we've got twenty-four hours left, we're not returning calls." I literally would not return any call related to the bill except from inside the Congress for those last twenty-four hours. We couldn't even concentrate on what we had to do to get the bill out because there was so much incoming.

Instead of considering S. 1980, the following Thursday the Senate took up the House bill and, without any fanfare or discussion, introduced two sets of amendments. In the first set, Senator Wendell Ford from Kentucky proposed revising the definitions of federal agency and museum to exclude the Smithsonian Institution from the bill's provisions.[117] In the version passed by the House, the Smithsonian Institution was explicitly included, "except as may be inconsistent with P.L. 101-185."[118] The definition of museum passed by the House could also be construed to include the Smithsonian, because the institution both receives federal funds and has possession or control of Native American cultural items.[119] The proposed Senate amendment inserted language in both definitions explicitly excluding the Smithsonian, thus relieving it from the bill's summary, inventory, notice, and repatriation provisions. "Had the Smithsonian stayed in," Eberhard recalled, "we would not have been able to get it passed, pure and simple. They had the political firepower to prevent the passage of the bill, and I think everybody who worked on this knew it."[120] The amendment passed.

Senator McCain introduced the second set of amendments, including several provisions specifically focused on Alaskan issues.[121] In the version of H.R. 5237 passed by the House, Indian tribe was defined by reference to the definition of Indian tribe in the Indian Self Determination and Education Assistance Act.[122] That definition, enacted in 1975, included "any

Indian tribe, band, nation, or other organized group or community, including any Alaska Native village *or regional or village corporation* as defined in or established pursuant to the Alaska Native Claims Settlement Act which is recognized as eligible for the special programs and services provided by the United States to Indians because of their status as Indians" (emphasis added).[123] The Senate amendment to H.R. 5237 replaced the citation with the actual text of the Self Determination Act definition, with the exception that Alaska Native village corporations and regional corporations were dropped. The remaining term, "native village" was defined in the Alaska Native Claims Settlement Act (ANCSA) to include any tribe, band, clan, group, village, community, or association in Alaska composed of twenty-five or more persons of one-quarter degree or more Alaska Indian, Eskimo, or Aleut blood, including 216 named native villages.[124] Under the Senate amendment, the 199 Alaska Native village corporations and 13 Alaska Native regional corporations established pursuant to ANCSA would not be able to claim cultural items in museum or federal agency collections, nor would museums or federal agencies be required to consult with Alaska Native village corporations or regional corporations. Another amendment related to the status of Alaska Native corporation lands. Under ANCSA, Alaska Native village corporations and regional corporations selected 44 million acres of lands to which the secretary of the Interior was directed to convey title.[125] However, the process of land conveyance was slow and complex and was still incomplete in 1990.[126] The House version of H.R. 5237 included both lands conveyed or subject to an interim conveyance under the definition of tribal lands,[127] and required the consent of the appropriate Alaska Native corporation prior to the excavation or removal of any Native American cultural items from those lands.[128] The proposed Senate amendment deleted ANCSA lands from the definition of tribal land and redefined federal lands to include those lands that had been selected but not yet conveyed.[129] As a result, the excavation and discovery provisions of bill, including the necessity of obtaining the consent of the appropriate Alaska Native village, would apply to selected lands until they were conveyed. Once the lands were conveyed to the appropriate Alaska Native village corporation or regional corporation, NAGPRA's excavation and discovery provisions no longer applied, with burial and site protection covered instead by state law. The amendment passed. "We always had to work with the concerns of the Alaska senators," Eberhard recalled.[130] "The Alaska senators were always looking for anything that they thought would negatively impact the balance that was struck in ANCSA, pure and simple. They would have been worried that in some way applying the provisions of NAGPRA to Alaska natives would acknowledge the existence of tribal government in Alaska, and they were not about to let that happen. It's that fundamental."

The Senate continued with its morning business, passing amendments to the Indian Arts and Crafts Act, National Capital Transportation Amendments Act, and Indian Child Protection and Family Violence Prevention Act, along with several bills providing specific relief to individual citizens. Unexpectedly, a motion was made to vitiate all actions taken with regard to H.R. 5237, and no objection was voiced. "Mr. President, if I may," offered Wyoming Senator Alan Simpson as explanation, "I will be able to resolve that tomorrow. But I have had contact from several national museums in connection with that particular legislation. Perhaps we can get that resolved."[131]

Eric Eberhard was in his office watching the floor debate on television.[132] The entire committee staff had worked hard to ensure that everyone was on board for the McCain's amendments to H.R. 5237 and Simpson's objection come out of the blue. Eberhard picked up the phone.

"What's your boss doing?" he asked Simpson's staffer, "I thought we were clear on this. We wouldn't have moved if we weren't."

"We're not sure. We'll find out and get back to you." Simpson had apparently heard from some of his Wyoming constituents who did not like the bill. "He's got some concerns," his staffer reported in a follow-up call. "We need to talk those through and see what we need to do by way of amendments."

"I need to understand the concerns," Eberhard responded, "but I don't think there is anything here we can amend. The bill is very finely balanced." Eberhard suggested that before they talk about any amendments, they should consider a colloquy.

H.R. 5237 was reintroduced for consideration by the Senate on Friday, but unlike the previous day, supporting statements were offered by Senators McCain, Inouye, Akaka, Moynihan, and Domenici. McCain characterized H.R. 5237 as a "true compromise," with each of the negotiating parties having to "give a little in order to strike a true balance," and he specifically recognized the diligent efforts of representatives of the AAM, SAA, NARF, and NCAI in developing the consensus.[133] Senator Inouye urged his colleagues to delay no longer in passing H.R. 5237 to undo over a century of injustice in the disparate treatment of Native American dead and restore Native American human rights. He offered that the legislation would not result in the wholesale reduction of museum collections, as some had argued, nor would the rights of antique collectors be taken away. "For museums that have dealt honestly and in good faith with Native Americans," Inouye concluded, "this legislation will have little effect. For museums and institutions which have consistently ignored the requests of Native Americans, this legislation will give Native Americans greater ability to negotiate."[134]

Senator Ford reintroduced the amendments excluding the Smithsonian Institution and explained that the Senate Committee on Rules and Administrative, which had jurisdiction over the Smithsonian Institution and which he chaired, had yet to consider H.R. 5327.[135] McCain added that the previous week he and Inouye had introduced a separate bill to apply the same standards for repatriation of Native American human remains, funerary objects, sacred objects, and objects of cultural patrimony to the Smithsonian Institution.[136] The amendment passed. The second set of amendments dealing with implementation of the bill in Alaska and other matters was introduced by McCain and passed without comment.

Senators Simpson and McCain then engaged in an extended colloquy to clarify the intent of some of the language of the proposed bill. The first concerned legal balances in the law to protect the interests of industries that would be critical to the economy. McCain assured Simpson that the excavation and discovery provisions of the bill did not apply to state or private lands. Furthermore, nothing in the bill would result in a permanent interruption of development activity on federal lands. "[The excavation and discovery] section of the bill is not intended as a bar to the development of Federal or tribal lands on which cultural items are found," McCain concluded. "Nor is this bill intended to significantly interrupt or impair development activities on Federal lands."[137]

Simpson asked whether the newly amended thirty-day time limitation in the inadvertent discovery section would begin from the time of the notice to the government or from the time the determination was made with respect to which Indian tribe was the rightful owner. McCain explained that the period started when the secretary with authority of the discovery site initially received notice, but that the "Secretary of the Interior will have responsibility to determine the ownership of cultural items found on Federal lands." He continued, "this process allows 30 days from the time notice is received by the Secretary for Indian tribes and Native Hawaiian organizations to provide for the appropriate disposition of cultural items found on Federal lands."[138]

Simpson explained that many good citizens in Wyoming enjoy walking and hiking on public lands, and some have small but important collections of artifacts. He wondered what potential liabilities the bill presented such private collectors. McCain explained that the bill would apply only to objects fitting the very narrow definitions of human remains, funerary objects, sacred objects, and objects of cultural patrimony on federal and tribal lands. Private collectors would still be able to pursue their hobby on state and private lands.[139]

Simpson asked if H.R. 5237 creates new property rights and whether lawful owners such as museums would be fairly compensated on the transfer of property to parties asserting rights under the bill. McCain explained that under the common law an individual may only acquire the title to property that is held by the transferor. McCain felt that the bill provides a clear standard for determining whether an item was originally acquired with the voluntary consent of an individual or Indian tribe that had authority to alienate the item in a manner that was consistent with general property law. He believed the bill was crafted in such a way as to avoid any problems with unconstitutional takings under the Fifth Amendment.[140]

H.R. 5237, with the various amendments, was passed by voice vote of the Senate on October 26, 1990.[141]

The House took up the Senate amendments on Friday, October 27, with the provisions excluding the Smithsonian Institution receiving the only substantive comment. "As evidenced by its inclusion in the House version," explained Representative Richardson, "it is clearly the intent of the House that the Smithsonian be held to the same provisions as all other Federal agencies and museums in the country regarding repatriation."[142] However, in the spirit of compromise, he agreed to exclude the Smithsonian Institution from H.R. 5237 in favor of similar legislation dealing specifically with the Smithsonian in the next Congress. Marie Howard recalled that representatives of many museums were livid that the "nation's attic" would not have to comply with the same requirements they faced.[143] Senator Inouye later acknowledged that "the other museums and scientific institutions that were to be covered under the Native American Graves Protection and Repatriation Act objected in the strongest possible terms . . . but ultimately agreed not to oppose passage of the act based in part upon my personal commitment that the Congress would subsequently enact legislation to assure that the Smithsonian Institution would be subject to Federal repatriation law."[144] The House agreed to the Senate amendments by unanimous consent. The bill was cleared for submission to the White House.

The 101st Congress adjourned on October 28, only nine days before the midterm elections. Senators Inouye, McCain, and Fowler were not running for reelection, but Representatives Bennett and Udall were re-elected on November 6. The Democrats gained one seat in the Senate and nine in the House, expanding their majorities in both bodies. The question remained as to whether Republican President George Bush would sign H.R. 5237 into law.

"Bush Weighs Bill on Tribal Remains," read a *New York Times* head-line.[145] The article pointed out that the administration had opposed an earlier version of the bill. Administration concerns that the bill would affect private property, and thereby call into play the Takings Clause of the Constitution, were addressed by refining the definition of right of possession and adding a clause stipulating that nothing in the bill could be construed to limit the application of any state or federal law pertaining to theft or stolen property. None of the administration's other demands were addressed in the final bill. The provision remained charging the review committee with compiling an inventory of culturally unidentifiable human remains and recommending specific actions for developing a process for their disposition. Disposition of cultural items discovered or excavated from federal or tribal land could still be made to an Indian tribe based on a cultural relationship or discovery on the tribe's aboriginal territory. Language allowing additional studies to ensure a correct determination of affinity had not been added, nor had provisions allowing federal agencies to apply for an extension to the inventory deadline. The bill still applied to sacred objects and objects of cultural patrimony. Congress had clearly rejected the administration's demands.

While the administration's position was being decided, the No-Name Alliance contacted representatives of the various tribal organizations to express a unified position on the pending legislation. On November 2, 1990, representatives of twelve national Native American and scientific organizations and three tribal organizations sent a letter urging President Bush to sign H.R. 5237 into law. The representatives identified the bill as "a vital piece of legislation that is the product of a carefully constructed compromise which has earned the support of Indian, museum, and historic preservation communities." The letter went on to predict that "the bill will create a workable framework fostering sensitivity and cooperation in achieving the appropriate repatriation of Native American human remains and cultural objects." The letter, on the letterhead of the SAA, was signed by representatives of the American Anthropological Association, American Association of Physical Anthropologists, Archaeological Institute of America, Association for American Indian Affairs, NARF, National

Conference of State Historic Preservation Officers, NCAI, National Trust for Historic Preservation, Preservation Action, SAA, Society for Historical Archaeology, and the Society of Professional Archaeologists.

On November 9, 1990, Assistant Secretary of the Interior Constance Harriman wrote to the Office of Management and Budget (OMB) regarding H.R. 5237.[146] Harriman explained that the bill incorporated many of the principles underlying the department's evolving approach to the treatment of human remains and funerary objects, and was generally better than other repatriation bills then under consideration. However, she pointed out that many issues outlined in Deputy Assistant Secretary Scott Sewall's October 2, 1990, letter to Representative Udall had not been addressed. "In light of the positive aspects of this legislation," Harriman concluded, "these concerns do not justify recommending disapproval of this legislation. Therefore, we recommend Presidential approval of enrolled bill H.R. 5237." In a November 14, 1990, memorandum to the president, OMB Director Richard Darman summarized agency recommendations regarding the enrolled bill.[147] The Departments of the Interior and Agriculture recommended approval, and the Department of Defense and the Smithsonian Institution did not provide comment.[148] The Department of Justice deferred to the other departments as to whether the bill should receive executive approval, but did raise concerns that Section 7(b), requiring the repatriation of culturally affiliated human remains and associated funerary objects, set forth no basis for private museums to lawfully decline. "While section 7 (b) is not unconstitutional, that provision may result in claims against the United States under the [Takings Clause of the] of the Constitution."[149] Darman's conclusion was to join the Departments of the Interior and Agriculture in recommending approval of H.R. 5237. His memorandum was circulated to the White House senior staff the next day with a 6 p.m. deadline for comments and recommendations.[150] President Bush signed the Native American Graves Protection and Repatriation Act into law on November 16, 1990. There was no signing ceremony or public announcement.

The Smaller Scope of Conscience

In the four years and twenty-nine days between the time when Senator Melcher introduced his first repatriation bill and President Bush signed the Native American Graves Protection and Repatriation Act into law, sixteen different numbered repatriation bills, some with several versions, were considered by leaders in both houses of Congress.[151] The various versions were used to negotiate and resolve most (though not all) of the important issues necessary to establish a national system for the disposition or repatriation of Native American human remains, funerary objects, sacred objects, and objects of cultural patrimony. Throughout the process, legislators and their staffers, along with representatives of the various constituency groups, selected specific issues for inclusion, refined the various terms and definitions, then refined them again, before stuffing them into two similar (but not identical) statutes that were passed by Congress without any opposition.

The Native American representatives were relieved. Congress had been scheduled to adjourn two weeks earlier so that the members could return to their districts to campaign for the November elections. An unrelated budget dispute kept them in session. "As it was, NAGPRA was the next to last bill passed in that session of Congress," recalled Jack Trope. "That's how close we came to not passing the bill in the 101st Congress. No one knows for sure what would have happened had we been forced to start again in the 102nd Congress." The Native American representatives were aware that opposition forces might better organize themselves and push back more strongly. "We probably would have passed something, but I have always believed that it would likely have been a weaker bill than the NAGPRA that was passed."[152]

Geoffrey Platt Jr., director of government affairs for the AAM, described the result as a true compromise. "Inflexible righteousness may be blessed," he wrote, "but principled flexibility is the key. Reaching a true compromise—in which each side has to give something to the other—always is difficult; deciding to attempt it and confront one's colleagues with that necessity, as happened at AAM, takes courage."[153]

The mood at the SAA was more reserved. Two days after NAGPRA was signed into law, SAA President Jeremy Sabloff's report to the executive board acknowledged the great amount of "psychic energy" that the reburial issue had taken from many people.[154] It "looked like we were going to get trampled," he reported, "but individuals count, as well as serendipity." He concluded that the final version of H.R. 5237 was better than he had hoped and would prove workable. In a commentary to the SAA membership titled "Repatriation We Can Live With," Keith Kintigh highlighted several features of the new law.[155] Under NAGPRA, repatriation is considered on a case-by-case basis contingent on a finding of cultural affiliation. The law does not mandate repatriation, it specifies the cases in which federally recognized Indian tribes or Native Hawaiian organizations have the right to determine the disposition of human remains or cultural items. Although Kintigh lamented that the final statute did not include provisions enhancing protection of Native American sites or for funding documentation of cultural items to be returned, he credited good-faith negotiations and compromise among the interested parties with leading to a bill that received broad support from the Indian, museum, scientific, and historic preservation communities. Kintigh concluded that NAGPRA creates a legal framework in which the balance between scientific importance and the cultural or religious values of related groups that was advocated in the SAA's 1986 Statement Concerning the Treatment of Human Remains can be achieved.

At some federal agencies, despair over repatriation legislation was manifest even as George H. W. Bush was about to sign NAGPRA into law. "I am not quite sure why the reburial issue should be included in a session entitled 'Restoration and Protection: Cutting Our Losses,'" began a National Park Service senior archeologist at a conference on November 15, 1990. "Reburial may in fact be contributing to and increasing our losses."[156]

Passage of H.R. 5237 involved the concentrated efforts of three members of Congress: Representative Morris Udall, Senator Daniel Inouye, and Senator John McCain. "If you look at them each as individuals," Eberhard recalled, "you couldn't find three more different folks by background, and personality, and everything else. Different reasons, different backgrounds, completely different people. But I think that they had a deep visceral reaction the more they learned about what was going on, and they formed a very, very powerful working team on these issues. It was really inevitable that you find a strong alliance between Mo, Inouye, and McCain on the legislation."[157]

Passage of NAGPRA represented the legislative process at its best, according to Marie Howard. "I think that this is a very good example of how laws should be made and can make a difference. From the legal side of things it comes down to property law. From the human side of it," she continued, "it was something very different and something that from Mr. Udall's perspective, from my perspective, is what government is good at."[158]

Udall hailed passage of the bill.

For decades, the skeletal remains of American Indians were removed from their burial sites, studied, catalogued, and relegated to the bins of museums and science. This legislation is about respecting the rights of the dead, the right to an undisturbed resting-place. It is a good bill, and long overdue. What we are saying to American Indians today, Mr. Speaker, is simply that your ancestors and their burial grounds are sacred, and will remain so.

In the larger scope of history, this is a very small thing. In the smaller scope of conscience, it may be the biggest thing we have ever done.[159]

Epilogue

Senator John McCain described H.R. 5237 as a "true compromise,"[160] and the past twenty years have shown it was an agreement that lasted. Amendments to NAGPRA have all been of a technical nature. In 1992, reference to the "United States Claims Court" in the definition of right of possession was changed to the "United States Court of Federal Claims."[161] In 1994, the capitalization in the title to the trafficking section was changed.[162] Other amendments have been proposed but have not received the necessary support in both houses of Congress to be enacted.[163]

In contrast, the repatriation provisions of the NMAI Act were clearly a work in progress. Even before H.R. 5237 was passed, Senators Inouye and McCain had already introduced an amendment to add definitions and summary, inventory, and notification provisions from the House bill to the NMAI Act.[164] Summaries were to be completed in three years. Inventories were to be completed within four years, with notification published in the *Federal Register*. The repatriation section of H.R. 5237 was included almost verbatim, as were definitions of "burial site," "cultural affiliation," "Indian tribe," "Native Hawaiian organization" (with an added provision requiring a membership of which a majority are Native Hawaiian), "associated funerary object," "unassociated funerary object," "sacred object," "Native American cultural patrimony," and "right of possession." However, the amendments were not voted on before the 101st Congress adjourned. A similar bill was introduced early in 1991, but likewise, it was not enacted.[165]

The matter of amending the NMAI Act arose again at a December 6, 1995, hearing before the Senate Indian Affairs Committee. Tessie Naranjo, chair of the Native American Graves Protection and Repatriation Review Committee, and committee member Dan Monroe presented the findings of the committee's Report to Congress for 1993–1994 which, among other recommendations, asked Congress to amend the NMAI Act to bring the Smithsonian repatriation process into line with practices under NAGPRA.[166] Inouye was curious about the review committee's recommendation and asked for detailed information as to how that institution was not complying with those provisions.[167] Monroe explained that various components of the Smithsonian were currently operating under different repatriation policies. The National Museum of the American Indian repatriation policy was "more liberal" than NAGPRA, whereas the rest of the Smithsonian Institution was operating under different policies. Monroe was particularly concerned that the Smithsonian was not required to complete summaries or inventories of its collections. Inouye agreed that the law must be applied evenly and without exception. "At the time of the passage of this Act," he recalled,

> the Smithsonian Institution prevailed upon the committee not to include the full institution in the act until such time as an overall institutional policy could be developed which might reconcile the differences between provisions addressing repatriation and the Native American Museum and other Smithsonian museums. We, in Congress, relied upon the representations of the Smithsonian at that time that recommendations for special legislation closely paralleling the provisions of the NAGPRA would be forthcoming. I will be calling upon the Secretary of the Institution to work with the committee to develop such legislation that we promised. I give you my pledge on that, sir.[168]

On July 18, 1996, Senator McCain fulfilled Inouye's promise by introducing S. 1970, a bill to amend the NMAI Act.[169] Senators Inouye, Ben Nighthorse Campbell, and Craig Thomas (Wyoming) were listed as cosponsors. McCain indicated that his intent was to ensure that the Smithsonian Institution carry out repatriation activities in a manner consistent with NAGPRA "so that these culturally important items can be returned to their rightful keepers and protectors, the Indian tribes."[170]

The bill proposed to amend Section 11 of the NMAI Act by defining the term "inventory" and establishing a deadline for its completion. It was defined as a simple, itemized list that, to the extent practicable, identifies, based on available information had by the Smithsonian Institution, the geographic and cultural affiliation of the Indian human remains and funerary objects in the possession or control of the Smithsonian Institution.[171] The proposed definition appears to have combined text from two sources in NAGPRA.[172] The one significant difference between the inventory as defined in NAGPRA and as defined in the amendment related to the range of evidence required. NAGPRA requires that the inventory be based on information "possessed by" the museum or federal agency.[173] The proposed amendment requires that the inventory be based on information "available" to the Smithsonian Institution. Regardless of the source of information, the proposed amendment set June 1, 1998, as the deadline.

The bill established a new Section 11(a) of the NMAI Act to require the secretary of the Smithsonian to develop a written summary of unassociated funerary objects, sacred objects, and objects of cultural patrimony by December 31, 1996.[174] The summary was defined by specific reference to the relevant provisions of NAGPRA,[175] as were the definitions of unassociated funerary objects, sacred objects, and objects of cultural patrimony.[176] Human remains and associated funerary objects were not defined.

The proposed amendments also required the Smithsonian to expeditiously return unassociated funerary objects, sacred objects, or objects of cultural patrimony to a requesting direct lineal descendant, Indian tribe, or Native Hawaiian organization when cultural affiliation has been established in the preparation of the summary or by information received from a requesting party.[177] Requests by direct lineal descendants were given priority over requests by culturally affiliated Indian tribes or Native Hawaiian organizations. The term "direct lineal descendant" was not defined.

The proposed amendments borrowed the "standard of repatriation" section from NAGPRA.[178] Unassociated funerary objects, sacred objects, or objects of cultural patrimony would be returned if a known lineal descendant or an Indian tribe or Native Hawaiian organization presented evidence that the Smithsonian Institution did not have right of possession, unless the Smithsonian could overcome that inference and prove it does have right of possession. However, right of possession was not defined. The amendments to the NMAI Act did not include the two additional exemptions contained in NAGPRA for situations in which there would be competing claims[179] or the cultural items would be indispensable for completion of a specific scientific study, the outcome of which would be of major benefit to the United States.[180]

Another proposed subsection mirrored the "museum obligation" section of NAGPRA,[181] exempting any museum of the Smithsonian Institution from liability for claims by an aggrieved party, or for claims of fiduciary duty, public trust, or violations of applicable law, if the museum repatriated any items in good faith pursuant to the act. The corresponding provisions in NAGPRA applied only to museums and provided no limitation of liability for federal agencies.

Another proposed subsection provided the secretary of the Smithsonian with the discretion to make an inventory, prepare a written summary, or carry out the repatriation of unassociated funerary objects, sacred objects, or objects of cultural patrimony in a manner that exceeds the requirements of the act. There is no corresponding section in the NAGPRA summary requirements, although the NAGPRA inventory requirements preclude construing the statute to be an authorization for the initiation of new scientific studies of human remains and associated funerary objects or other means of acquiring or preserving additional scientific information.[182]

The bill proposed to amend Section 12 of the NMAI Act to expand membership of the special committee from five to seven persons, including two traditional religious leaders.[183] The committee report made it clear that the expansion of the special committee by two members and its additional responsibility for unassociated funerary objects, sacred objects, and objects of cultural patrimony in the National Museum of Natural History would not alter or interfere with the sole authority of the board of trustees of the National Museum of the American Indian concerning repatriation at that institution.[184]

Finally, included in the proposed amendments was a definition of Native Hawaiian organization by specific reference to the term in NAGPRA. The original NMAI Act used the term without definition but included specific definitions for two such organizations, the Office of Hawaiian Affairs and Hui Malama I Na Kupuna O Hawai'i Nei.

On August 2, 1996, the bill was reported to the Senate by the Committee on Indian Affairs.[185] Senator Orrin Hatch from Utah added his name as a cosponsor on September 5, the same day the bill passed with the unanimous consent of the Senate. The House concurred on September 26, and President Bill Clinton signed the bill into law on October 9, 1996.[186]

The 1996 amendments to the NMAI Act that finally required the Smithsonian to expeditiously return sacred objects to direct lineal descendants came too late for William Tallbull. He passed away seven months before and, as the first hints of spring caressed the snow-covered Montana hills, was laid to rest in the Busby cemetery on the Northern Cheyenne Reservation. Father Peter Powell—the Episcopal priest, scholar, author, and honorary member of the Northern Cheyenne Tribe who had corroborated the sincerity of Tallbull's efforts to the Smithsonian researcher—traveled from Chicago to conduct the funeral service. Tallbull's face was painted with the distinctive markings of the Dog Soldier Society. His quest to reclaim his grandfather's pipe remains unfulfilled.

CHAPTER EIGHT

Legislative History in Interpretive Context

President George H. W. Bush's signature on the final page of the National Museum of the American Indian (NMAI) Act and on the Native American Graves Protection and Repatriation Act (NAGPRA) ended the opening stage of the legislative process covered in the first seven chapters of this book. Legal scholars remind us, however, that codification of statutes is not the end of lawmaking but only the beginning.[1] Consistent with the separation of powers established by the U.S. Constitution, the federal courts are granted the final and authoritative interpretation of what a statute means, and executive agencies may conduct formal rulemaking and adjudication of the meaning of statutory language, subject to judicial review.[2] This final chapter briefly explores the role legislative history has had and will continue to have in the second life of the repatriation provisions of the NMAI Act and NAGPRA.

The interpretation of statutes is not done in a vacuum. To aid in the process, the courts have developed an array of informal "intrinsic" rules to guide how statutory text should be read. Supreme Court Justice Felix Frankfurter (1882–1965) is credited with the most succinct articulation of the primary extrinsic rule of statutory interpretation. First, read the statute. Next, read the statute again. Then, read the statute another time.[3] A thorough review of the text within the "four corners" of a statute is a mandatory initial step in the process of statutory interpretation. The basic components of the legislative text—the individual words, phrases, and sentences—must each be given legal effect, if possible, so that no part of the text will be made inoperative, superfluous, void, or insignificant.[4]

Words and phrases that are used more than once are presumed to have the same meaning each time they are used, whereas different terms in the statute may not be construed to have the same meaning.[5] Words or phrases that are not specifically defined are presumed to have their common meaning, which may be discerned by reference to their dictionary definitions.[6] Some intrinsic rules have a much broader purview, such as the canon that each part or section of a statute should be interpreted in a fashion that is consistent with the entire legislative scheme of which it is a part. Mediating any inherent contradictions between the specific and general intrinsic rules is an overarching presumption that the general purpose of the legislative scheme always controls, with all specific parts considered subsidiary to the general intent of the legislation.[7]

Individual words are the basic building blocks of a statute. The repatriation provisions of the NMAI Act—Sections 11 through 14 and parts of Sections 2 and 16—include 369 unique words, which are used a cumulative total of 1,445 times. Typical of most English-language texts, the most common word in these sections is the definite article "the," which is used 125 times, accounting for nearly 9 percent of the total number of words. Nearly 30 percent of the words are articles ("the," "a," "an"), conjunctions ("and," "or," "but," "so"), or prepositions ("of," "to," "in," "with," "for," "by"). On the other end of the spectrum, over half of the total words in the NMAI Act repatriation provisions are used only once. Some of the 369 unique words are combined to form phrases that are used repeatedly throughout these provisions. One word and six multiword phrases are defined specifically, including "Indian," "Hui Malama I Na Kupuna O Hawai'i Nei," "Office of Hawaiian Affairs," "burial site," "funerary object," "Indian tribe," "Native American," and "Native Hawaiian." Phrases that are frequently used in the repatriation provisions but are not separately defined include "human remains" and "preponderance of the evidence."

NAGPRA includes 773 unique words—about twice as many as are in the NMAI Act repatriation provisions, in a text that is more than three times the other act's length. However, the comparative prevalence of words is similar. The definite article "the" is likewise the most common word, used 310 times or almost 7 percent of the total words. Almost half of the total words in NAGPRA are used only once. Nineteen of the multiword phrases are defined specifically, including "burial site," "cultural affiliation," "cultural items," "associated funerary objects," "unassociated funerary objects," "sacred objects," "cultural patrimony," "Federal agency," "Federal lands," "Hui Malama I Na Kupuna O Hawai'i Nei," "Indian tribe," "museum," "Native American," "Native Hawaiian," "Native Hawaiian organization," "Office of Hawaiian Affairs," "right of possession," "Secretary," and "tribal land." Five phrases used frequently in NAGPRA that are not separately defined are "human remains," "preponderance of the evidence," "lineal descendant," "religious leader," and "good faith."

Following the rules of statutory interpretation, all 1,445 words in the NMAI repatriation provisions and 4,575 words in NAGPRA must be given legal effect. Within the NMAI Act, the 369 unique words in the repatriation provisions are presumed to have the same meaning each time they are use; the same goes for the 773 unique words in NAGPRA. The majority of terms and phrases in both statutes are not defined specifically, meaning that the same common meaning applies. Typical of the differences between the meaning of terms in the NMAI Act and NAGPRA are those that are defined specifically in one statute but not the other.

A frequently invoked rule of statutory interpretation asserts that a statute that is clear and unambiguous on its face may not be interpreted by a court.[8] Legislation is considered ambiguous when well-informed persons can reasonably disagree about its meaning. Questions regarding statutory construction are matters of law and are decided by a judge, not by a jury. However, the court should never exclude relevant and probative evidence in determining the statutory meaning, included legislative history.

Legislative History

Legislative history is commonly used by the courts and executive agencies to interpret statutory meaning, particularly when ambiguous language is identified. An important distinction must be made between a "history of legislation," such as in this book, and a "legislative history," which is used by the courts and executive branch to interpret the meaning of a statute. A history of legislation typically begins at the beginning: exploring the issues in need of legislative remedy; chronicling the actions of lobbying groups' documenting the introduced bills, congressional hearings, and reports over several Congresses; and ending with the enacted statute. A history of legislation also relies on a wide range of sources: the bills themselves and related committee and hearing reports prepared prior to passage, handwritten meeting notes, emails, postenactment recollections, even sticky notes—basically, any and all relevant information. A legislative history, on the other hand, starts at the end—the enacted bill—and then isolates its constituent parts and applies specific parts of the available historical documentation to the singular task of understanding the meaning of specific words, phrases, or provisions of the statute. Similarly, a legislative history relies on much narrower range of sources, typically defined to include only those documents readily available to and relied on by the legislators in passing the bill.[9]

The primary source of legislative history is the report issued by the sponsoring congressional committee(s) prior to consideration by Congress as a whole. Such a report is typically issued when the bill is voted out by the sponsoring committee, and it is reasonable to assume that the legislature as a whole adopted the intent of the committee for those parts of a bill passed as discussed in the committee report without change.[10] Conversely, committee reports for rejected or failed bills, or for portions of bills that were changed before they were passed by Congress as a whole, are considered meaningless and cannot be used as extrinsic aids.[11]

Although the enacted bill number typically provides a link to the appropriate committee report, the NMAI Act, identified as S. 978 in the *Congressional Record*, provides a counterexample. During the first session of the 101st Congress, there were two parallel bills to establish the National Museum of the American Indian. Senator Daniel Inouye introduced S. 978 in the Senate on May 11, 1989; four weeks later, Representative Ben Nighthorse Campbell introduced H.R. 2668 in the House of Representatives.[12] The Senate Select Committee on Indian Affairs reported out Inouye's bill first, issuing its report on September 27, 1989.[13] S. 978 passed the whole Senate on October 3, 1989, and was then referred for consideration to the House of Representatives.[14] Instead of taking up the Senate bill, however, the House continued consideration of H.R. 2668, with the Committee on Public Works and Transportation and the Committee on House Administration issuing separate reports.[15] On November 13, 1989, the House passed H.R. 2668, and then turned to S. 978 by striking all of the Senate language and replacing it with the text from H.R. 2668.[16] Although the bill that was eventually signed into law by President Bush bears the Senate number, all of the text is from the House bill, including the codification of the repatriation provisions resulting from the August 1989 agreement between Secretary of the Smithsonian Robert Adams and the Native American negotiators. Thus, the two House committee reports, identified as parts 1 and 2 of House Report 101-340, provide the most accurate reflection of congressional intent. The two parts of the report are nearly identical, providing the same version of the bill and almost verbatim purpose, background, and discussion sections. Both legislative background sections mention three previous bills considered in the 101st Congress—Byron Dorgan's H.R. 1124, Morris Udall's H.R. 1646, and Campbell's H.R. 2668—as well as two House bills considered during the 100th Congress (Udall's H.R. 3480 and Dorgan's H.R. 5411). Both reports highlight the August 1989 agreement between representatives of the Smithsonian and the Indian community with respect to the repatriation of human remains and funerary objects.

The primary source of legislative history for NAGPRA is the report issued for H.R. 5237 by the House Committee on Interior and Insular Affairs on October 15, 1990.[17] Besides providing the then-current version of the bill, the report summarizes the bill's purpose and provides an outline of the background history, including the July 29, 1988, hearing before the Senate Select Committee on Indian Affairs on John Melcher's S. 187; the November 28, 1989, passage of the NMAI Act; the February 28, 1990, issuance of the final report of the National Dialogue on Museum/Native American Relations; the June 17, 1990, hearing before the House Committee on Interior and Insular Affairs regarding Bennett's H.R. 1381 and Udall's H.R. 1646 and H.R. 5237; and the October 10, 1990, committee markup of H.R. 5237.

Although H.R. 5237 was under consideration in the House, the Senate Select Committee on Indian Affairs was working on a parallel bill. The committee report on S. 1980 was issued on September 26, 1990, but the bill was eventually abandoned in lieu of H.R. 5237. Although committee reports for rejected or failed bills are considered meaningless and cannot be used as extrinsic aids, the regulations promulgated by the secretary of the Interior and the court in one particular case mistakenly relied on Senate Report 101-473 in reaching their conclusions.

In addition to committee reports, courts have considered statements made by some members of Congress during deliberations to confirm a bill's purpose, meaning, and intended effect. The greatest deference is given to statements by the chairperson and other members of the sponsoring committee after the bill is reported out by the committee.[18] Such post–committee report statements are often viewed as supplements to the committee report and are accorded the same weight. Consideration may also be given to statements made by the sponsor of the bill or an amendment.[19] Isolated remarks by other members of Congress are generally not considered when interpreting the statutory text.[20] Statements by individual members of Congress, regardless of role, are not given effect to override a clear and unambiguous meaning in the language of the statute.

For the NMAI Act, four different committees were involved in deliberations on various versions. The bill reported out by the Senate Rules Committee and the Select Committee on Indian Affairs on September

27, 1989, included rudimentary repatriation provisions that received no comment from the respective committee chairs, Wendell Ford from Kentucky and Inouye. Senator John McCain from Arizona, vice chair of the Indian Affairs Committee, described the repatriation provisions as reflecting an agreement by the Smithsonian Institution to inventory and repatriate Native American human remains and associated grave offerings.[21] When elaborated repatriation provisions were added to the corresponding House bill, neither Udall, chair of the Insular and Interior Affairs Committee, nor Frank Annunzio from Illinois, chair of the Administration Committee, commented on the revision. However, Representative Campbell, sponsor of the House bill, indicated that he felt the revised provisions meant that "many of the skeletal remains and funerary objects currently held by the Smithsonian Institution will be available for return to Indian tribes."[22] Other comments regarding the House repatriation language came from Representative Dorgan,[23] Eni F. H. Faleomvaega from American Samoa,[24] and James T. Walsh from New York.[25] When the Senate again considered S. 978, with the House repatriation amendments, Inouye acknowledged the resolution of the repatriation issue but did not elaborate on any of the details of that resolution.[26]

Udall, who was both the sponsor of H.R. 5237 and the chair of the House Interior and Insular Affairs Committee, did not comment on the bill prior to passage. Six representatives addressed the House prior to the initial passage of the bill on October 22, 1990, including Campbell,[27] John Rhodes from Illinois,[28] Cardiss Collins from Illinois,[29] Bill Richardson from New Mexico,[30] Charles Bennett from Florida,[31] and Patsy Mink from Hawaii.[32] The most extensive on-the-record discussion of H.R. 5237 occurred following introduction of the two Senate amendments on October 26, 1990, including comments and colloquies involving McCain,[33] Ford,[34] Inouye,[35] Daniel Akaka from Hawaii,[36] Daniel Patrick Moynihan from New York,[37] Alan Simpson from Wyoming,[38] and Pete Domenici from New Mexico.[39]

The various versions of a bill considered by the relevant committee or the whole legislature are also important in determining how specific provisions are to be construed or applied. The general pattern is that the statutory language becomes more detailed and specific over time as alternative situations are considered by the legislature. Language that was considered and rejected by the legislature provides an indication that the body did not want the issue considered and that the provisions should not be subsequently adopted by the court or executive agency.[40] Five versions of S. 978 were considered by the Senate or House in 1989. The initial bill was introduced by Senator Inouye on May 11 and was referred to the Committee on Rules and the Select Committee on Indian Affairs.[41] An amended version was introduced by the Committee on Rules on May 17.[42] Another amended version was introduced on September 27 by the Select Committee on Indian Affairs.[43] A fourth version was passed by the Senate on October 3.[44] The repatriation provisions in these early versions directed the Smithsonian to conduct a study, in consultation with tradition Indian religious leaders, that would identify the identity of all Indian skeletal remains and associated grave offerings in its possession and recommended a policy for their return, repatriation, or final disposition. The report would be provided to Congress within three years of enactment of the statute. On November 13, the House struck all of the Senate language and inserted language from H.R. 2668, with the Senate agreeing to the House amendments the next day. The so-called Santa Fe agreement, which was formalized in the November 9, 1989, version of H.R. 2669 and subsequent versions of S. 978, greatly expanded the repatriation provisions by shifting the Smithsonian's mandate from one of conducting a study and recommending action to Congress to determining the identity or cultural affiliation of Indian and Native Hawaiian human remains and associated funerary objects and, on request, expeditiously repatriating them to the descendant or culturally affiliated Indian tribe or Native Hawaiian organization.

Seven versions of H.R. 5237 were considered by the House or Senate in 1990. The initial bill was introduced by Udall on July 10 and was referred for consideration by the House Committee on Interior and Insular Affairs.[45] Udall introduced an amended version September 24.[46] A third version was provided to the House committee prior to markup on October 10 with a revised fourth version included in the House committee's October 15 report.[47] The House passed a fifth version of H.R. 5237 on October 22.[48] A sixth version was considered and amended by the Senate on October 25, vitiated, then passed again on October 26.[49] The seventh and final version of H.R. 5237 was passed by the House a second time on October 27.[50]

Federal courts occasionally consider statements made at congressional hearings as aids for determining legislative intent. Such statements may include those of a sponsor concerning a bill's nature and effect or those of a witness urging adoption of an amendment if Congress then adopts the witness's view. Statements made by others at committee hearings are generally not accorded any weight.[51] At the joint hearing held by the Select Committee on Indian Affairs and the Committee on Rules and Administration on S. 978, five senators spoke, including the bill's sponsor, along with twelve other individuals representing the Museum of the American Indian, city and state of New York, Smithsonian Institution, and several Native American organizations.[52] Only one interchange occurred regarding S. 978's repatriation provisions, between Onondaga Chief Oren Lyons and Senator Inouye about the prospect for the Onondaga repatriating wampum belts at the Smithsonian.[53] The joint hearings held by the House Committee on Interior and Insular Affairs, House Administration, and Public Works and the Committee on Transportation include statements from thirteen representatives, including the bill's sponsor, along with nineteen other individuals representing the Museum of the American Indian, city and state of New York, Smithsonian Institution, several Indian tribes and Native American organizations, a museum, a university, and the Society for American Archaeology (SAA).[54] A number of representatives and witnesses specifically addressed the issue of repatriation. The following year, the House Committee on Interior and Insular Affairs hearing on three repatriation bills—Bennett's H.R. 1381 and Udall's H.R. 1646 and 5237—included statements by Bennett and two other representatives, one senator, and eleven other individuals representing several Indian tribes and Native American organizations, the SAA and American Association of Museums (AAM), a museum, and the Antique Tribal Art Dealers Association.[55]

Finally, though not considered part of the legislative history per se, statutory interpretation may also rely on other external sources, such as other statutes and the common law. The NMAI Act includes explicit reference to five other statutes, three of which relate directly to the repatriation provisions.[56] The term "Indian tribe" is defined by specific reference to the same term in the Indian Self Determination and Education Assistance Act.[57] The special committee established to monitor and review the inventory, identification, and return of Indian human remains and funerary objects is explicitly exempted from provisions of the Federal Advisory Committee Act.[58] The 1996 amendments to the act define "unassociated funerary objects," "sacred objects," "objects of cultural patrimony," "summary," and "Native Hawaiian organization" by specific reference to the same terms in NAGPRA.[59] NAGPRA includes reference to five other laws. The Alaska Native Claims Settlement Act is relied on to define "federal lands" to include land selected but not yet conveyed to an Alaska Native corporation, and "Indian tribe" to include Alaska Native villages (but not Alaska Native corporations).[60] "Tribal land" is defined to include lands administered for the benefit of Native Hawaiians pursuant to the Hawaiian Homes Commission Act and the Act to Provide for the Admission of the State of Hawaii into the Union.[61] The U.S. Court of Federal Claims is assigned jurisdiction to determine if the definition of "right of possession" results in Fifth Amendment taking by the United States.[62] Cultural items may only be removed or excavated from federal or tribal land pursuant to a permit issued under provisions of the Archaeological Resources Protection Act (ARPA).[63] Interpretation of statutes included by reference is guided by several rules. Two statutes dealing with the same subject should be harmonized if possible. A provision of a new statute is presumed to be in accord with the legislative policy in prior statutes in the absence of an expressed repeal or amendment with the body of statutes dealing with the same subject being construed together.[64] If there remains conflict in meaning, the latter, more specialized statute prevails.[65] When specific reference is made to some provision or definition in another statute, only the appropriate parts of the referenced statute are considered.[66]

Common law—the body of usages and customs of immemorial antiquity and the judgments and decrees of the courts—can also influence how statutes are interpreted. For federal civil statutes, the common law consists of the body of English law at the time of the Declaration of Independence and court opinions of the various states at the time the federal statute was enacted. In cases where the clear language of a federal civil statute conflicts with the common law, the statutory language governs as the latest expression of law. Conversely, in cases where the language of a federal civil statute is ambiguous, the common law is presumed to prevail.[67] Although Congress is presumed to already know the relevant common law before a statute is enacted, the Native American Rights Fund (NARF) outlined relevant common law provisions during the various House and Senate hearings.[68] One cannot have an ownership interest in a dead body, but the next of kin retain a right to control its disposition. Any ownership interest that may be recognized in funerary objects would be with the next of kin. A thief cannot acquire any title to stolen property and cannot confer title to any purchaser.

Against the rich background of sources of legislative history for the NMAI Act and NAGPRA, the amount of postenactment interpretation of the statutes is actually quite unequal. The NMAI Act is rarely cited in published court opinions, with most of these citations relating to broader issues of federal acknowledgment of certain rights to Native Hawaiians and not to repatriation issues. Although the NMAI Act does require administrative rulemaking, it only relates to the activities of the special repatriation advisory committee. Internal policies and guidelines formulated without notice and comment rulemaking are generally not accorded any deference by the courts. Deliberations of the special committee are explicitly exempted from government-wide requirements for open meetings and publicly available detailed minutes. Overall, there is only a minimal public record of how the NMAI Act is being interpreted. On the other hand, NAGPRA, which applies to more than 1,000 museums and federal entities as well as criminal defendants, has been repeatedly litigated. The Department of the Interior used notice and comment rulemaking to promulgated interpretive regulations in 1995, 1997, 2003, 2007, and 2010. Proceedings of the Native American Graves Protection and Repatriation Review Committee are transcribed, and all of their findings and recommendations are published in the *Federal Register*. As a result, there are considerably more examples of judicial and executive interpretation of specific terms in NAGPRA than there are for corresponding terms in the NMAI Act. Despite this disparity, review of these statutes can identify areas of potential ambiguity that could be litigated in the future and for which the legislative history and external sources can be used to clarify. These issues fall into four broad categories. Who must comply with the statutes? Who has standing to make a request? What items are covered? What activities are required?

Who Must Comply with the Statutes?

Identifying the parties that must comply is typically the first question asked of any legislation. The repatriation provisions of the NMAI Act and NAGPRA collectively define three mutually exclusive jurisdictional categories—the Smithsonian Institution, federal agencies, and museums.

Though most of the NMAI Act is devoted to the establishment and management of the National Museum of the American Indian, the repatriation provisions apply more broadly to the Smithsonian Institution as a whole.[69] The findings section of the NMAI Act address specifically the 4,000 Indian remains acquired from the Army Medical Museum, as well as the approximately 14,000 additional Indian remains acquired through archeological excavations, individual donations, and museum donations.[70] These 18,000 remains were in the collections of the National Museum of Natural History when the NMAI Act was enacted.

The repatriation provisions of NAGPRA apply to two categories of institutions: federal agencies and museums. The statute defines a federal agency as "any department, agency, or instrumentality of the United States."[71] Although the Smithsonian Institution is a congressionally chartered instrumentality of the United States, Congress chose to explicitly exclude it from NAGPRA's definition of federal agency.[72] Regulations promulgated by the Department of the Interior clarify that the definition of federal agency includes all components of the executive, legislative, and judicial branches of the U.S. government that either manage land or have possession or control of collections of Native American human remains or cultural items.[73] All federal agencies are responsible for completing summaries and inventories of Native American collections in their control.[74] Federal agencies are responsible for the appropriate treatment and care of all collections from federal lands being held by nongovernmental repositories.[75]

A museum is defined in NAGPRA as "any institution or State or local government agency (including any institution of higher learning) that has possession of, or control over, human remains or cultural items and receives Federal funds."[76] Although the Smithsonian Institution has possession of or control over human remains or cultural items and receives federal funds, Congress chose to explicitly exclude it from NAGPRA's definition of museum.[77] In an early version of H.R. 5237, the definition of museum also applied to "any person" who received federal funds and had possession or control of Native American cultural items, but the phrase was changed to "institution" in a subsequent version.[78] Such institutions generally include any corporation, association, partnership, or trust, but exclude individual persons even if they have possession of or control over human remains or cultural items and receive federal funds.[79] Prior to passage by the House, Representative Bennett lamented that H.R. 5237 did not go far enough and hoped that Congress would soon consider the protection of Native American burial sites and sacred objects held in the private sector.[80] Regulations promulgated by the Department of the Interior clarify several terms in the statutory definition. Possession is defined to mean having physical custody of such objects with sufficient legal interest to lawfully treat them as part of the museum's collection. Generally, a museum would not be considered to have possession of human remains or cultural items on loan from another individual, museum, or federal agency.[81] The term "control" is defined to mean having a legal interest in human remains or cultural items sufficient to lawfully permit the museum to treat the objects as part of its collection, whether or not the objects are in the physical custody of the museum. Generally, a museum that has loaned human remains or cultural items to another individual, museum, or federal agency is considered to retain control of those objects.[82] The phrase "receives federal funds" is defined by regulation to mean the receipt of funds by a museum after November 16, 1990, from a federal agency through any grant, loan, contract (other than a procurement contract), or other arrangement by which a federal agency makes or made available to a museum assistance in the form of funds. Procurement contracts are not considered a form of federally based assistance but are provided to a contractor in exchange for a specific service or product. Federal funds provided for any purpose that are received by a larger entity of which the museum is a part are considered federal funds for purposes of these regulations. For example, if a museum is a part of a state or local government or private university that receives federal funds for any purpose, it is considered to receive federal funds. The statute covers tribal museums if the Indian tribe of which the museum is a part receives federal funds through any grant, loan, or contract (other than a procurement contract).[83]

The jurisdictional requirements of the excavation or discovery provisions in Section 3 of NAGPRA apply differently than the repatriation provisions. Section 3 applies only to federal or tribal lands with implementation responsibilities falling to "any person who knows, or has reason to know, that such person has discovered Native American cultural items on Federal or tribal lands"; "the Secretary of the Department, or head of any other agency or instrumentality of the United States, having primary management authority" over the federal lands where the discovery was made; and the secretary of the Interior. The person making the discovery is required to cease activity in the area of the discovery, make a reasonable effort to protect the items discovered, and provide written notification to the appropriate land-managing authority.[84] The land-managing authority is required to certify that notification of a discovery has been received.[85] The secretary of the Interior is required to promulgate regulations regarding the disposition of cultural items not claimed under the ownership or control provisions of Section 3(a).[86] The statutory text does not explicitly identify who is responsible for determining the disposition of or control over any excavated or discovered cultural items,[87] although a separate section on delegation implies that that duty is assigned to the land-managing authority.[88] However, Senator McCain's explanation to his colleagues prior to Senate passage of H.R. 5237 indicates that he thought the secretary of the Interior is responsible for determining the ownership of all cultural items discovered on all federal lands.[89]

Who Has Standing to Make a Request?

The NMAI Act and NAGPRA provide certain individuals and organizations with the opportunity to request human remains, funerary objects, or cultural items. The NMAI Act, as passed in 1989, provided standing to claim human remains and associated funerary objects to descendants of particular Indian individuals and culturally affiliated Indian tribes and Native Hawaiian organizations.[90] A descendant is not defined in the statute, nor is the term clarified in the legislative history. Indian tribe is defined in the NMAI Act by explicit reference to the Indian Self Determination and Education Assistance Act,[91] which defines the term to mean "any Indian tribe, band, nation, or other organized group or community, including any Alaska Native village or regional or village corporation as defined in or established pursuant to the Alaska Native Claims Settlement Act, which is recognized as eligible for the special programs and services provided by the United States to Indians because of their status as Indians."[92] The House committee report makes it clear that the term "Indian tribe" in the repatriation provisions refers to federally recognized tribes.[93] The NMAI Act's definition of Indian tribe includes 336 Indian tribes located in the contiguous forty-eight states and, in Alaska, 229 Alaska Native villages, 175 village corporations, and 13 regional corporations. There is no specific definition of Native Hawaiian organization in the NMAI Act, although by context it is clear that such organizations must have expertise in Native Hawaiian affairs and include Hui Malama I Na Kupuna O Hawai'i Nei and the Office of Hawaiian Affairs.[94]

In explaining the NMAI Act's definition of Indian tribe—which includes only those Indian tribes, bands, nations, or other organized groups or communities recognized as eligible for the special programs and services provided by the United States to Indians because of their status as Indians—the House committee report adds that "the limitation of this formal [repatriation] process to federally recognized Indian tribes is not meant to preclude the Smithsonian from returning remains and objects to non-federally recognized tribes, groups, or other Native entities."[95] Within the Smithsonian, this congressional direction has been implemented in different ways. The National Museum of the American Indian repatriation policy takes a permissive approach by considering all claims "submitted by descendants and those who can demonstrate a cultural affiliation to the materials," without reference to the restricting definition of Indian tribe at all.[96] The National Museum of Natural History repatriation policy takes a more restrictive approach, focusing on claims submitted by lineal descendants and federally recognized tribes, bands, nations, and organized groups or communities of Native Americans, including Alaska Native villages and regional or village corporations, with requests submitted by state-recognized Native American groups initially considered on a case-by-case basis.[97] More recently, this policy was revised to not consider any claims submitted nonfederally recognized groups, although such groups will be included in consultation and repatriations if a federally recognized Indian tribe provides the museum with a letter of support.[98]

Finally, regarding the scope of the repatriation procedures in the NMAI Act, the House committees explain that it "believes that H.R. 2668 provides a reasonable method and policy for the repatriation of Indian bones and funerary objects in the possession of the Smithsonian Institution. However, many human remains in the collection of unknown origin and will, therefore, remain in the collection."[99] Again, within the Smithsonian this congressional direction has been implemented in different ways, with the National Museum of Natural History retaining culturally unidentifiable Native American human remains in its collections, whereas the National Museum of the American Indian chose to rebury a group of undocumented and unaffiliated human remains on tribal land in upstate New York.[100]

NAGPRA also provides standing to claim Native American cultural items to lineal descendants, Indian tribes, and Native Hawaiian organizations. As with the term "descendant" in the NMAI Act, "lineal descendant" is not defined in NAGPRA. The statute does make clear, however, that lineal descendants have priority over Indian tribes or Native Hawaiian organizations in making requests for human remains, funerary objects, and sacred objects.[101] Regulations promulgated by the Department of the Interior define lineal descendant as an "individual tracing his or her ancestry directly and without interruption by means of the traditional kinship system of the appropriate Indian tribe or Native Hawaiian organization or by the American common law system of descendance to a known Native American individual whose remains, funerary objects, or sacred objects are being requested."[102] The necessity of a direct and unbroken line of ancestry between the individual making the request and a known individual is a high standard, but it is consistent with the preference for disposition or repatriation to lineal descendants required by the statute. Reference to traditional kinship systems in the regulatory definition is designed to accommodate the different systems that individual Indian tribes and Native Hawaiian organizations use to reckon kinship.[103]

Indian tribe is defined in NAGPRA to mean "any tribe, band, nation, or other organized Indian group or community of Indians, including any Alaska Native village as defined in or established by the Alaska Native Claims Settlement Act,[104] which is recognized as eligible for the special programs and services provided by the United States to Indians because of their status as Indians."[105] The legislative history provides no additional guidance regarding the meaning of the term. NAGPRA's statutory definition of Indian tribe includes 336 Indian tribes located in the contiguous forty-eight states and 229 Alaska Native villages. The definition of Indian tribe has been a target of repeated judicial and executive interpretation. The first court case to grapple with the statutory definition of Indian tribe was filed in 1992 by the Abenaki Nation of Mississquoi and Abenaki Tribal Council.[106] The plaintiffs made multiple allegations regarding the involvement of the U.S. Army Corps of Engineers in a project located on nonfederal land, particularly claiming violations of provisions of National Historic Preservation Act (NHPA) and NAGPRA. The court was faced with two different definitions of Indian tribe in evaluating the Abenaki claims. The NHPA requires federal agencies to consult with "interested parties," including representatives of Indian tribes,[107] which the statute defines as "the governing body of any Indian tribe, band, nation, or other group that is recognized as an Indian tribe by the Secretary of the Interior."[108] Because neither Abenaki group was included on the Bureau of Indian Affairs list of federally recognized Indian tribes,[109] the court ruled that the plaintiffs were not "interested parties" under the NHPA and were not entitled to participate as consulting parties.[110] However, in reviewing NAGPRA's definition of Indian tribe, the court found that the Abenaki Nation of Mississquoi received federal funds and was an "Indian group" as defined by regulations for establishing that an American Indian group exists as an Indian tribe,[111] and thus "falls squarely within [the NAGPRA] definition."[112]

In 1995, the Department of the Interior promulgated NAGPRA regulations that attempted to clarify the definition of Indian tribe.[113] In response to public comment and a recommendation from the review committee that the definition should include Indian groups recognized by any federal agency and not just those recognized by the secretary of the Interior, the Department of the Interior removed reference to the Bureau of Indian Affairs' acknowledgment procedures, which had been included in the proposed rule, and simply stated that the department would promulgate a listing of such Indian tribes.[114] However, the list, initially distributed on paper and later posted to a website, ultimately only included those Indian tribes identified by the Bureau of Indian Affairs. However, in reiterating the definition of Indian tribe from the Indian Self Determination and Education Act, the 1995 regulations mistakenly concludes that "the final language of the Act is verbatim from the American Indian Self Determination and Education Act (25 U.S.C. 450b)," but then goes on to explain that "the American Indian Self Determination and Education Act, the source for the definition of Indian tribe in the Act, explicitly applies to Alaska Native corporations and, as such, supports their inclusion under the Act."[115] NAGPRA's statutory definition clearly excludes Alaska Native corporations from the definition of Indian tribe. Adding them by regulation, particularly when the sequence of bills indicated they were originally included but were dropped in the last-minute Senate amendment, appears to be counter to the plain meaning of the statutory language as well as to the sequence of changes made to H.R. 5237 prior to enactment. In 2011, the Department of the Interior's Office of the Solicitor reversed its 1995 approval of the definition of Indian tribe and concluded that Congress intentionally omitted Alaska Native regional and village corporations and recommended that the regulatory definition of the term be changed as soon as feasible.[116] The regulatory definition was subsequently removed and reserved.[117] The regulatory revision did not address the department's potential liability regarding museums that repatriated Native American human remains, funerary objects, sacred objects, or objects of cultural patrimony to an Alaska Native regional or village corporation between 1996 and 2010, as required by the then-current regulations and subject to civil penalty for failure to comply.

Though early repatriation bills defined Indian tribe to include a number of Indian groups that are not recognized by the United States, including tribes terminated by federal law after 1940[118] and state-recognized Indian groups,[119] both the NMAI Act and NAGPRA ultimately excluded nonfederally recognized groups from the definition of Indian tribe. However, neither statute explicitly forbids repatriation to such groups. The committee report based on the final NMAI Act language noted that although the formal repatriation process was defined in terms of repatriations to federally recognized Indian tribes, this did not preclude the Smithsonian from returning human remains and funerary objects to nonfederally recognized Indian groups or other Native entities.[120]

Regarding the status of nonfederally recognized Indian groups under NAGPRA, the regulatory preamble relies on another statutory provision, explaining that Section 12 of NAGPRA makes it clear that Congress based the act on the unique relationship between the United States and Indian tribes and should not be construed to establish a precedent with respect to any other individual or organization.[121] "The statutory definition of Indian tribe," explains the preamble, "precludes extending applicability of the Act to Indian tribes that have been terminated, that are current applicants for recognition, or have only State or local jurisdiction legal status."[122] Since promulgation of the regulations, courts have consistently denied standing to claim items under NAGPRA to nonfederally recognized Indian groups.[123] Under NAGPRA's repatriation provisions, human remains in federal agency or museum collections for which a relationship of shared group identity can be shown with a particular nonfederally recognized Indian group are considered "culturally unidentifiable." Federal agencies and museums were initially required to retain possession of all culturally unidentifiable human remains pending promulgation of specific regulations which were finally promulgated in 2010, unless legally required to do otherwise or recommended to do otherwise by the secretary of the Interior.[124] The regulations promulgated in 2010 lifted the restriction on disposition of culturally unidentifiable human remains to Indian tribes or Native Hawaiian organizations, but still required Federal agencies and museums to obtain the recommendation of the secretary of the Interior prior to disposition of such remains to appropriate nonfederally recognized Indian groups.[125] The administration of this process is currently handled by the National Park Service.

NAGPRA defines a Native Hawaiian organization differently than the NMAI Act does. The NMAI Act definition only required that such organizations have expertise in Native Hawaiian affairs. The NAGPRA definition of Native Hawaiian organization requires that such an organization (1) serves and represents the interests of Native Hawaiians, (2) has as a primary and stated purpose the provision of services to Native Hawaiians, and (3) has expertise in Native Hawaiian affairs. Like the NMAI Act, NAGPRA's statutory definition specifically identifies the Office of Hawaiian Affairs and Hui Malama I Na Kupuna O Hawai'i Nei as being Native Hawaiian organizations.[126] NAGPRA's parallel Senate bill included a provision requiring Native Hawaiian organizations to have a membership of which a majority is Native Hawaiian.[127] However, this provision was not included in H.R. 5237, and the legislative history must be interpreted to mean that Congress considered the additional criterion and decided it should not be included. The congressional rejection of the Native Hawaiian membership criterion seems prescient in light of the Supreme Court's subsequent decision that a state law restricting non-Native Hawaiians from voting for trustees of the Office of Hawaiian Affairs was unconstitutional.[128]

What Items Are Covered?

As enacted in 1989, the NMAI Act provided descendants, Indian tribes, and Native Hawaiian organizations with the opportunity to claim "Indian" and "Native Hawaiian" human remains and associated funerary objects. The NMAI Act defined Indian as "a member of an Indian tribe,"[129] which is consistent with usage of the term as a noun, such as when proscribing membership on the new museum's board of trustees.[130] Use of the term as an adjective, such as in the phrase "Indian human remains," is more problematic. For human remains to be "a member of an Indian tribe," the date of death would necessarily be after 1789, when the United States first gained the authority to recognize Indian tribes under the Indian Commerce Clause of the Constitution.[131] This narrow interpretation has generally been ignored by the Smithsonian Institution, which instead concentrates on human remains and associated funerary objects that are culturally affiliated with an Indian tribe regardless of the age of the human remains or funerary objects. Native Hawaiian, on the other hand, is defined by the NMAI Act in a more expansive fashion to include any "member or descendant of the aboriginal people who, before 1778, occupied and exercised sovereignty in the area that now comprises the State of Hawaii."[132]

Instead of distinguishing between Indian and Native Hawaiian human remains and associated funerary objects, as was done in the NMAI Act, NAGPRA covers Native American cultural items, with the term defined as "of, or relating to, a tribe, people, or culture that is indigenous to the United States."[133] Using Native American as an adjective to refer to both Indian and Native Hawaiian cultural items was first introduced in Senator Inouye's S. 1980 but with a different definition.[134] NAGPRA's definition of Native American was introduced in the first version of H.R. 5237 and was not changed in subsequent versions of the bill.[135] Through notice and comment rulemaking, the Department of the Interior modified the statutory definition. First, the department added the phrase "including Alaska and Hawaii" in response to a comment requesting clarification that the definition applied to those areas.[136] Second, the department dropped the words "that is," so that the regulatory definitions reads "of, or relating to, a tribe, people, or culture indigenous to the United States, including Alaska and Hawaii."[137]

Interpretation of NAGPRA's definition of Native American was the focus in *Bonnichsen v. United States*. Following the 1996 discovery of a 9,000-year-old human skeleton on land controlled by the U.S. Army Corps of Engineers, the agency announced its decision that the remains were of

Native American ancestry and culturally affiliated with five Indian tribes and bands.[138] A group of eight physical anthropologists, whose request to study the remains was denied by the Corps, requested that the district court review of the agency's decision under provisions of the Administrative Procedure Act.[139] In its June 27, 1997, order, the district court vacated the agency's decision and remanded the matter with a list of seventeen issues to be considered by the Corps, including explaining what is meant by the terms "Native American" and "indigenous." In a footnote, U.S. Magistrate Judge John Jelderks references the dictionary definition of indigenous — "occurring or living naturally in an area, not introduced; native" — and concluded that "it is not easy to apply the concept of 'indigenous' to remains as ancient as those at issues here, at least given the present state of knowledge regarding the origin of humanity in the Americas."[140]

The Corps asked the National Park Service, the agency delegated by the secretary of the Interior with the responsibility for implementing some provisions of NAGPRA, to respond to the questions. In a December 23, 1997, letter to the Corps,[141] the Park Service took issue with the court's interpretation of indigenous, considering it implausible that Congress intended the term to exclude tribes, peoples, or cultures descending from immigrants coming to the Americas from other continents. As an example, the Park Service pointed out that use of the dictionary definition of "indigenous" cited by the court would exclude Native Hawaiians who are recognized by both Native Hawaiian tradition and historical evidence as having migrated to the Hawaiian Islands sometime between 200 BC and AD 800. The Park Service further considered the term "Native American" to be "clear and self-explanatory," and to apply to:

> human remains and cultural items relating to tribes, peoples, or cultures that resided within the area now encompassed by the United States prior to the historically documented arrival of European explorers, irrespective of when a particular group may have begun to reside in this area, and, irrespective of whether some or all of these groups were or were not culturally affiliated or biologically related to present-day Indian tribes.

With Jelderks retaining jurisdiction over the matter, the Corps decided to delegate responsibility to the Department of the Interior for determining if the human remains were Native American and, if it was determined they were, to provide for their disposition.[142] Following completion of additional radiocarbon dating, sedimentary analysis, lithic analysis, and geomorphologic analysis, the Department of the Interior determined that the human remains were Native American.[143] The following September, Secretary of the Interior Bruce Babbitt determined that disposition of the human remains to the tribal claimants was supported by evidence of cultural continuity sufficient to show cultural affiliation and the location of the original discovery site within the tribes' aboriginal territory.[144] The plaintiffs immediately resumed their litigation.

In his August 30, 2002, opinion, Jelderks set aside Interior's decision, enjoined the transfer of the remains to the tribal claimants, and required the Corps to allow the scientists to study the remains, based in part on a reconsideration of the term "Native American."[145] Whereas his earlier opinion raised concerns about the meaning of the term "indigenous," he now shifted his focus to two different words in the statutory definition. "Giving the 'plain language' of this provision its ordinary meaning," Jelderks wrote, "use of the words 'is' and 'relating' in the present tense requires a relationship to a presently existing tribe, people, or culture."[146] He then proceeded to review and dismiss the Department of the Interior's determinations that the human remains were culturally affiliated and found within the aboriginal lands of the claiming tribes.

Both the government and plaintiffs appealed the case. The 9th Circuit Court of Appeals affirmed Jelderk's opinion, agreeing that use of the present tense in the definition of Native American unambiguously requires that human remains bear some relationship to a presently existing tribe, people, or culture to be considered Native American. The circuit court also concluded that use of the phrase "of, or relating to" in the definition of Native American means that NAGPRA protects graves of persons not shown to be of current tribes in a different way than graves of persons related to presently existing tribes, peoples, or cultures. "Congress enacted NAGPRA to give American Indians control over the remains of their genetic and cultural forbearers, not over the remains of people bearing no special and significant genetic or cultural relationship to some presently existing indigenous tribe, people, or culture."

Human remains are not defined in either the NMAI Act or NAGPRA. The findings section of the NMAI Act specifically addresses the human remains in the collection of the National Museum of Natural History, including 4,000 Indian remains acquired from the Army Medical Museum, as well as the approximately 14,000 Indian remains acquired through archeological excavations, individual donations, and museum donations.[147] NAGPRA's implementing regulations define human remains as the physical remains of a body of a person of Native American ancestry.[148] The term was interpreted broadly to include bones, teeth, hair, ashes, or mummi-fied or otherwise preserved soft tissues. The regulations make no distinc-tion between fully articulated burials and isolated bones and teeth. The term applies equally to recent and ancient Native American human re-mains. It does not include remains or portions of remains freely given or naturally shed by the individual from whose body they were obtained, such as hair made into ropes or nets.[149] Purposefully disposed human re-mains should not be considered either freely given or naturally shed.[150] For the purposes of determining cultural affiliation, human remains in-corporated into funerary objects, sacred objects, or objects of cultural pat-rimony are considered as part of that object. This provision is intended to prevent the destruction of a cultural item that is affiliated with one Indian tribe but incorporates human remains affiliated with another tribe.

The NMAI Act defines a funerary object as "an object that, as part of a death rite or ceremony of a culture, is intentionally placed with individual human remains, either at the time of burial or later."[151] While the NMAI Act requires the Smithsonian to repatriate Native American human re-mains recovered from a mass grave, such as the Cheyenne victims of the Fort Robinson outbreak described by Bill Tallbull at the February 20, 1987 hearing on Senator Melcher's S. 187, objects found with those re-mains are not subject to return. Similarly, the NMAI Act excludes from repatriation funerary objects that can only be associated with a general cemetery site and not with individual human remains or a specific burial site into which individual human remains were deposited.

NAGPRA's definition of associated funerary object is essentially the same as that in the NMAI Act, with added clarifications that funerary ob-jects also include items placed near, but not necessarily with, individual human remains, and that the relevant standard of proof is one of reason-able belief.[152] NAGPRA distinguishes between "associated" and "unassoci-ated" funerary objects. Both definitions describe funerary objects in the same way—"objects that, as a part of the death rite or ceremony of a cul-ture, are reasonably believed to have been placed with individual human remains either at the time of death or later."[153] The two definitions are distinguished by the relationship between the funerary objects and hu-man remains with which they were originally placed. When "the remains are not in the possession or control of *the* Federal agency or museum," (emphasis added) the funerary objects are considered to be unassoci-ated.[154] The definite article "the" indicates that the noun "Federal agency or museum" is a particular one identifiable to the reader, typically the one already mentioned. When "the human remains and associated funerary objects are presently in the possession or control of *a* Federal agency or museum," (emphasis added) the funerary objects are considered to be associated.[155] The indefinite article "a" indicates that the noun "Federal agency or museum" is not yet a particular one identifiable to the reader.

The potential ambiguity arises when one museum or federal agency has possession or control of human remains for which the associated funerary objects are in the possession or control of another museum or federal agency. This is not just a hypothetical situation. Between 1929 and 1931, archeologists at the University of Minnesota conducted extensive excavations at several sites in New Mexico, recovering the remains of 186 individuals and a number of funerary objects. These items were believed to have been interred between AD 1000 and 1150 by a group known in the archeological literature as the Mimbres tradition. Three years before NAGPRA was enacted, the human remains were transferred from the university to the Minnesota Indian Affairs Council, another state entity, pursuant to provisions of Minnesota statute 307.08, and the funerary objects remained at the university's Frederick R. Weisman Art Museum.[156] When NAGPRA was enacted, the museum was faced with the conundrum of how to classify the funerary objects in its possession and control and which document to prepare. Because the human remains were not in the possession or control of *the* Weisman Art Museum, the funerary objects could be considered unassociated and the museum should prepare a summary and provide it to Indian tribes that may be culturally affiliated with the collection. Conversely, because the human remains were in the possession or control of *a* museum, the Minnesota Indian Affairs Council, the funerary objects could be considered associated and the Weisman Art Museum should prepare an inventory and determine their cultural affiliation.

The first step in solving this puzzle is to take the statutory language on its face. Applying the canons of construction, the distinction between the definite article and indefinite article in the two definitions must be given effect. One interpretation is that there is in fact no ambiguity and the Weisman Art Museum should prepare both a summary and an inventory of the funerary objects. However, this interpretation would appear to run counter to the legislative history. H.R. 5237 originally defined funerary objects with no distinction based on whether they were associated with individual human remains.[157] The distinction between associated and unassociated funerary objects, as well as the procedural requirement to prepare a summary, were a major component of the negotiations between the AAM and tribal negotiations that resulted in the October 4, 1990, agreement.[158] The agreement language was introduced verbatim in the October 10, 1990, version of the bill.[159] The House committee report issued on October 15, 1990, did not highlight the distinction between associated and unassociated funerary objects, instead focusing on the new summary provision "intended to make it easier for the Federal agencies, museums, and institutions of higher education to compile and survey the objects they have in their possession or under their control."[160] This issue was raised by a commenter during the public comment period prior to promulgation of the final NAGPRA regulations in 1995, to which the drafters responded that such items should be considered as associated funerary objects and placed on the inventory, not on the summary.[161]

NAGPRA's implementing regulations effect another small but significant shift in meaning regarding the categories of associated and unassociated funerary objects. The statutory definition of unassociated funerary object includes a requirement that—in addition a reasonable belief that they were placed with individual human remains as part of the death rite or ceremony of a culture—such objects must be identified by a preponderance of the evidence in one of three additional ways: either as (1) relating to specific individuals or families, (2) relating to known human remains, or (3) having been removed from a specific burial site of an individual culturally affiliated with a particular Indian tribe. The latter requirements are not included in the statutory definition of associated funerary object. The Department of the Interior's regulations shift this requirement to apply to both associated and unassociated funerary objects.[162]

When originally enacted in 1989, the NMAI Act did not distinguish between "associated" and "unassociated" funerary objects in terms of documentation or reporting. Instead, the Smithsonian was required to inventory and identify the origin of all Indian funerary objects, regardless of whether they were associated with Native American human remains in their collections and, if the object's tribal origin could be identified, notify the affected Indian tribe.[163] The 1996 amendments to the NMAI Act defined the inventory as a simple, itemized list and added a summary requirement that included NAGPRA's definition of unassociated funerary object by specific reference.[164] However, the amendment did not change the scope of the inventory requirement, which still mandates the Smithsonian to inventory and identify the origin of all Indian funerary objects, both associated and unassociated.

The definition of sacred object was controversial throughout the development of the various repatriation bills. In Udall's initial version of H.R.

5237, the term was defined as an "item whose primary purpose when possessed by Native Americans *was devoted* to a traditional Native American religious ceremony or ritual and which *may have* a religious significance or function in the continued observance or renewal of such ceremony or ritual" (emphasis added).[165] However, the October 10, 1990, version of the bill included a revised version of the definition. Sacred object was defined to mean "specific ceremonial objects which *are needed* by traditional Native American religious leaders for the practice of traditional Native American religions by their present day adherents" (emphasis added).[166] "The operative part of the definition," explains the House committee report, "is that there must be 'present day adherents.'"[167] However, when the Department of the Interior promulgated implementing regulations in 1995, it chose to add an additional criteria requiring that such objects were previously devoted to a traditional Native American religious ceremony or ritual.[168] The new language was drawn from the Senate committee report,[169] but also had been included in earlier versions of H.R. 5237 and was subsequently stricken in the final version of the bill.[170] The contradiction between the statutory definition emphasizing a present-day need for the items and the regulatory addition requiring evidence of previous use in a religious ceremony was highlighted in a 1998 hearing before the Native American Graves Protection and Repatriation Review Committee. Several years before, two traditional religious leaders from the Pueblo of Cochiti had reviewed the archeological collections at Bandelier National Monument in New Mexico and identified fifty-three projectile points as needed for the practice of traditional Cochiti religion by present-day adherents. The Pueblo received a response to their repatriation claim from the National Park Service highlighting the regulatory clause requiring evidence of previous use. After considering testimony from both parties, the Nreview committee recommended that the projectile points be reclassified as sacred objects and repatriated to the Pueblo.[171]

Cultural patrimony is defined in NAGPRA as:

> an object having ongoing historical, traditional, or cultural importance central to the Native American group or culture itself, rather than property owned by an individual Native American, and which, therefore, cannot be alienated, appropriated, or conveyed by any individual regardless of whether or not the individual is a member of the Indian tribe or Native Hawaiian organization and such object shall have been considered inalienable by such Native American group at the time the object was separated from such group.[172]

This definition was added in the September 24, 1990, version of H.R. 5237 and was not changed in subsequent versions.[173] The 1996 amendment to the NMAI Act added a requirement to prepare a summary of objects of cultural patrimony, with the term defined by explicit reference to the NAGPRA definition.[174]

What Activities Are Required?

The NMAI Act requires the secretary of the Smithsonian to inventory the Indian and Native Hawaiian human remains and funerary objects in the possession or control of the institution.[175] As enacted in 1989, the term "inventory" was not defined, so the common meaning of a detailed, itemized list, report, or record of things in one's possession likely applies. The statute also requires the secretary of the Smithsonian to identify the origin of the Indian human remains and funerary objects using the best available scientific and historical documentation, notify any affected Indian tribe at the earliest opportunity, and expeditiously return such human remains and associated funerary objects on the request of the descendant or culturally affiliated Indian tribe.[176] The meaning of "best available scientific and historical documentation" was clarified in the House committee report to include accession records, field notes, and research findings. Although not specifically required, the House committees stressed that they do not intend to preclude the use of tribal oral tradition and history in the inventory process.[177] Indian funerary objects removed from a specific burial site but not associated with Indian human remains are to be returned expeditiously on the request of the Indian tribe that is culturally affiliated with the burial site.[178] The House committee report also clarifies that "only those [nonassociated funerary] objects from the burial of an individual person, as opposed to mass burial or entire cemeteries, are subject to return."[179] Although the purpose of the repatriation provisions is to establish the origin or cultural affiliation of Indian human remains and funerary objects, a savings provisions stipulates that the section may not be interpreted to limit the Smithsonian's existing authority to return such remains or objects to Indian tribes or individuals.[180] For example, the repatriation provisions are not meant to preclude the return of human remains and funerary objects to nonfederally recognized tribes, groups, or other Native entities.[181] Regarding Native Hawaiian human remains and funerary objects, the secretary of the Smithsonian is directed to enter into an agreement to return them to the appropriate Native Hawaiian organizations.[182]

NAGPRA's inventory requirements are more broadly applicable but more narrowly focused than those in the NMAI Act. All federal agencies and museums that have possession or control over holdings or collections of Native American human remains and associated funerary objects are required to compile an inventory.[183] The statute specifically defines the inventory as a "simple itemized list" summarizing existing museum or federal agency records—including inventories or catalogs, relevant studies, or other pertinent data—for the limited purpose of determining the geographical origin, cultural affiliation, and basic facts surrounding acquisition of Native American human remains and associated funerary objects.[184] The original version of H.R. 5237 also required that the inventory be based on the best available scientific and historical documentation.[185] In the final version, this requirement was reduced to reliance on "existing" records. NAGPRA's reliance on existing records to compile the inventory (instead of the best available documentation required by the NMAI Act requirements) is further restricted by a stipulation that nothing in NAGPRA may be construed to authorize the initiation of new scientific studies or other means of acquiring or preserving additional scientific information from Native American human remains and associated funerary objects.[186] Unlike the 1989 version of the NMAI Act, which had no deadline for completing the inventory, NAGPRA requires inventory completion no later than November 16, 1995, although a museum that made a good-faith effort could apply to the secretary of the Interior for an extension.[187] No later than six months after completion of the inventory, the museum or federal agency must notify the appropriate Indian tribes or Native Hawaiian organizations that culturally affiliated human remains and associated funerary objects were identified, with a copy of the notice sent to the secretary of the Interior for publication in the *Federal Register*.[188] If an inventory establishes the cultural affiliation of these items, then the federal agency or museum must expeditiously return the items on the request of a known lineal descendant or cultural affiliated Indian tribe or Native Hawaiian organization.[189]

In the original version of H.R. 5237, unassociated funerary objects, sacred objects, and objects of inalienable communal property were to be included in the item-by-item inventory.[190] Following negotiations between museum and tribal representatives, a new section was proposed to make it easier for federal agencies and museums to compile and survey the potentially large number of such items.[191] Each federal agency or museum is required to prepare a written summary of holdings or collections of Native American unassociated funerary objects, sacred objects, or objects of cultural patrimony.[192] The summary must describe the scope of the collection, including the kinds of objects included; the means, period, and geographical source of acquisition; and cultural affiliation, where readily ascertainable.[193] The summaries must be completed no later than November 16, 1993.[194] Following completion of the summary, each federal agency or museum must consult with the representatives of the appropriate Indian tribes and Native Hawaiian organizations regarding the future disposition of the items.[195] If a summary shows the cultural affiliation of the items, then the agency or museum must expeditiously return them on the request of the culturally affiliated Indian tribe or Native Hawaiian organization.[196] When Congress amended the NMAI Act in 1996, it added a section requiring the Smithsonian Institution to also prepare a summary, which, at a minimum, includes the same information as required in NAGPRA's summary provisions.[197] The Smithsonian summaries were to be completed by December 31, 1996.

The 1996 amendments also required the Smithsonian to complete an inventory of Indian human remains and Indian funerary objects in its possession or control by June 1, 1998. Although the amended text was based on the NAGPRA inventory requirements (which require museums and federal agencies to consult with Indian tribes and Native Hawaiian organizations and identify the geographical and cultural affiliation of human remains and associated funerary objects as part of completing the inventory), the Smithsonian interpreted the new requirements to establish a two-step process.[198] The first step involves preparation of a detailed listing of human remains and funerary objects using information in the electronic catalog. The second step, generally undertaken only when an Indian tribe submits a repatriation claim, involves consultation with Indian tribes and preparation of a repatriation case report based on the best available scientific and historical documentation. Under this interpretation, only the first step was required to be completed by the 1998 deadline, and there is no statutory deadline to complete the remaining consultations and make the remaining cultural affiliation determinations. The U.S. Government Accountability Office concluded that the two-step inventory interpretation raised questions about the Smithsonian's compliance with the NMAI Act and recommended that Congress consider ways to expedite the repatriation process by directing the Smithsonian to make cultural affiliation determinations as efficiently and effectively as possible.[199]

Under both the NMAI Act and NAGPRA, completion of the inventory or summary is just the first step in determining whether human remains, funerary objects, sacred objects, or objects of cultural patrimony are to be returned to a requesting lineal descendant, Indian tribe, or Native Hawaiian organization. However, potential subsequent steps differ under the two statutes. Under NAGPRA, human remains and funerary objects for which cultural affiliation has not been established in an inventory or summary must also be expeditiously returned where the requesting Indian tribe or Native Hawaiian organization can show cultural affiliation by a preponderance of the evidence based on geographical, kinship, biological, archeological, anthropological, linguistic, folkloric, oral traditional, historical, or other relevant information or expert opinion. There is no corresponding provision in the NMAI Act.[200] Both statutes include provisions requiring the expeditious return of sacred objects and objects of cultural patrimony when the requesting party is the direct lineal descendant of an individual who owned the sacred object, the requesting Indian tribe or Native Hawaiian organization can show that the object was owned or controlled by the tribe or organization, or the requesting tribe or organization can show that the sacred object was owned or controlled by a one of its members.[201] The NMAI Act provisions also apply to unassociated funerary objects and require the requesting Indian tribe or Native Hawaiian organization to show cultural affiliation by the preponderance of the evidence. Both statutes establish advisory committees to assist in resolving disputes. The Smithsonian committee is charged with reviewing findings, presumably prepared by the Smithsonian staff, related to the origin or return of such remains or objects and facilitating the resolution of disputes that may arise between Indian tribes.[202] NAGPRA authorizes its review committee to make its own findings relating to the origin or the return of such remains and objects and extends the dispute resolution role to the full range of affected parties, including lineal descendants, Native Hawaiian organizations, federal agencies, and museums, as well as Indian tribes.[203]

There was much discussion during the legislative process regarding the disposition of human remains for which no descendant or culturally affiliated Indian tribe or Native Hawaiian organizations could be identified. The NMAI Act is silent on this matter, but the House committee report makes it clear that human remains of unknown origin are to remain in the Smithsonian collections.[204] NAGPRA takes a different approach, charging the review committee with compiling an inventory of culturally unidentifiable human remains that are in the possession or control of each federal agency and museum and recommending specific actions for developing a process for their disposition. NAGPRA does not specify to whom the review committee's recommendation is to be delivered, although the House Committee on Interior and Insular Affairs states in its report that it looks forward to those recommendations.[205] NAGPRA's ambiguity on this issue stands in marked contrast to specificity of the corresponding Senate bill that would require the review committee to compile its inventory of unidentifiable human remains and make a final report to Congress and the president within six years of the committee's establishment.[206]

Both the NMAI Act and NAGPRA include a provision allowing the Smithsonian Institution, a federal agency, or a museum to retain control of Native American unassociated funerary objects, sacred objects, or objects of cultural patrimony if it can prove it has right of possession to the objects.[207] Right of possession is not defined in the NMAI Act, so the common meaning of the phrase applies. Right of possession is commonly used in discussing real property and means a "right which may reside in one man while another has actual possession, being the right to enter and turn out such actual occupant."[208] In this common meaning, the right of possession is retained by the non-possessing party. NAGPRA, on the other hand, specifically defines right of possession to mean "possession obtained with the voluntary consent of an individual or group that had authority of alienation."[209] NAGPRA's definition of right of possession shifts the focus from a right retained by the non-possessing party to a right that can be gained by the possessor under certain circumstances. In particular, NAGPRA stipulates that a federal agency or museum has right of possession to an unassociated funerary object, sacred object, or object of cultural patrimony if the object was originally acquired with the voluntary consent of an individual or group with authority to alienate it.[210]

In a September 17, 1990, letter to Udall, the Department of Justice raised concerns about the way right of possession was defined in H.R. 5237.[211] By focusing exclusively on consent obtained from Native Americans, the department argued, the definition did not address private museums that might have a property interest in objects excavated with the consent of government or private landowners. The department offered two alternatives to avoid the problem: either amend the bill to exclude private museums—and thus private property—from the repatriation provisions or broaden the right of possession to include all objects with which a private museum has a property interest cognizable under federal or state law. To address the Department of Justice's concerns, the October 15, 1990, version of H.R. 5237 added language stipulating that nothing in the definition of right of possession would affect the application of relevant state law to the right of ownership of unassociated funerary objects, sacred objects, or objects of cultural patrimony.[212] The committee report explained that the definition of right of possession would supplement, not confer or detract, from existing federal, state, or tribal law regarding ownership.[213] However, the legislators were still not satisfied with the compromise, because when the House considered the bill the next week, the text added on October 15 had been stricken and replaced with a new provision stipulating that the definition of right of possession would apply—and by implication supersede—otherwise applicable property law, unless such an interpretation would result in a Fifth Amendment taking by the United States as determined by the U.S. Court of Federal Claims. Only on such a court determination does other property law apply.

Beyond establishing the Court of Federal Claims as the venue for adjudicating disputed right of possession claims, NAGPRA also sets the standard for the court to use in weighing the evidence provided by the various parties. Section 7(c) of the act stipulates that if a known lineal descendant or an Indian tribe or Native Hawaiian organization requests the return of Native American unassociated funerary objects, sacred objects, or objects of cultural patrimony and presents evidence that, if standing alone before the introduction of evidence to the contrary, would support a finding that the federal agency or museum did not have the right of possession, then the agency or museum must return the object unless it can overcome such inference and prove that it has a right of possession.[214] This provision does two things. First, consistent with long-standing federal law, it establishes that the federal agency or museum has the ultimate burden of persuading the court that that agency or museum holds right of possession to the contested unassociated funerary object, sacred object, or object of cultural patrimony.[215] A provision in an earlier version of H.R. 5237 that shifted the burden of proving the claim to the lineal descendant, Indian tribe, or Native Hawaiian organization once right of possession was established was also deleted in the final version.[216] Second, unlike some situations where the party not carrying the burden of proof carries the so-called benefit of assumption (meaning they need present no evidence to support their claim), the statutory provision establishes that a lineal descendant, Indian tribe, or Native Hawaiian organization must make an initial showing of evidence that the federal agency or museum does not have right of possession. In his October 26, 1990, colloquy, Senator McCain responded to a question from Senator Simpson about property rights that the bill seemed to be creating as well as whether lawful owners would be fairly compensated for repatriated cultural items.[217] McCain explained that H.R. 5237 requires that before a cultural item is subject to repatriation, an Indian tribe or Native Hawaiian organization must establish a prima facie case—"evidence which, if standing alone before the introduction of evidence to the contrary, would support a finding"—that a federal agency or museum does not have right of possession to a cultural item. He also pointed out that under the common law an individual may only acquire title to property that is actually held by the transferor. Last, McCain pointed out that if a taking of property under the Fifth Amendment to the Constitution is found to have occurred, an individual could seek redress in the Court of Federal Claims.

NAGPRA includes two other provisions allowing a federal agency or museum to retain control of Native American cultural items. Neither are included in the NMAI Act. In the first, a federal agency or museum may retain possession of cultural items if they are indispensable for completion of a specific scientific study, the outcome of which will be of major benefit to the United States.[218] Such items must be returned no later than ninety days after the study is completed. The House committee report recognizes the importance of scientific studies and urges the scientific community to enter into mutually agreeable situations with culturally affiliated tribes in such matters.[219] However, the legislative history does not clarify what type of study might meet the major benefit standard. The context makes it clear that such a study would necessarily need to be of sufficient importance to overcome the rights of an individual to claim a parent's body.[220] Courts have long held that the federal government may substantially burden sincerely held religious beliefs only after it demonstrates that the federal action is in furtherance of a compelling governmental interest and is the least restrictive means of furthering that interest.[221] The major benefit standard in NAGPRA would appear to be much higher than the compelling interest standard. Furthermore, any such determination that the outcome of a specific scientific study is of major benefit to the United States would necessarily be made by the United States, most likely by the secretary of the Interior.

The second provision that allows a federal agency or museum to temporarily retain control of Native American cultural items applies to situations in which the agency or museum cannot clearly determine which of multiple requesting parties is the most appropriate claimant.[222] This provision was introduced in the October 10, 1990, version of H.R. 5237.[223] The House committee report clarifies that to invoke this provision each of the multiple requests must be determined to be "legitimate"—that is, not spurious or unjustified—implying that the standard of lineal descent or cultural affiliation has been met by each of the requesting parties.[224] The agency or museum may retain the item until the requesting parties agree on its disposition or the dispute is otherwise resolved.

A provision in ARPA provides another complication when determining the disposition of Native American cultural items recovered from tribal lands. In 1979, ARPA authorized the secretary of the Interior to issue regulations providing for the ultimate disposition of objects collected under three different laws: the Antiquities Act, the Reservoir Salvage Act, and ARPA itself.[225] Starting in 1906, the Antiquities Act permitted the excavation or gathering of objects of antiquity from lands owned or controlled by the United States and directed the permanent preservation of such objects in public museums.[226] The Reservoir Salvage Act, passed in 1960, charged the secretary of the Interior to determine the ownership of and the most appropriate repository for any relics and specimens recovered as a result of any federally funded or licensed project.[227] ARPA stipulated that all archeological resources from public or Indian lands, including graves and human skeletal materials, would remain the property of the United States but would be preserved by a suitable university, museum, or other scientific or educational institution, with the caveat that the ultimate disposition of archaeological resources excavated or removed from Indian lands could only occur with the consent of the individual Indian or Indian tribe that owns or has jurisdiction over those lands.[228] In 1993, the Bureau of Indian Affairs promulgated regulations governing the custody of archaeological resources from Indian lands generally, but specifically exempted the disposition of Native American cultural items as defined by NAGPRA. NAGPRA regulations issued in 1995 did not specifically rely on the ARPA authority. Finally, over thirty years after ARPA's implementation, the Department of the Interior finally revised the NAGPRA regulations initially promulgated in 1996 to partially fulfill ARPA's authorization regarding the ultimate disposition of objects of antiquity, relics and specimens, and archaeological resources.[229] Of note, the NAGPRA regulations fail to address ARPA's specific statutory requirement that the ultimate disposition of archaeological resources excavated or removed from Indian lands may only occur with the consent of the individual Indian or Indian tribe that owns or has jurisdiction over those lands despite the canon of statutory interpretation that earlier legislation may not be indirectly repealed without evidence of a particular intention to do so.

Although both the NMAI Act and NAGPRA include similar (but not identical) provisions regarding the repatriation of cultural items from the collections of the Smithsonian, federal agencies, and museums, only NAGPRA includes an additional set of procedures dealing with the disposition of cultural items discovered or excavated prospectively. Though earlier bills had applied to all lands, NAGPRA's discovery and excavation provisions apply only to lands under some type of federal jurisdiction, with special provisions applying to the subset of those federal lands that are held in trust for Indian tribes.[230] Federal lands are defined as any lands, other than tribal lands, that are controlled or owned by the United States. In 1990, the United States controlled or owned 649,802,000 acres of non-trust federal lands, or approximately 28.6 percent of the country's total land area.[231] This includes the approximately 44 million acres in Alaska that had been selected by but not yet conveyed to Alaska Native corporations and groups organized pursuant to the Alaska Native Claims Settlement Act, which were identified as tribal lands in earlier versions of H.R. 5237. The Bureau of Land Management is responsible for managing approximately 40 percent of federal lands, followed by the Forest Service (29 percent), the Fish and Wildlife Service (14 percent), and the National Park Service (13 percent), and at least thirty-six other federal agencies.[232] Tribal lands are defined to include all lands within the exterior boundaries of any Indian reservation, all dependent Indian communities, and any lands administered for the benefit of Native Hawaiians pursuant to the Hawaiian Homes Commission Act and Section 4 of Public Law 86-3. In 1990, lands held in trust for Indian tribes by the United States comprised 55,737,451 acres, or approximately 2.4 percent of the country's total land area.[233] The amount of privately owned land situated within the exterior boundaries of Indian reservations to which NAGPRA's discovery and excavation provisions also apply is not known. In addition, the discovery and excavation provisions also apply to the 201,660 acres of land on the islands of Hawai'i, Kaua'i, Lana'i, Maui, Molokai, and O'ahu that are administered by the Department of Hawaiian Home Lands, a department of the Hawaiian state government.[234]

Starting in 1990, Native American cultural items may only be intentionally removed or excavated from federal or tribal lands if four criteria are met. First, the excavation or removal must be conducted in a manner consistent with the permitting provisions of the Archaeological Resources Protection Act. Under ARPA, a federal land manager may only grant a permit if the individual carrying out the proposed activity is qualified and competent in archeological theory and methods and in collecting, handling, analyzing, evaluating, and reporting archeological data, and the proposed work furthers the purpose of archeological knowledge in the public interest and is not inconsistent with any requirements applicable to the management of public lands.[235]

Although the statutory language indicates that ARPA requirements establish minimum qualifications and methodologies for the excavation or

removal of Native American cultural items, one court used the requirement to exempt recently buried Native American human remains from
NAGPRA's provisions entirely. In *Kickapoo Traditional Tribe v. Chacon*,
the tribe had taken the body of one of its recently deceased members from
a mortuary and buried it on tribal land.[236] When the coroner ordered an
autopsy, with the concurrence of the next of kin, the tribe requested and
initially received a temporary restraining order. The court subsequently
vacated its order, finding in part that the ARPA permit requirement meant
that NAGPRA was not intended to apply to a recently buried Native
American corpse, which, being less than 100 years old and of no particular cultural or anthropological interest, was not an archeological resource
as defined by ARPA. Such tortured logic was not necessary because the
statute gives preference to lineal descent claims and explicitly protects the
applicability of state and federal law pertaining to theft or stolen property.
In 2011, another federal court disregarded the Kickapoo ruling, determining that the corpse of Jim Thorpe, the famous Native American athlete
who died in 1953, was clearly "Native American human remains" under
NAGPRA.[237]

Second, the cultural items may only be excavated or removed from
federal lands after consultation with the appropriate Indian tribe or Native
Hawaiian organization. For tribal lands, excavation or removal of cultural
items requires the consent of the appropriate Indian tribe or Native Hawaiian organization. In the original version of H.R. 5237, tribal consent
was required prior to excavation on both federal and tribal lands.[238] The
U.S. Army Corps of Engineers wrote to Representative Udall warning that
such a requirement could virtually stop all federal projects.[239] The consent
requirement in the committee markup version of H.R. 5237 was limited
to excavations or removals occurring on tribal lands, with only consultation being required prior to permitting excavation or removal of cultural
items from federal lands.[240] The third related requirement is that proof of
consultation or consent must be shown by the federal agency.

The fourth prerequisite for the intentional removal or excavation of
cultural items from federal or tribal lands is that the ownership and right
of control of the disposition of any cultural items must be determined according to the priority listing in the act. Consistent with the common law,
the first priority for the control of Native American human remains and
associated funerary objects is with lineal descendants. If the lineal descendants cannot be ascertained, the act identifies additional priority levels for
human remains, funerary objects, sacred objects, or objects of cultural

patrimony. The next priority is with the Indian tribe or Native Hawaiian organization on whose tribal land the cultural items were discovered. Third priority is with the Indian tribe or Native Hawaiian organization that has the closest cultural affiliation with the cultural items. In this section, cultural affiliation is used as a continuous variable meaning that any distinction, however slight, can give preference to one claimant over another as long as it is "closer." This stands in contrast to the usage of "cultural affiliation" in the repatriation provisions of the act, which is either reasonably or clearly shown. If cultural affiliation cannot be demonstrated, the next priority for determining ownership or control of cultural items removed or excavated from federal or tribal lands is with an Indian tribe that is recognized as aboriginally occupying the area in which the objects were discovered, unless a different tribe can be shown to have a stronger cultural relationship to the cultural items. The original version of H.R. 5237 included only the aboriginal occupation requirement.[241] This was expanded during House committee markup to identify final judgments of the Indian Claims Commission as the source for identifying aboriginal occupation and adding the cultural relationship provision.[242] Final judgments of the U.S. Court of Federal Claims were identified as another source for identifying aboriginal occupation just before enactment of the final bill.[243] In promulgating regulations, the Department of the Interior acknowledged that final judgments of the Indian Claims Commission are valuable tools for identifying areas occupied by a present-day Indian tribe, but recommended that other sources of information should also be consulted.[244] Regulations promulgated in 2011 clarify that aboriginal land may also be recognized by a treaty, act of Congress, executive order, or other relevant and authoritative governmental determination.[245] Ownership or control based on lineal descent or tribal lands are considered inherent in that no claim is required. On the other hand, an Indian tribe or Native Hawaiian organization must state a claim for cultural items based on cultural affiliation, aboriginal land, or cultural relationship.

In *Bonnichsen v. U.S.*, the Federal District Court explored the definition of cultural affiliation and its application to the remains of an individual discovered in 1996 on federal lands in Washington state. Cultural affiliation is defined as a relationship of shared group identity that can be reasonably traced historically or prehistorically between a present-day Indian tribe or Native Hawaiian organization and an identifiable earlier group. In *Bonnichsen*, the magistrate's efforts to clarify the meaning of cultural affiliation ignored the House committee report on H.R. 5237, although that report contains explicit language indicating that cultural affiliation must be "based upon an overall evaluation of the totality of the circumstances and evidence pertaining to the connection between the claimant and the material being claimed and should not be precluded solely because of some gaps in the record."[246] Instead, the *Bonnichsen* court relied on language in the Senate committee report on S. 1980 emphasizing the need for "continuity" between the present-day Indian tribes and material from historic or prehistoric Indian tribes.[247] The term "continuity"—meaning an uninterrupted succession or flow—does not appear in either H.R. 5237 or in the House committee report, but it was part of the definition of cultural affiliation in S. 1980. Not surprisingly after raising the bar from a reasonable relationship to one requiring continuity, the *Bonnichsen* court found that the record did not support a finding of cultural affiliation.

The *Bonnichsen* court also offers a unique interpretation of the provision establishing ownership or control of Native American cultural items discovered on federal land with the Indian tribe that aboriginally occupied the area as recognized by a final judgment of the Indian Claims Commission or the U.S. Court of Claims. The human remains were found on land controlled by the Army Corps of Engineers that was ceded to the United States in 1855 by the Walla-Walla, Cayuse, and Umatilla tribes.[248] In 1951, the Confederated Tribes of the Umatilla Indian Reservation filed a petition with the Indian Claims Commission (ICC) for additional compensation for the lands ceded by the 1855 treaty. After over a decade of deliberation, the ICC issued a finding of fact identifying three separate tracts of land to which the Walla-Walla, Cayuse, and Umatilla tribes had held "original Indian title" when the treaty was signed.[249] For the remaining ceded lands, including the area in which the human remains in the *Bonnichsen* case were found, the ICC found substantial evidence that several tribes, including the Walla-Walla, Cayuse, and Umatilla, traveled, gathered, fished, and hunted in the area. The ICC ultimately granted a joint motion for a final judgment against the government for $2.4 million in compensation to the Confederated Tribes of the Umatilla Indian Reservation.[250] In *Bonnichsen*, the district court ruled that the government misconstrued NAGPRA's aboriginal occupation provision "to include cases in which no valid final judgment established aboriginal title, and misinterpreted the statute by applying it to cases in which the ICC had specifically found that the tribe *failed* to establish its aboriginal title."[251] The court supported its opinion by referencing the October 2, 1990, letter from the Department of the Interior to Representative Udall, included in the House committee report, which recommended deletion of the aboriginal occupation clause in its entirety.[252] The *Bonnichsen* court erred on at least two points. First, the opinion that the final judgment in the Umatilla case was in some way invalid, because it was based on a settlement, is counter to the ICC establishing legislation that authorized the U.S. attorney general to compromise claims, with the approval of the ICC, and stipulated that such compromise claims have the effect of a final judgment.[253] Second, the *Bonnichsen* court pulls a classic bait-and-switch, subtly substituting the ICC's standard of "aboriginal title" in lieu of NAGPRA's "aboriginal occupation" requirement. Aboriginal title, as used by the ICC, "must rest on actual, exclusive, and continuous use and occupation for a long time prior to the loss of the property."[254] NAGPRA, on the other hand, requires only aboriginal "occupation," which need not be continuous, exclusive, or for a long time. The ICC's findings of fact provide ample documentation that the Walla-Walla, Cayuse, and Umatilla, along with several other tribes, "occupied" the area where the human remains were found.

Any person who discovers cultural items on lands under federal jurisdiction must notify the appropriate land manager: the departmental secretary or agency head with primary management authority for federal lands; the appropriate Indian tribe or Native Hawaiian organization for tribal lands; and, for land selected pursuant to the Alaska Native Claims Settlement Act, the appropriate Alaska Native corporation or group. If the discovery occurs in connection with construction, mining, logging, agriculture, or other activity, the person must also cease activity in the area of discovery for a minimum of thirty days and protect the discovered items. In his colloquy with Senator Simpson just before Senate passage of the amended bill, Senator McCain explained that his section of the bill "is not intended as a bar to the development of Federal or tribal lands on which cultural items are found. Nor is this bill intended to significantly interrupt or impair development activities on Federal or tribal lands."[255] Regulations promulgated by the Department of the Interior circumvented notification of Alaska Native corporations regarding discoveries of cultural items on lands selected pursuant to the Alaska Native Claims Settlement Act but not yet conveyed.[256] In *Yankton Sioux Tribe v. U.S. Army Corps of Engineers*, the court ruled that the type of "activities" described in this section are not limited to "development" but also include regulation of a lake's water level that resulted in the exposure of human remains along the shore.[257] In a related case involving the same litigants, the court found an injury in fact when human remains embedded in frozen soil, but known to the U.S. Army Corps of Engineers, were not protected adequately.[258]

NAGPRA requires museums and federal agency to consult with Indian tribes and Native Hawaiian organizations prior to initiating the excavation or removal of cultural items from tribal lands; prior to completing an inventory of Native American human remains and associated funerary objects; following completion of a summary of unassociated funerary objects, sacred objects, or objects of cultural patrimony; and prior to the return of cultural items to determine the place and manner of delivery. Although the statute uses the term without definition, the House committee report clarifies that "the term 'consultation,' wherever it appears in the bill, means a process involving the open discussion and joint deliberations with respect to potential issues, changes, or actions by all interested parties."[259] Attempts to include the House committee definition of consultation in the Department of the Interior's regulations were repeatedly rebuffed by the department's solicitors. The one court case that directly addressed NAGPRA's consultation requirements did not reference the House committee definition when it found that the Bureau of Land Management's refusal to meet or consult with the Fallon Paiute Tribe after the tribe retained experts and sought to introduce evidence into the agency's decision-making process was not an error under NAGPRA.[260]

Section 4 of NAGPRA amends Title 18 of the federal Criminal Code, making it illegal to traffic in Native American human remains and cultural items. The initial version of H.R. 5237 included a single section prohibiting anyone from knowingly selling, purchasing, using for profit, or transporting for sale or profit any Native American human remains, funerary object, sacred object, or object of inalienable communal property obtained in violation of the act. This section applies to all cultural items, other than human remains, and is narrowed to actions done in violation of the statute. The statute may be violated by (1) removing cultural items from federal or Indian lands without a permit or otherwise in accordance with the ownership determination requirements; or (2) failing to complete the summary, inventory, consultation, and repatriation provisions for cultural items in federal agency or museum collections. The September 24, 1990, version of H.R. 5237 added a second section precluding the sale, purchase, use for profit, or transport for sale or profit of Native human remains without the right of possession.[261] Conviction for a first offense is a misdemeanor; subsequent convictions are felonies.

Legislative History Going Forward

The legal principle of *stare decisis* obliges federal judges to respect the precedents established by prior decisions of superior federal courts.[262] Only one repatriation case has been considered by the Supreme Court. In *United States v. Corrow*, the Supreme Court declined to reconsider an appeals court opinion that NAGPRA's definition of cultural patrimony provided the defendant with fair notice that sale of a Navajo medicine bundle was prohibited and did not encourage arbitrary and discriminatory enforcement.[263] Several appeals have resulted in judicial opinions with precedential application limited to a single federal circuit. Most notably, in *Bonnichsen v. United States*, the 9th Circuit Coart of Appeals ruled that NAGPRA's definition of Native American requires that human remains bear some relationship to a presently existing tribe, people, or culture.[264]

Critical use of the legislative history of the two statutes can be expected to continue as the courts and the executive branch grapple with new and evolving issues. Although the details of specific controversies are impossible to anticipate, the legislative texts themselves, along with twenty years of implementation, make it possible to predict where a review of the legislative history is likely to arise. The repatriation provisions of the NMAI Act have yet to receive any judicial attention, but it is likely that the Smithsonian's two-step interpretation of the statutory inventory process will eventually be challenged by a rebuffed tribal claimant. There has been more judicial consideration of NAGPRA, but several critical areas remain unexplored. The 9th Circuit Court's opinion regarding the meaning of the definition of Native American is likely to again receive more attention as issues are raised in other judicial circuits. The definitions of sacred object and object of cultural patrimony, which apply to both NAGPRA and the NMAI Act, are also likely be receive judicial review as claims continue for such items. The exemption that allows a museum or federal agency to retain possession or control of Native American cultural items to which it can prove right of possession is also likely to receive judicial review.

The intent of this book is to provide museums, federal agencies, lineal descendants, Indian tribes, Native Hawaiian organizations, and, ultimately, the courts with a thorough understanding of the legislative history of the two acts in the hope that these and other questions that may arise can be answered in a way that is consistent with both the intent and meaning of the law.

The sixteen different numbered bills regarding repatriation introduced in Congress between 1986 and 1990 reflect the progressive refinement of the system of definitions and processes that became the federal repatriation laws of 1989 and 1990. They also reflect the evolving confrontations, negotiations, and eventual agreements between the various constituency groups involved intimately in crafting the legislation. The statutory text, along with the associated reports, drafts, statements, and hearings, provide each new generation with the references needed to apply a law to new situations.

Judge Harold Leventhal described the use of legislative history as the equivalent of entering a crowded cocktail party and looking over the heads of the guests for one's friends.[265] Review of the second life of the repatriation provisions of the NMAI Act and NAGPRA shows that Leventhal's concern is valid—the legislative history has occasionally been misused to skew the plain meaning of the statutes. Some interpreters appear more susceptible to this type of manipulation, whether it is relying on executive commentary opposing the bill, or versions or reports on other bills that were considered and rejected by the legislature, or interpreting previous legislation to limit the repatriation provisions of the NMAI Act and NAGPRA. Such misapplication of legislative history has most often been used in a way that is detrimental to claims made by lineal descendants, Indian tribes, or Native Hawaiian organizations.

Other parts of the legislative history that were readily available to and relied on by the legislators in passing the bill are critical to understanding the full intent of the legislature. Of particular note are the House committee report on H.R. 2668 memorializing the agreement between the Smithsonian and tribal representatives, the House committee report on H.R. 5237 that clarifies the nature of consultation, and Senator McCain's extended colloquy explaining the last-minute changes to H.R. 5237.

Notes

Prologue

1. "Je weniger die Leute darüber wissen, wie Würste und Gesetze gemacht werden, desto besser schlafen sie nachts." Commonly (mis)attributed to Otto von Bismarck (1815–1898). According to Fred R. Shapiro in "Quote . . . Misquote," *New York Times Magazine* (July 21, 2009), the more likely source is John Godfrey Saxe in *Daily Cleveland Herald* (March 29, 1869): "Laws, like sausages, cease to inspire respect in proportion as we know how they are made."

2. John V. Sullivan, How Our Laws are Made. H.R. Doc. No. 110-49 (July 24, 2007). Riddick's Senate Procedure, Precedents, and Practices, S. Doc. No. 101-28 (1992).

3. Jack F. Trope and Walter R. Echo-Hawk, *The Native American Graves Protection and Repatriation Act: Background and Legislative History*. 24 Ariz. St. L.J. 35 (1992). Reprinted in *Repatriation Reader: Who Owns American Indian Remains?* 123 (Devon Abbott Mihesuah ed., 2000); *The Future of the Past: Archaeologists, Native Americans, and Repatriation* 9 (Tamara Bray ed., 2001). Cited in *Na Iwi O Na Kupuna O Mokapu v. Dalton*, 894 F. Supp. 1397, 1417 (D. Haw. 1995); *U.S. v. Corrow*, 119 F.3d 796, 800 (10th Cir. 1997); *Bonnichsen v. U.S.*, 969 F. Supp. 614, 625 (D. Or. 1997); *Bonnichsen v. U.S.*, 969 F. Supp. 628, 649 (D. Or. 1997); *Kickapoo Traditional Tribe v. Chacon*, 46 F. Supp. 2d 644, 654 (D. W.Tex. 1999); *Yankton Sioux Tribe v. U.S. Army Corps of Engineers*, 83 F. Supp. 2d 1047, 1054 (D. S.D. 2000); *Yankton Sioux Tribe v. U.S. Army Corps of Engineers*, 209 F. Supp. 2d 1008, 1016 (D. S.D. 2002); *San Carlos Apache Tribe v. U.S.*, 272 F. Supp. 2d 860, 887 (D. Ariz 2003); *Hawk v. Danforth*, No. 06-223, slip op. at 3 (D. Wis. Aug. 17, 2006).

4. Oswald Werner and G. Mark Schoepfle, *Systematic Fieldwork* (Sage, 1987).

Chapter 1: Tallbull's Quest

1. *Tallbull's Life Journey Completes its Circle*, Earth Medicine (Apr. 1996), at 3.

2. Peter J. Powell, *Sweet Medicine: The Continuing Role of the Sacred Arrows, the Sun Dance, and the Sacred Buffalo Hat in the Northern Cheyenne History* (University of Oklahoma Press, 1969).

3. Native American Cultural Preservation Act: Hearing on S. 187 before the Senate Select Committee on Indian Affairs, 100th Cong. 28 (May 20, 1987) (hereafter S. Hrg. 100-90).

4. General Carr's July 25, 1869, report to General Ruggles included an inventory of material captured, including moccasins, war shields, and war bonnets. Frank J. North, *Journal of an Indian Fighter*, Nebraska History, June 1958, at 140. A drawing of "Tall Bull's Tobacco Pipe, Ornamented with Feathers and Scalp-Locks" appears in Richard Irving Dodge's *Our Wild Indians: Thirty-Three Years Personal Experience among the Red Man of the Great West* 128 (A. D. Worthington, 1882). "Tall Bull was chief of a band of outlaw Cheyenne and Sioux. He was killed at the battle of Summit Springs, Colorado. His wife, who was captured at the time, said the scalps attached to the pipe were those of white settlers on the Salina River, Kansas, taken only two weeks previously," at ix. A photograph of the pipe was also included in John Ewers, *Plains Indian Sculpture: A Traditional Art from America's Heartland* (1986).

5. S. Hrg. 100-90, *supra*, note 3, at 30.

6. "When you were here you saw the photograph showing the pipe with a stone bowl. Later we looked at the pipe and could not find the bowl. After you left I looked at the photograph again and on the back it listed the bowl as a Mandan bowl, catalogued separately. Apparently it was placed with the pipestem just for photographic effect, but does not belong to it. So we do not actually have a bowl for the pipe. The catalog card for the pipe in fact does not mention a bowl." Letter from Susan Crawford, National Museum of Natural History to Mark Elk Shoulder, Northern Cheyenne Tribe (April 15, 1986).

7. Clara Spotted Elk, *Skeletons in the Attic*, N.Y. Times (Mar. 8, 1989).

8. Stephen Loring and Miroslav Prokopec, *A Most Peculiar Man: The Life and Times of Aleš Hrdlička*, in *Reckoning with the Dead* 27 (Tamara Bray and Thomas Killion ed., 1994).

9. Aleš Hrdlička, *Catalogue of Human Crania in the United States National Museum*, Proceedings of the United States National Museum (Government Printing Office, 1944).

10. Douglas J. Preston, *Skeletons in Our Museums' Closets*, Harper's Magazine, Feb. 1989, at 68 (hereafter Preston).

11. Transcript of Meeting, Native American Graves Protection and Repatriation Review Committee, May 14, 1994, at 74.

12. Report of the Official Canvass of the Vote Cast at the General Election Held in the State of Montana, Nov. 2, 1976, Nov. 2, 1982, Nov. 8, 1988. http://cdm15018 .contentdm.oclc.org. Accessed April 7, 2011.

13. Memorandum from Don Fowler, president, Society for American Archaeology to Interested Parties, Re. Reburial and Related Issues (June 2, 1986). Undated notes in the files of the SAA Government Affairs Committee indicate that Spotted Elk would begin drafting during the May 21–29, 1986, congressional recess after meeting with representatives of interested groups. The notes outlined a three-step "defense": (1) meet with Spotted Elk and present the official SAA statement on reburial; (2) distribute the statement to archeologists, urging them to send it to their congressional repre-

sentatives; and (3) meet with representatives of museums, physical anthropologists, archeological societies, historic preservation groups, and other interested groups to discuss and detail approaches to dealing with the legislation.

14. Unpublished and undated draft on file with the author.

15. Alan Jabbour, *The American Folklife Center: A Twenty-Year Retrospective*, pt. 2. Folklife Center News, American Folklife Center, The Library of Congress, Summer–Fall 1996, vol. 18, nos. 3 and 4.

16. S. 2952, 99th Cong. §1 (Oct. 18, 1986).

17. Iveing Molotsky and Warren Weaver Jr., *Briefing: Of Bones*, N.Y. Times, Oct. 25, 1986, section 1, at 1.

18. Ron Martz, *The Forgotten Indians*, Atlanta Journal & Atlanta Constitution, Nov. 16, 1986, at A15.

19. S. 2952, 99th Cong. §6 (d) (Oct. 18, 1986).

20. S. 2952, 99th Cong. §3 (10) (Oct. 18, 1986).

21. S. 2952, 99th Cong. §6 (b)(1) (Oct. 18, 1986).

22. S. 2952, 99th Cong. §2 (3) (Oct. 18, 1986).

23. S. 2952, 99th Cong. §4 (b)(1) (Oct. 18, 1986). The bill stated that the board included seventeen members, but then listed only fifteen positions. Nonvoting positions were provided for one representative from the Institute for American Indian Arts, Smithsonian Institution, Department of the Interior, Department of Agriculture, and Advisory Council on Historic Preservation. An earlier draft of the bill listed only fourteen members, including two fewer Indians, and no members of the House or Senate. Unpublished draft on file with the author.

24. S. 2952, 99th Cong. §5 (a)(2) (Oct. 18, 1986).

25. S. 2952, 99th Cong. §5 (a)(1) (Oct. 18, 1986).

26. S. 2952, 99th Cong. §5 (b) (Oct. 18, 1986).

27. S. 2952, 99th Cong. §5 (c)(2) (Oct. 18, 1986).

28. S. 2952, 99th Cong. §5 (d)(1) (Oct. 18, 1986).

29. S. 2952, 99th Cong. § 5(d)(2) (Oct. 18, 1986).

30. S. 2952, 99th Cong. § 5(e) (Oct. 18, 1986).

31. Indian Claims Commission Act, Pub. L. No. 79-726, §2, 60 Stat. 1049 (1946).

32. Nancy Oestreich Lurie, *The Indians Claims Commission*, 436 Annals Am. Acad. Pol. & Soc. Sci 99 (1978) (hereafter Lurie).

33. Indian Claims Commission Act, Pub. L. No. 79-726, §13(b), 60 Stat. 1049 (1946).

34. Lurie, *supra* note 33, at 103–104.

35. Archaeological Resources Protection Act, PL 96-95 (2)(b).

36. Antiquities Act, 34 Stat. 225, 16 U.S.C. 431–433.

37. Archaeological Resources Protection Act, Pub. L. 96-95 §(3)(1).

38. Archaeological Resources Protection Act, Pub. L. 96-95 §(4)(b)(3).

39. S. 2952, 99th Congress §(7)(d) (Oct. 18, 1986).

40. Letter from Senator John Melcher to Michele Aubry, archeologist, National Park Service (Nov. 10, 1986).

41. Ron Martz, *The Forgotten Indians*, Atlanta Journal & Atlanta Constitution, Nov. 16, 1986, at A15.

42. 133 Cong. Rec. S435 (daily ed., Jan. 6, 1987).

43. S. 187, 100th Cong. §(6)(c)(1) (Jan. 6, 1987).

44. 133 Cong. Rec. S435 (daily ed., Jan. 6, 1987).

45. *Argument on Reburial of Excavated Bones Expected to Heat Up*, Arizona Republic, Jan. 25, 1987, at B2.

46. S. Hrg. 100-90, *supra* note 3, at 1. Inouye's name was formally added as a co-sponsor on Mar. 3, 1987.

47. Frank Oliveri, Senator Cites "Shameful" U.S. History, Honolulu Advertiser (Aug. 29, 2004). Senator Byrd reportedly recommended Inouye consider the position since he "looked like an Indian."

48. S. Hrg. 100-90, *supra* note 3, at 26.

49. Letter from Suzan Harjo, executive director, National Congress of American Indians, to Robert M. Adams, secretary, Smithsonian Institution (July 22, 1985).

50. Letter from James C. Tyler, acting director, National Museum of Natural History, to Karen Funk, National Congress of American Indians (Aug. 29, 1985). Alaska and Hawaii were not included.

51. Letter from Karen Funk to James Tyler (Sept. 11, 1985).

52. NCAI Newsletter (Feb. 6, 1986). The letter was drafted by physical anthropologist Douglas Ubelaker, who consulted with visiting scholar Russell Thornton. Thornton predicted that tribes would show little interest because the demands for repatriation were mainly articulated by "urban" Native Americans. Russell Thornton, *Who Owns Our Past?*, in *Studying Native America* 396 (Russell Thornton, ed.) University of Wisconsin Press (1999).

53. Department of the Interior and Related Appropriations for 1987: Hearings before a Subcommittee of the Committee on Appropriations, House of Representatives, 99th Congress, Mar. 6–7, 1986, at 112.

54. 42 U.S.C. §1996.

55. Peter H. Lewis, *Indian Bones: Balancing Research Goals and Tribes' Rights*, Washington Post, May 20, 1986, at C3.

56. Jan Hammil, statement before the House of Representatives, Interior and Insular Affairs Committee, Public Lands Subcommittee (July 30, 1985).

57. S. Hrg. 100-90, *supra* note 3, at 26.

58. Circular No. 2, May 21, 1862, from Surgeon General William A. Hammond to all medical directors and medical officers. In Robert S. Henry, *The Armed Forces Institute of Pathology: Its First Century 1862–1962*. Washington, DC: Office of the Surgeon General (1964) at 12.

59. *The Medical and Surgical History of the War of the Rebellion (1861–1865)*. Washington, DC: Government Printing Office (1870–1888).

60. George A. Otis, Surgeon General's Office, Washington, DC. Circular no. 2, Apr. 4, 1867.

61. S. Hrg. 100-90, *supra* note 3, at 26. "I secured his head in the night of the day he was buried. From the fact he was buried so near these lodges, I did not know but what I was suspected in this business and that it was their intention to sleep watch over the body. Believing that they would hardly think that I would steal his head before he was cold in his grave, I early in the evening with two of my hospital attendants secured this specimen."

62. Army Medical Museum records concerning skeletal material transferred to the Smithsonian Institution 1868–1897. http://siris-archives.si.edu/ipac20/ipac.jsp?uri=full=3100001~!220395!0&term=#focus. Accessed April 7, 2011.

63. S. Hrg. 100-90, *supra* note 3, at 27.

64. S. 187, 100th Cong. §(5)(c)(2) (Jan. 6, 1987).

65. S. 187, 100th Cong. §(5)(a)(1)(A) and (5)(a)(1)(B) (Jan. 6, 1987).

66. S. 187, 100th Cong. §(5)(b)(1) (Jan. 6, 1987).

67. S. 187, 100th Cong. §(7)(d) (Jan. 6, 1987).

68. S. Hrg. 100-90, *supra* note 3, at 50. The Neanderthal, an extinct species of the genus Homo, is generally believed to have lived from 130,000 to 24,000 years ago in Europe and Asia. The Mesozoic Era is a geologic period extending from 265–65 million years ago. The witness, Thomas King of the staff of the Advisory Council for Historic Preservation, contradicted Inouye's assumption by responding that Indian tribes could make a plausible claim of cultural ancestry or descent extending back 2,000 years.

69. S. Hrg. 100-90, *supra* note 3, at 27.

70. S. Hrg. 100-90, *supra* note 3, at 82. Letter from Cindy Darcy, Native American Advocacy Project, Friends Committee on National Legislation to Senator John Melcher (Feb. 20, 1987).

71. Letter from William Merrill, associate curator, National Museum of Natural History, to William Tallbull (Feb. 17, 1990).

72. S. Hrg. 100-90, *supra* note 3, at 28, 90.

73. Unsigned letter on letterhead of the Saint Augustine's Center in Chicago (probably Father Peter Powell) to the keepers of the Cheyenne Sacred Arrows and Sacred Buffalo Hat (March 19, 1987).

74. S. Hrg. 100-90, *supra* note 3, at 28.

75. S. Hrg. 100-90, *supra* note 3, at 29.

76. S. Hrg. 100-90, *supra* note 3, at 46.

77. S. Hrg. 100-90, *supra* note 3, at 47.

78. S. Hrg. 100-90, *supra* note 3, at 50.

79. S. Hrg. 100-90, *supra* note 3, at 176.

80. SAA Executive Board Meeting minutes no. 55 (May 4, 1985).

81. SAA Executive Board Meeting minutes no. 57 (Dec. 6, 1985).

82. Polly M. Quick, *Proceedings: Conference on Reburial Issues, Newberry Library, Chicago, June 14–15, 1985* (Society for American Archaeology 1985).

83. Society for American Archaeology, Statement Concerning the Treatment of Human Remains (1986).

84. Adams assumed the position of secretary of the Smithsonian in 1984, after a distinguished career at the University of Chicago. While serving on the university faculty and in the administration, he continued several decades of archeological fieldwork investigating long-term changes in settlement and land-use patterns in Middle Eastern urban societies, especially in Iraq. Adams also brought an interest in contemporary science and research policies to the secretary's job. http://www.anthro.ucsd.edu/Faculty_Profiles/adams.html. Accessed April 7, 2011.

85. S. Hrg. 100-90, *supra* note 3, at 189.

86. S. Hrg. 100-90, *supra* note 3, at 65.

87. S. Hrg. 100-90, *supra* note 3, at 70.

88. S. Hrg. 100-90, *supra* note 3, at 72.

89. S. Hrg. 100-90, *supra* note 3, at 73.

90. S. Hrg. 100-90, *supra* note 3, at 201.

91. S. Hrg. 100-90, *supra* note 3, at 71.

92. S. Hrg. 100-90, *supra* note 3, at 68.

93. S. Hrg. 100-90, supra note 3, at 68.

94. Interview with Patricia Zell, chief counsel, Senate Select Committee on Indian Affairs in Washington, DC (May 5, 1998) (hereafter Zell).

95. *Decent Burial*, Fresno Bee, May 13, 1987: B6.

96. S. 187, 100th Cong. (Jan. 6, 1987).

97. S. Con. Res. 76, 100th Cong. (Sept. 16, 1987).

98. S. 187, 100th Cong. §(2)(c) (May 28, 1988).

99. S. 187, 100th Cong. §(3)(g) (May 28, 1988).

100. S. 187, 100th Cong. §(3)(h) (May 28, 1988).

101. S. 187, 100th Cong. §(3)(b) (May 28, 1988).

102. S. 187, 100th Cong. §(3)(d) (May 28, 1988).

103. S. 187, 100th Cong. §(4)(b) (May 28, 1988).

104. S. 187, 100th Cong. §(4)(c) (May 28, 1988).

105. S. 187, 100th Cong. §(4)(d) (May 28, 1988).

106. S. 187, 100th Cong. §(20) (May 28, 1988).

107. S. 187, 100th Cong. §(22) (May 28, 1988).

108. 134 Cong. Rec. S12421 (daily ed. May 25, 1988).

109. Native American Museum Claims Commission Act: Hearing on S. 187 before the Senate Select Committee on Indian Affairs, 100th Cong. (July 29, 1988) (hereafter S. Hrg. 100-931). The bill was now cosponsored by Senators Burdick, Bradley, McCain, Inouye, Baucus, and Mitchell.

110. S. Hrg. 100-931, *supra* note 109, at 47.

111. S. Hrg. 100-931, *supra* note 109, at 49.

112. S. Hrg. 100-931, *supra* note 109, at 61.

113. S. Hrg. 100-931, *supra* note 109, at 65.

114. S. Hrg. 100-931, *supra* note 109, at 60.

115. S. Hrg. 100-931, *supra* note 109, at 47.

116. Human Remains Attributed to the Blackfeet at the National Museum of Natural History. http://anthropology.si.edu/repatriation/reports/regional/plains/blackfeet.htm. Accessed Apr. 7, 2011.

117. Robert E. Bieder, *A Brief Historical Survey of the Expropriation of American Indian Remains.* Boulder: Native American Rights Fund, 1990, at 45–46.

118. House Report 101-340, Pt. 2, at 14.

119. S. Hrg. 100-931, *supra* note 109, at 55.

120. S. Hrg. 100-931, *supra* note 109, at 56.

121. S. Hrg. 100-931, *supra* note 109, at 57.

122. Zell, *supra* note 93.

123. S. Hrg. 100-931, *supra* note 109, at 73.

124. S. Hrg. 100-931, *supra* note 109, at 140.

125. Memorandum from M. C. Meigs to Smithsonian Secretary Joseph Henry (March 21, 1874).

126. Notes from discussions with Fr. Peter Powell (June 9, 1988).

127. Notes from phone conversation with John Moore (June 9, 1988).

128. Letter from Robert M. Adams, secretary of the Smithsonian, to William Tallbull (June 29, 1988).

129. S. Hrg. 100-931, *supra* note 109, at 71.

130. S. Hrg. 100-931, *supra* note 109, at 79.

131. S. Hrg. 100-931, *supra* note 109, at 196.

132. S. Hrg. 100-931, *supra* note 109, at 85.

133. Walter R. Echo-Hawk, *Museum Rights vs. Indian Rights: Guidelines for Assessing Competing Legal Interests in Native Cultural Resources,* 14 N.Y.U. Rev. L & Soc. Change 437 (1986).

134. S. Hrg. 100-931, *supra* note 109, at 88.

135. Memorandum from Assistant Secretary for Fish and Wildlife and Parks Bill Horn to other assistant secretaries of the Department of the Interior (April 22, 1988). S. Rept. No. 101-952 at 267.

136. Memo from Gayle E. Manges, field solicitor, Office of the Solicitor, Department of the Interior, to Regional Director, Southwest Region, National Park Service (Nov. 30, 1987). Two weeks earlier, the departmental consulting archeologist, along with representatives of the Bureau of Indian Affairs, discussed the same issues with attorneys from the Office of the Solicitor's Division of Indian Affairs.

137. "Every collection made under the authority of the act and of this part shall be preserved in the public museum designated in the permit and shall be accessible to the public. No such collection shall be removed from such public museum without the written authority of the Secretary of the Smithsonian Institution, and then only to another public museum, where it shall be accessible to the public; and when any public museum, which is a depository of any collection made under the provisions of the act and this part, shall cease to exist, every such collection in such public museum shall thereupon revert to the national collections and be placed in the proper national depository." 43 CFR §3.17.

138. Memo from NPS Assistant Director—Archeology to NPS Regional Director, Southwest Region (Jan. 27, 1988).

139. *The Tall Bull Pipe: A Chronology of Recent Events* (n.d.).

140. Letter from Thomas M. Boyd, acting assistant attorney general, U.S. Dept. of Justice, to Senator Daniel K. Inouye (Sept. 7, 1988), in S. Rep. No. 100-601, at 13.

141. Letter from Morton Rosenberg, specialist in American Public Law, Congressional Research Service, to Senator Daniel K. Inouye (Sept. 7, 1988), in S. Rept. No. 101-601, at 15.

142. S. Rept. No. 100-601, at 8.

143. S. 187, 100th Cong. §(3)(4) (Oct. 21, 1988).

144. S. 187, 100th Cong. §(4)(c) (Oct. 21, 1988).

145. S. 187, 100th Cong. §(4)(d) (Oct. 21, 1988).

146. S. 187, 100th Cong. §(4)(e) (Oct. 21, 1988).

147. Preston, *supra* note 10, at 69.

148. Preston, *supra* note 10, at 69.

149. Bill McAllister, *GOP Gunning for Montana Senate Seat,* Wash. Post, Oct. 28, 1988, at A16.

150. Bill McAllister, *Montana Wilderness Bill Pocket-Vetoed; Politics Is Charged after President's Action against Sen. Melcher's Legislation,* Wash. Post, Nov. 4, 1988, at A11.

151. Bill McAllister, *Montana Negative Ads, Visits by Bush Helped Produce Victory for Burns,* Wash. Post, Nov. 10, 1988, at A47.

152. Sara Lowen, *Indians and Smithsonian Clash over Fate of Remains*, Orange County Register, June 5, 1988, at G10.

153. Preston, *supra* note 10, at 68.

154. Preston, *supra* note 10, at 70.

Chapter 2: The Green Boxes

1. S. Rept. No. 101-143, at 2 (1989).

2. Roland W. Force, *Politics and the Museum of the American Indian: The Heye & The Mighty* 371 (Mechas Press, 1999) (hereafter Force).

3. H. Rept. No. 101-340, pt. 2 at 9 (1989).

4. Douglas Cole, *Captured Heritage: The Scramble for Northwest Coast Artifacts* 216 (Douglas & McIntyre, 1985).

5. National American Museum Act: Joint Hearing Before S. Select Comm. on Indian Affairs and S. Comm. Rules and Administration, 100th Cong., part 2 at 59 (Nov. 12 and 18, 1987) (hereafter S. Hrg. 100-547).

6. H. Rept. No. 101-340, pt. 2 at 10 (1989).

7. S. Hrg. 100-547, *supra* note 5, pt. 2 at 59.

8. H. Rept. No. 101-340, pt. 2 at 10 (1989).

9. George G. Heye and George H. Pepper, *Exploration of a Munsee Cemetery Near Montague, New Jersey* 3 (Museum of the American Indian, 1915).

10. Cole, *supra* note 4, at 217.

11. H. Rept. No. 101-340, pt. 2 at 9 (1989). The Smithsonian and the Peabody Museum at Harvard University were first and second in size.

12. H. Rept. No. 101-340, pt. 2 at 9 (1989).

13. Mary Heng, *The Power of Publicity*, American Indian Ritual Object Repatriation Foundations, 5 News and Notes, spring–summer, 1998, at 1.

14. *Indians' Talisman Returns to Tribe: Museum Here Will Restore Sacred Bundle to Elders of Gros Ventre*, New York Times, Dec. 7, 1937; *The Sacred Bundle*, New York Times, Dec. 8, 1937; Scott Hart, *Indians Here to Recover Totem Puzzled by Beasts in Jail (Zoo)*, Washington Post, Jan. 12, 1938, at 28; *Medicine Men See White Father*, Washington Post, Jan. 14, 1938, at 20; *Indian Chiefs Visit President at the White House*, New York Times, Jan. 14, 1938; *Indians Get Relics as Skies Threaten: Foolish Bear and Drags Wolf Reclaim Sacred Bundle of Thunderbird*, New York Times, Jan. 15, 1938; *Indian Fetish Back to North Dakota and Lo! It Rains*, July 21, 1938, at 12; Edmund Carpenter, *Two Essays: Chief & Greed* 98 (Persimmon Press, 2005).

15. Annual Report of the Board of Trustees of the Museum of the American Indian, Heye Foundation (for the period from Mar. 31, 1955 to Apr. 1, 1956).

16. H. Rept. No. 101-340, at 11 (1989).

17. Establishment of the National Museum of the American Indian: Joint Hearing on H.R. 2668 Before the H. Comm. on Interior and Insular Affairs, Comm. on House Administration, and Comm. on Public Works and Transportation, 101st Cong, 27 (1989) (hereafter H.R. Hrg. 101-53).

18. H. Rept. No. 101-340, pt. 2 at 10 (1989).

19. H. Rept. No. 101-53, *supra* note 17, at 100 (1989).

20. 133 Cong. Rec. S25320 (daily ed. Sept. 25, 1987).

21. H. Rept. No. 101-53, *supra* note 17, at 100 (1989).

22. Interview with Patricia Zell, chief counsel, Senate Select Committee on Indian Affairs, in Washington, DC (May 5, 1998).

23. Interview with Patricia Zell.

24. S. 1722, 100th Cong. §(202) (Sept. 25, 1987).

25. S. 1722, 100th Cong. §(203)(a) (Sept. 25, 1987).

26. S. 1722, 100th Cong. §(203)(b) (Sept. 25, 1987).

27. S. 1722, 100th Cong. §(206)(3) (Sept. 25, 1987).

28. S. 1722, 100th Cong. §(206)(2) (Sept. 25, 1987).

29. Patricia Pierce Erickson, *Decolonizing the "Nation's Attic": The National Museum of the American Indian and the Politics of Knowledge-Making in a National Space*, in *The National Museum of the American Indian: Critical Conversations* 59 (Amy Lonetree & Amanda Cobb, eds., 2008).

30. *Larsen Bay Tribal Council Resolution No. 87-09, May 29, 1987*, in *Reckoning with the Dead* 187 (Tamara Bray & Thomas Killion eds., Smithsonian Institution Press, 1994).

31. Stephen Loring and Miroslav Prokopec, *A Most Peculiar Man: The Life and Times of Aleš Hrdlička*, in *Reckoning with the Dead* 32 (Tamara Bray & Thomas Killion eds., Smithsonian Institution Press, 1994).

32. Letter from Anthropology Department Chair to Larsen Bay Tribal Council (Sept. 25, 1987), in *Reckoning with the Dead* 188 (Tamara Bray & Thomas Killion, eds., Smithsonian Institution Press, 1994).

33. S. Hrg. 100-547, *supra* note 5, pt. 1 at 1.

34. S. Hrg. 100-547, *supra* note 5, pt. 1 at 3.

35. S. Hrg. 100-547, *supra* note 5, pt. 1 at 2.

36. S. Rept. No. 100-494, at 3.

37. S. Hrg. 100-547, *supra* note 5, pt. 2 at 47.

38. H.R. 3414, 100th Cong. (Oct. 1, 1987).

39. S. Rept. No. 100-494, pt. 2 at 36–37.

40. S. Rept. No. 100-494, pt. 2 at 71.

41. S. Rept. No. 100-494, pt. 2 at 71.

42. S. Rept. No. 100-494, pt. 2 at 77.

43. Force, *supra* note 2, at 375.

44. S. Rept. No. 100-494, pt. 1, at 30.

45. S. Rept. No. 100-494, pt. 1, at 29.

46. S. Hrg. 100-547, *supra* note 5, pt. 1 at 77–78.

47. S. Hrg. 100-547, *supra* note 5, pt. 1 at 78–79.

48. S. Hrg. 100-547, *supra* note 5, pt. 1 at 80.

49. S. Hrg. 100-547, *supra* note 5, pt. 1 at 81.

50. S. Hrg. 100-547, *supra* note 5, pt. 1 at 81–82.

51. S. Hrg. 100-547, *supra* note 5, pt. 1 at 82.

52. S. Hrg. 100-547, *supra* note 5, pt. 1 at 84–85.

53. S. Hrg. 100-547, *supra* note 5, pt. 1 at 87–88.

54. S. Hrg. 100-547, *supra* note 5, pt. 2 at 171.

55. S. Hrg. 100-547, *supra* note 5, pt. 1 at 114–115.

56. S. Hrg. 100-547, *supra* note 5, pt. 2 at 84–85.

57. S. Hrg. 100-547, *supra* note 5, pt. 2 at 171.

58. S. Hrg. 100-547, *supra* note 5, pt. 2 at 108.

59. S. Hrg. 100-547, *supra* note 5, pt. 2 at 71.

60. S. Hrg. 100-547, *supra* note 5, pt. 2 at 171.
61. S. Hrg. 100-547, *supra* note 5, pt. 2 at 71.
62. S. Hrg. 100-547, *supra* note 5, pt. 2 at 93.
63. S. Hrg. 100-547, *supra* note 5, pt. 2 at 71.
64. S. Hrg. 100-547, *supra* note 5, pt. 2 at 78.
65. S. Hrg. 100-547, *supra* note 5, pt. 2 at 172.
66. S. Hrg. 100-547, *supra* note 5, pt. 2 at 78.
67. S. Hrg. 100-547, *supra* note 5, pt. 2 at 79.
68. S. Hrg. 100-547, *supra* note 5, pt. 2 at 80.
69. Harjo left the position of executive director of the National Congress of American Indians shortly after Wayne Ducheneaux was elected as its president. Harjo was reportedly furious with both Clara Spotted Elk and Karen Funk for joining the "Ducheneaux faction." Mario Gonzalez and Elizabeth Cook-Lynn, *The Politics of Hallowed Ground: Wounded Knee and the Struggle for Indian Sovereignty* 56 (U. of Ill. Press, 1998).
70. S. Hrg. 100-547, *supra* note 5, pt. 1 at 42.
71. S. Hrg. 100-547, *supra* note 5, pt. 2 at 81.
72. S. Hrg. 100-547, *supra* note 5, pt. 2 at 84.
73. S. Rept. No. 100-494, at 4.
74. S. Rept. No. 100-494, at 37.
75. S. Rept. No. 100-494, at 4.
76. S. 1722, 100th Cong. §(101)(c)(2) (April 13, 1988).
77. S. 1722, 100th Cong. §(105) (April 13, 1988).
78. S. 1722, 100th Cong. §(106)(b) (April 13, 1988).
79. S. 1722, 100th Cong. §(106)(a) (April 13, 1988).
80. S. 1722, 100th Cong. §(2) (April 13, 1988).
81. S. 1722, 100th Cong. Title II (April 13, 1988).
82. S. 1722, 100th Cong. §(101)(c)(4) (April 13, 1988).
83. S. Rept. No. 101-143, at 3 (1989).
84. S. Rept. No. 100-494, at 43 (1989).
85. S. Rept. No. 100-494, at 40 (1989).
86. S. Rept. No. 100-494, at 41 (1989).
87. S. Rept. No. 100-494, at 5 (1989).
88. S. Rept. No. 100-494, at 4 (1989).
89. S. Rept. No. 100-494 (1989).
90. Force, *supra* note 2, at 432.
91. H.R. 5411, 100th Cong. §(2)(a) (Sept. 28,1988).
92. H.R. 5411, 100th Cong. §(2)(b) (Sept. 28,1988).
93. H.R. 5411, 100th Cong. §(2)(c)(1) (Sept. 28, 1988).
94. H.R. 5411, 100th Cong. §(2)(c)(2) (Sept. 28, 1988).

Chapter 3: The Political Dynamics of Public Awareness

1. Jane Hubert, *The Disposition of the Dead*, World Archaeological Bulletin, no. 2 (1988). King's draft, which include a possible new statute titled the American Indian Reinterment Act, along with proposed amendments to the American Indian Freedom

of Religion Act, National Historic Preservation Act, Archaeological Resources Protection Act, and National Environmental Policy Act, elicited firm objections from several archeologists. *See* Memorandum from Bruce D. Smith, secretary, Society for American Archaeology, to the SAA Executive Board (Feb. 13, 1986).

2. 16 U.S.C. §470bb (1).

3. 16 U.S.C. §470dd.

4. 49 Fed. Reg. 1016 (Jan. 6, 1984).

5. Proposed Amendment to the Archaeological Resources Protection Act of 1979, Advisory Council on Historic Preservation (Oct. 5, 1988).

6. Letter from Robert D. Bush, executive director, Advisory Council on Historic Preservation, to Jerry Rogers, associate director, National Park Service (Oct. 24, 1988).

7. S. 2912, 100th Cong. (Oct. 18, 1988).

8. S. 2912, 100th Cong. §(920)(d) (Oct. 18, 1988).

9. 134 Cong. Rec. S31551 (Oct. 18, 1988).

10. S. 2912, 100th Cong. §(3)(8) (Oct. 18, 1988). An undated draft of uncertain authorship is titled "Rough Cut #1: Language for Disposal of Deadfolk Section."

11. Senator Fowler's interest in the disposition of Native American human remains seems to have caught the attention of at least some in his home state. In January 1989, the newly elected representative from Georgia's Fourth District, former actor Ben Jones, explained that he had "more skeleton's in [his] closet than the Smithsonian Institution." Montgomery Brower and Margie Bonnett Sellinger, *En Route to Congress, Actor Ben Jones First Beat the Bottle, Then the Incumbent*, People (Jan. 30, 1989).

12. Comments on S. 2912, the Comprehensive Preservation Act of 1988 Introduced by Senator Wyche Fowler in the 100th Congress (March 6, 1989).

13. Clara Spotted Elk, *Skeletons in the Attic*, N.Y. Times (March 8, 1989). Also published in the N.Y. Times, *Scholastic Update*, vol. 121, no. 18, at 25 (May 26, 1989).

14. The National Museum of Health and Medicine and the National Archives do in fact contain the remains of Holocaust victims in their collections. These human remains, including pieces of skin bearing tattoos, were introduced at the Nuremberg trial as evidence of the atrocities at Buchenwald. Discussions regarding the ultimate disposition of these human remains are ongoing.

15. Archaeological and Historic Preservation Act of 1974 (16 U.S.C. §469-469c, Pub. L. No. 93-291).

16. Ruthann Knudsen, record of telephone conversation with Jody H. (Jay) Mooney, Office of Congressman Charles E. Bennett (March 16, 1989), "CEB read the *National Geographic* article on Slack Farm and came in last week and told JHM to put together a bill that would prohibit interstate commerce of materials taken from graves of AIRFA significance."

17. Brian Fagan, *Black Day at Slack Farm*, Archaeology 41(4) (1988), at 15.

18. Native American Museum Claims Commission Act: Hearing on S. 187 before the Senate Select Committee on Indian Affairs, 100th Cong., at 79 (July 29, 1988).

19. Harvey Arden, *Who Owns Our Past?*, National Geographic, vol. 75, no. 3, at 378 (March 1989).

20. Protection of Native American Graves and the Repatriation of Human Remains and Sacred Objects: Hearing on H.R. 1381, H.R. 1646 and H.R. 5237 before the House Committee on Interior and Insular Affairs, 101st Cong. 62 (1990) (hereafter H.R. Hrg. 101-62), at 47.

21. H.R. Hrg. 101-62, *supra* note 20, at 47.

22. H.R. Hrg. 101-62, *supra* note 20, at 46.

23. H.R. 1381, 101st Cong. §(2) (March 14, 1989).

24. H.R. 1381, 101st Cong. §(3)(a) (March 14, 1989).

25. H.R. 1381, 101st Cong. §(5) (March 14, 1989).

26. H.R. 1381, 101st Cong. §(4) (March 14, 1989).

27. H.R. Hrg. 101-62, *supra* note 20, at 46.

28. 135 Cong. Rec. H893 (March 23, 1989).

29. H.R. 1646, 101st Cong. §(2) (March 23, 1989).

30. H.R. 1646, 101st Cong. §(3)(1) (March 23, 1989).

31. H.R. 1646, 101st Cong. §(3)(5) (March 23, 1989).

32. H.R. 1646, 101st Cong. §(3)(6) (March 23, 1989).

33. H.R. 1646, 101st Cong. §(4)(a) (March 23, 1989).

34. H.R. 1646, 101st Cong. §(4)(b) (March 23, 1989).

35. H.R. 1646, 101st Cong. §(4)(b) (March 23, 1989).

36. H.R. 1646, 101st Cong. §(5) (March 23, 1989).

37. H.R. 1646, 101st Cong. §(5)(c) (March 23, 1989).

38. H.R. 1646, 101st Cong. §(5)(d) (March 23, 1989).

39. H.R. 1646, 101st Cong. §(6)(2) (March 23, 1989).

40. Letter from Representative Morris Udall to House colleagues (April 11, 1989).

41. Letter from Henry Sockbeson, Steven Moore, and Walter R. Echo-Hawk, Native American Rights Fund (no date).

42. Letter from Loretta Neumann to Jerry Sabloff, Keith Kintigh, Bill Lovis, Lynne Goldstein (May 24, 1989).

43. Interview with Karen Funk, legislative analyst, Hobbs, Straus Dean & Walker LLP (April 20, 2012).

44. Letter from Loretta Neumann to Morris K. Udall (April 28, 1989).

45. Letter from Senator John McCain to Richard L. Johnes, president, Board of Trustees, Heard Museum (April 24, 1989).

46. Interview with Eric Eberhard, distinguished Indian law practitioner in residence, Seattle University Law School (Jan. 2011).

47. Memorandum from Keith Kintigh to SAA Task Force on Repatriation and Reburial: Dick Ford, Vin Steponaitis, Phil Walker, Lynne Goldstein (ex officio), Bill Lovis (ex officio), Startup (May 1, 1989).

48. S. 1021, 101st Cong. §(4) (May 17, 1989).

49. .S. 1021, 101st Cong. §(5)(a) (May 17, 1989).

50. S. 1021, 101st Cong. §(5)(b) (May 17, 1989).

51. S. 1021, 101st Cong. §(5)(b) (May 17, 1989).

52. S. 1021, 101st Cong. §(6)(b)(2) (May 17, 1989).

53. S. 1021, 101st Cong. §(6)(c)(3) (May 17, 1989).

54. Memorandum from Keith Kintigh to Dick Ford, Vin Steponaitis, Phil Walker, Lynne Goldstein, Bill Lovis, Jeremy Sabloff, Prudence Rice, Loretta Neumann, Frank McManamon (June 1, 1989).

55. Sec. 120. Human Remains and Associated Grave Goods (June 20, 1989).

56. The Inside Story of Section 120 of S. 1579 and Why Karen Funk Is Backing Away from It. Memo from Tom (King) to Pat (Parker) (Feb. 23, 1990).

57. S. 1579, 101st Cong (Aug. 4, 1989).

58. S. 1579, 101st Cong. §(120) (Aug. 4, 1989).

59. S. 1579, 101st Cong. §(113)(a)(14) (Aug. 4, 1989).

60. S. 1579, 101st Cong. §(113)(a)(13) (Aug. 4, 1989).

61. S. 1579, 101st Cong. §(113)(a)(11) (Aug. 4, 1989).

62. Not all were as impressed as King was with the Vermillion Accord. Ellis Neiburger, an Illinois dentist writing on behalf of the Ethnic Minority Council of America, described the Vermillion meeting as "a scientific sham, a media event for the advocates of reburial. The burial movement," according to Ellis, "often motivated by media attention, politics and money, masquerades as a religious or racial rights movement" (*Profiting from Reburial* 344 Nature 297 [March 22, 1990]). Neiburger was no stranger to politics and masquerades. From 1985 to 1987, he provided advice to the leadership of the Paleopathology Association, including "mak[ing] a claim that there 'appears' to be Caucasian specimens in the group," creating lobbying groups with names like Indians Against Destruction of Native American Heritages and Citizens for Religious Freedoms to write letters to government officials demanding forensic analysis of skeletal remains, and "personally attack[ing] 'professionals' who advocate reburial on ethical/scientific grounds." "There is also the old trick of mixing bones & letting the newspeople know that the Indians are doing pagan things to those poor white people. This will stop 'em in their tracks." Letters from Ellis Neiburger to John (last name unknown) (April 12, 1985); John (last name unknown) (Sept. 5, 1985); Doug Ubelaker (April 11, 1987).

63. Point-by-point comparison: Vermillion Accord and Section 120, S. 1579, no author or date identified.

64. The Inside Story of Section 120 of S. 1579 and Why Karen Funk Is Backing Away from It. Memo from Tom (King) to Pat (Parker) (Feb. 23, 1990).

65. H.R. 3412, 101st Cong. (Oct. 5, 1989).

66. Letter from Representative Charles E. Bennett to Jeremy Sabloff (Nov. 29, 1989).

67. Interview with Patricia Zell, chief counsel, Senate Select Committee on Indian Affairs, in Washington, DC (May 5, 1998).

Chapter 4: The Way of the Coyote

1. H.R. Rept. No. 101-340, pt. 2 at 12 (1989).

2. S. Rept. No. 101-143, at 3 (1989).

3. H.R. 5411, 100th Cong. (Sept. 28, 1988).

4. H.R. 1124, 101st Cong. §(2)(a) (Feb. 27, 1989).

5. Establishment of the National Museum of the American Indian: Joint Hearing on H.R. 2668 Before the H. Comm. on Interior and Insular Affairs, Comm. on House Administration, and Comm. on Public Works and Transportation, 101st Cong, 117 (1989) (hereafter H.R. Hrg. 101-53).

6. 135 Cong. Rec. H2807 (Feb. 27, 1989).

7. H.R. Hrg. 101-53, *supra* note 5, at 1 (1989).

8. The majority of the Native American human remains in the Heye Foundation collection were transferred to the New York University School of Dentistry in 1956.

9. H.R. Hrg. 101-53, *supra* note 5, at 17 (1989).

10. National Memorial Museum of the American Indian: Joint Hearing before the Senate Select Committee on Indian Affairs and the Senate Committee on Rules and Administration on S. 978 to Authorize the Establishment within the Smithsonian Institution of the National Museum of the American Indian and to Establish a Memorial to the American Indian, 101st Cong 79-93 (1989) (hereafter S. Hrg. 101-203).

11. H.R. Rept. No. 101-340, pt. 2, at 13 (1989).

12. S. 978, 101th Cong. § (9)(1) (May 11, 1989). The Smithsonian Institution objected to the provision requiring their board of regents to consult with the National Museum of the American Indian board of trustees in conducting the study and making recommendations. In a May 12, 1989, memorandum, Senate Indian Affairs chief counsel recommended deleting the consultation requirement. Memorandum from Patricia Zell to Senator Daniel Inouye, re. May 16, 1989 Mark-Up of S. 978 (May 12, 1989).

13. S. 978, 101th Cong. §§(9)(3) and (9)(4) (May 11, 1989).

14. S. Hrg. 101-203, *supra* note 10, at 57.

15. S. Hrg. 101-203, *supra* note 10, at 59.

16. Interview with Jack Trope, counsel, Association for American Indian Affairs (May 7, 1998).

17. Interview with Jack Trope.

18. H.R. Hrg. 101-53, *supra* note 5, at 88 (1989).

19. H.R. Hrg. 101-53, *supra* note 5, at 101 (1989).

20. H.R. Hrg. 101-53, *supra* note 5, at 106 (1989).

21. H.R. Hrg. 101-53, *supra* note 5, at 115 (1989).

22. H.R. Hrg. 101-53, *supra* note 5, at 115 (1989).

23. H.R. Hrg. 101-53, *supra* note 5, at 166–167 (1989).

24. H.R. Hrg. 101-53, *supra* note 5, at 168 (1989).

25. H.R. Hrg. 101-53, *supra* note 5, at 50 (1989).

26. Unmarked Human Burial Sites and Skeletal Remains Protection Act, Neb. Rev. Stat. §12-1201 to 1212 (1989); Kansas Unmarked Burial Site Preservation Act, Kan. Stat. Ann. §75-2741–75-2754 (1989).

27. Jane Gross, *Stanford Agrees to Return Ancient Bones to Indians*, N.Y. Times (June 24, 1989). Patrick Sweeney, Indians Win Battle to Bury Ancestors, St. Paul Pioneer Press Dispatch, July 16, 1989, at 1B. Rogers Worthington, *Where Archeologists See Discovery, Indians See Only Lost Souls*, Chicago Tribune, July 24, 1988, at 6.

28. H.R. Hrg. 101-53, *supra* note 5, at 173 (1989).

29. Although Echo-Hawk's testimony is dated July 20, 1989, it appears that the requested changes had already been made in the June 15, 1989, version of H.R. 2668.

30. 547 F. Supp. 580 (M.D.La 1982); 496 SO. 2d 601 (La. Ct. App.). writ denied, 498 SO. 2d 753 (La. 1986).

31. H.R. Hrg. 101-53, *supra* note 5, at 174 (1989).

32. *Christensen v. Superior Court*, 54 Cal. 3d 868, 2 Cal. Rptr. 2d 79, 820 P.2d 181 (1991).

33. H.R. Hrg. 101-53, *supra* note 5, at 175–176 (1989).

34. H.R. Hrg. 101-53, *supra* note 5, at 177–178 (1989).

35. H.R. Hrg. 101-53, *supra* note 5, at 178 (1989).

36. H.R. Hrg. 101-53, *supra* note 5, at 179–180 (1989).

37. H.R. Hrg. 101-53, *supra* note 5, at 181 (1989).

38. H.R. Hrg. 101-53, *supra* note 5, at 182 (1989).
39. H.R. Hrg. 101-53, *supra* note 5, at 189 (1989).
40. H.R. Hrg. 101-53, *supra* note 5, at 183 (1989).
41. H.R. Hrg. 101-53, *supra* note 5, at 184 (1989).
42. H.R. Hrg. 101-53, *supra* note 5, at 191 (1989).
43. H.R. Hrg. 101-53, *supra* note 5, at 191 (1989).
44. H.R. Hrg. 101-53, *supra* note 5, at 191 (1989).
45. H.R. Hrg. 101-53, *supra* note 5, at 191 (1989).
46. H.R. Hrg. 101-53, *supra* note 5, at 191 (1989).
47. H.R. Hrg. 101-53, *supra* note 5, at 184 (1989).
48. H.R. Hrg. 101-53, *supra* note 5, at 195 (1989).
49. H.R. Hrg. 101-53, *supra* note 5, at 195 (1989).
50. H.R. Hrg. 101-53, *supra* note 5, at 195 (1989).
51. H.R. Hrg. 101-53, *supra* note 5, at 196 (1989).
52. H.R. Hrg. 101-53, *supra* note 5, at 197–201 (1989).
53. Annual Report of the Board of Trustees of the Museum of the American Indian, Heye Foundation (for the period from March 31, 1955, to April 1, 1956).
54. H.R. Hrg. 101-53, *supra* note 5, at 219 (1989).
55. H.R. Hrg. 101-53, *supra* note 5, at 221 (1989).
56. H.R. Hrg. 101-53, *supra* note 5, at 226 (1989).
57. H.R. Hrg. 101-53, *supra* note 5, at 224 (1989). By "glutinous," Harjo probably meant "gluttonous."
58. H.R. Hrg. 101-53, *supra* note 5, at 225 (1989).
59. H.R. Hrg. 101-53, *supra* note 5, at 225 (1989).
60. H.R. Hrg. 101-53, *supra* note 5, at 226 (1989).
61. H.R. Hrg. 101-53, *supra* note 5, at 226 (1989).
62. H.R. Hrg. 101-53, *supra* note 5, at 226 (1989).
63. H.R. Hrg. 101-53, *supra* note 5, at 228 (1989).
64. H.R. Hrg. 101-53, *supra* note 5, at 228 (1989).
65. H.R. Hrg. 101-53, *supra* note 5, at 238 (1989).
66. H.R. Hrg. 101-53, *supra* note 5, at 265 (1989).
67. H.R. Hrg. 101-53, *supra* note 5, at 267 (1989).
68. H.R. Hrg. 101-53, *supra* note 5, at 268 (1989).
69. H.R. Hrg. 101-53, *supra* note 5, at 268 (1989).
70. H.R. Hrg. 101-53, *supra* note 5, at 271 (1989).
71. H.R. Hrg. 101-53, *supra* note 5, at 273 (1989).
72. H.R. Hrg. 101-53, *supra* note 5, at 271 (1989).
73. H.R. Hrg. 101-53, *supra* note 5, at 272 (1989).
74. H.R. Hrg. 101-53, *supra* note 5, at 276 (1989).
75. H.R. Hrg. 101-53, *supra* note 5, at 277 (1989).
76. H.R. Hrg. 101-53, *supra* note 5, at 277 (1989).
77. H.R. Hrg. 101-53, *supra* note 5, at 288 (1989).
78. H.R. Hrg. 101-53, *supra* note 5, at 289 (1989).
79. H.R. Hrg. 101-53, *supra* note 5, at 290 (1989).
80. H.R. Hrg. 101-53, *supra* note 5, at 311 (1989).
81. H.R. Hrg. 101-53, *supra* note 5, at 307 (1989).
82. *Lyng v. Northwest Indian Cemetery Protective Association*, 485 U.S. 439 (1988).

On April 19, 1988, the Supreme Court reversed a lower court ruling and held that the First Amendment provides no protection for Indian people to practice traditional religions unless (1) there was specific governmental intent to infringe on a religion, or (2) the government's action coerces individuals to act contrary to their spiritual beliefs.

83. H.R. Hrg. 101-53, *supra* note 5, at 308 (1989).

84. Memorandum from Bob Adams to Sam Hughes, "Oversight" mechanisms on Indian skeletons, etc. (Aug. 11, 1989).

85. A Dialogue on NAGPRA: The Issue of "Culturally Unidentifiable" Remains 213 (Arizona State University School of Law & Heard Museum June 14, 2002) (hereafter Dialogue on NAGPRA).

86. Dialogue on NAGPRA, *supra* note 85, at 215.

87. Dialogue on NAGPRA, *supra* note 85, at 217.

88. Dialogue on NAGPRA, *supra* note 85, at 217.

89. H.R. Rept. No. 101-340, pt. 2, at 15 (1989).

90. Dialogue on NAGPRA, *supra* note 85, at 218.

91. Felicity Barringer, *Major Accord Likely on Indian Remains*, N.Y. Times, Aug. 20, 1989 (hereafter Barringer).

92. Barringer, *supra* note 91. A correction printed the next day clarified that the American Anthropological Association, most of whose members are cultural anthropologists who do not work with physical materials, had designated a commission to recommend a policy position for adoption at it next annual meeting.

93. *Smithsonian, Indians Near Pact on Remains*, Arizona Republic, Aug. 20, 1989, at A14.

94. Kara Swisher, *Smithsonian to Surrender Indian Bones, Accord Sets Stage for New Museum*, Washington Post, Sept. 12, 1989, at A1.

95. Barringer, *supra* note 91.

96. Memorandum from Bob Adams to Sam Hughes (Aug. 22, 1989).

97. Barringer, *supra* note 91.

98. Press Conference, Smithsonian Institution (Sept. 12, 1989).

99. Memorandum from Bob Adams to Sam Hughes (Aug. 22, 1990).

100. Interview of Representative Ben Nighthorse Campbell by Jane Pauley, *Today Show*, NBC (Sept. 13, 1989).

101. *Plunder of Sacred Graves*, San Diego Union, Sept. 11, 1989; *Last Rites for Indian Dead*, Los Angeles Time, Sept. 16, 1989; *A Barbaric Way to Treat American Indians*, St. Louis Post-Dispatch (Sept. 20, 1989).

102. H.R. Rept. No. 101-340, pt. 2, at 9.

103. Society for American Archaeology Suggested Revisions to H.R. 2668 (Sept. 17, 1989).

104. Memorandum from Loretta Neumann to Keith Kintigh (Sept. 18, 1989).

105. Kathleen Reinburg, telephone notes (Sept. 20, 1989).

106. Memorandum from Loretta Neumann to Jerry Sabloff, Pru Rice, Bill Lovis, and Keith Kintigh (Sept. 28, 1989).

107. Memorandum from Loretta Neumann to Jerry Sabloff, Smithsonian Bill—Public Works/House Administration (Oct. 13, 1989).

108. 135 Cong. Rec. S12397 (1989).

109. Email from Vincas Steponaitis to Keith Kintigh (Oct. 21, 1989).

110. H.R. Rept. No. 101-340, pt. 1, at 1 (1989).

111. H.R. Rept. No. 101-340, pt. 1, at 15 (1989).
112. H.R. 2668, 101st Cong. §11 (a) (Oct. 9, 1989).
113. H.R. 2668, 101st Cong. §11(b), (c), and (d) (Oct. 9, 1989).
114. H.R. Rept. No. 101-340, pt. 1, at 15 (1989).
115. H.R. Rept. No. 101-340, pt. 1, at 16 (1989).
116. H.R. Rept. No. 101-340, pt. 1, at 15 (1989).
117. H.R. 2668, 101st Cong. §12 (a) (Oct. 9, 1989).
118. H.R. 2668, 101st Cong. §13 (Oct. 9, 1989).
119. Letter from Robert D. Reischauer, director, Congressional Budget Office, to Representative Glenn M. Anderson (cost estimate for H.R. 2668) (Nov. 2, 1989) in H.R. Rept. No. 101-340, pt. 1, at 33 (1989). Letter from Robert D. Reischauer, director, Congressional Budget Office, to Representative Frank Annunzio (cost estimates for H.R. 2668) (Nov. 2, 1989) in H.R. Rept. No. 101-340, pt. 2, at 42 (1989).
120. H.R. 2668, 101st Cong. §13 (Nov. 13, 1989).
121. 135 Cong. Rec. H8448 (Nov. 13, 1989).
122. 135 Cong. Rec. E3926 (daily ed., Nov. 13, 1989).
123. 135 Cong. Rec. H8451 (Nov. 13, 1989).
124. 135 Cong. Rec. E3803 (Nov. 13, 1989).
125. 135 Cong. Rec. H8449 (Nov. 13, 1989).
126. 135 Cong. Rec. H8452 (Nov. 13, 1989).
127. Memorandum from Bill Merrill to Don Ortner (Nov. 15, 1989).
128. Note from Don Ortner to Frank Talbot (Nov. 16, 1989).
129. President's Statement on Signing the National Museum of the American Indian Act (Nov. 28, 1989).

Chapter 5: Two Practices, No Policy

1. 135 Cong. Rec. S16799 (daily ed., Nov. 21, 1989).
2. S. 1980, 101st Cong. §(3)(a)(1) (Nov. 21, 1989).
3. S. 1980, 101st Cong. §(2)(13) (Nov. 21, 1989).
4. S. 1980, 101st Cong. §(2)(12) (Nov. 21, 1989).
5. S. 1980, 101st Cong. §(3)(a)(1) (Nov. 21, 1989).
6. S. 1980, 101st Cong. §(3)(a)(3) and (3)(a)(4) (Nov. 21, 1989).
7. S. 1980, 101st Cong. §(3)(b)(1)(A) and (3)(b)(1)(B) (Nov. 21, 1989).
8. S. 1980, 101st Cong. §(3)(b)(2)(A) and (3)(b)(2)(B) (Nov. 21, 1989).
9. S. 1980, 101st Cong. §(3)(c)(1) (Nov. 21, 1989).
10. S. 1980, 101st Cong. §(3)(c)(2) (Nov. 21, 1989).
11. S. 1980, 101st Cong. §(3)(c)(3) (Nov. 21, 1989).
12. 25 U.S.C. §194, derived from R.S. §2126, derived from act June 30, 1834, ch. 161, §22, 4 Stat. 733. "In all trials about the right of property in which an Indian may be a party on one side, and a white person on the other, the burden of proof shall rest upon the white person, whenever the Indian shall make out a presumption of title in himself from the fact of previous possession or ownership."
13. Memorandum from Walter Echo-Hawk and Henry Sockbeson, Native American Rights Fund, to Marie Howard and Cathy Wilson, H.R. Comm. on Interior and Insular Affairs (Aug. 18, 1990).

14. S. 1980, 101st Cong. §(3)(a) (Nov. 21, 1989).

15. S. 1980, 101st Cong. §(3)(b) (Nov. 21, 1989).

16. S. 1980, 101st Cong. §(3)(b)(1) (Nov. 21, 1989).

17. S. 1980, 101st Cong. §(3)(d)(1) (Nov. 21, 1989).

18. S. 1980, 101st Cong. §(3)(d)(2) (Nov. 21, 1989).

19. S. 1980, 101st Cong. §(3)(d)(6) (Nov. 21, 1989).

20. S. 1980, 101st Cong. §(3)(d)(3) (Nov. 21, 1989).

21. S. 1980, 101st Cong. §(3)(d)(7) (Nov. 21, 1989).

22. S. 1980, 101st Cong. §(3)(f) (Nov. 21, 1989).

23. S. 1980, 101st Cong. §(4)(b)(1) (Nov. 21, 1989).

24. S. 1980, 101st Cong. §(4)(b)(2) (Nov. 21, 1989).

25. Letter from Loretta Neumann to Jerry Sabloff, Pru Rice, Keith Kintigh, Bill Lovis, Mark Leone, Lynne Goldstein, Mark Lynott, and Bill Stini, with copies to Geoffrey Platt, Mary Beaudry, and Frank McManamon (Dec. 15, 1989).

26. Walter Echo-Hawk, Memorandum to File: Proposed Strategy and Division of Labor for the Second Session of the 101st Congress (n.d.). See also Memorandum from Jack Trope to Gary Kimble and Jerry Flute, Association for American Indian Affairs, AIRFA/Repatriation Legislation (Dec. 14, 1990).

27. Summary of Meeting Jan. 24 on Reburial/Repatriation. Society for American Archaeology, Office of Government Relations (Jan. 29, 1990).

28. S. 1579, 101st Cong. §(120) (Aug. 4, 1989).

29. Historic Preservation Administration Act of 1989 (S. 1578) and the National Historic Preservation Policy Act of 1989 (S. 1579): Hearings before the S. Subcommittee on Public Lands, National Parks, and Forests of the Committee on Energy and Natural Resources, 101st Cong., at 101 (Feb. 22 and May 19, 1990) (hereafter S. Hrg. 101-721).

30. S. Hrg. 101-721, *supra* note 29, at 103.

31. S. Hrg. 101-721, *supra* note 29, at 103.

32. S. Hrg. 101-721, *supra* note 29, at 159.

33. S. Hrg. 101-721, *supra* note 29, at 163.

34. S. Hrg. 101-721, *supra* note 29, at 166.

35. S. Hrg. 101-721, *supra* note 29, at 173.

36. Memorandum from Tom [King] to Pat [Parker] (Feb. 23, 1990).

37. *Lyng v. Northwest Indian Cemetery Protective Association*, 485 U.S. 439 (Apr. 19, 1988).

38. *Burying Bones of Contention: Tradition Challenges Research over Rites for the Dead*, Time, Sept. 10, 1984, at 32.

39. Note from Jerry Rogers to Bennie Keel (Sept. 26, 1984).

40. Guidelines for the Disposition of Archeological and Historical Human Remains. Department of the Interior (July 23, 1982).

41. Letter from Bennie Keel, National Park Service, to Leslie Wildesen, Colorado Historical Society (Feb. 28, 1985), in *Proceedings of the Conference on Reburial Issues* (June 14–15, 1985). Washington, DC: Society for American Archaeology.

42. Letter from Bennie Keel, National Park Service, to William Bass, University of Tennessee (Feb. 13, 1985), in *Proceedings of the Conference on Reburial Issues* (June 14–15, 1985). Washington, DC: Society for American Archaeology.

43. Ron Martz, *The Forgotten Indians*, Atlanta Journal & Atlanta Constitution, Nov. 16, 1986, at A15.

44. "Jerry's performance standards," Rowland Bowers handwritten notes, undated [believed to be from Sept., 1989].

45. "Southwest Region Has Policy Regarding Return of Skeletal Remains," undated draft.

46. Comments on Proposed Press Release, Walter Wait (Sept. 18, 1989).

47. "Southwest Region Has Policy Regarding Return of Skeletal Remains," News Release (Sept. 27, 1989).

48. Note from Ron Ice to Cal Calabres (Sept. 27, 1989).

49. Memorandum from Robert C. Heyder to Lorraine Mintzmeyer regarding Mesa Verde Material Located in the Smithsonian (Nov. 1, 1989).

50. Memorandum from Lorraine Mintzmeyer to John Ridenour regarding Return of Rocky Mountain Region Parks' Collections Housed in the United States National Museum (Smithsonian Institution) (Nov. 21, 1989).

51. Note from Jerry Rogers to 430, 434, 436, 408, 413 (Dec. 12, 1989).

52. Letter from John E. Echohawk to members of the Native American Rights Fund (Dec. 4, 1989). A handwritten note passing the letter on to the SAA's Bill Lovis read: "Bill—This arrived today. I thought you . . . should be aware of what's in the future." Note from Kathleen (Reinburg) to Bill (Lovis) (Dec. 19, 1989).

53. Jerry Rogers talking points (Jan. 22, 1990).

54. Orlan Love, Federal Investigation Launched into Missing Bones at Effigy Mounds, http://www.kcrg.com/news/local/Federal-Investigation-Launched-into-Missing-Bones-at-Effigy-Mounds-147051845.html. Accessed May 5, 2012.

55. Memorandum from Loretta Neumann, Society for American Archaeology, to Jerry Sabloff, Pru Rice, Keith Kintigh, Bill Lovis, Mark Leone, Lynn Goldstein, Mark Lynott, and Bill Stini (Feb. [probably March] 2, 1990). Copy to Frank McManamon (March 2, 1990).

56. The Panel for National Dialogue on Museum/Native American Relations, Michael J. Fox (Feb. 1, 1989).

57. Report of the Panel for a National Dialogue on Museum/Native American Relations (Feb. 28, 1990).

58. The Panel for National Dialogue on Museum/Native American Relations, Apr. 1, 1989. meeting.

59. Interview with Marie Howard, House Committee on Natural Resources (Jan. 29, 1999).

60. Interview with Patricia Zell, chief counsel, Senate Select Committee on Indian Affairs in Washington, DC (May 5, 1998) (hereafter Zell).

61. Suzan Harjo, *Protecting Native American Human Remains, Burial Grounds, and Sacred Places: Panel Discussion*, 19 Wicazo Sa Review 2, at 181 (2004).

62. Native American Grave and Burial Protection Act (S. 1021), Native American Repatriation of Cultural Patrimony Act (S. 1980), and Heard Museum Report: Hearing before the S. Select Committee on Indian Affairs, 101st Congress (May 14, 1990), at 371 (hereafter S. Hrg. 101-952).

63. S. Hrg. 101-952, *supra* note 62, at 368. The Panel for a National Dialogue on Museum/Native American Relations: A Minority View. Undated document.

64. Minutes of SAA Executive Board Meeting no. 77, April 18, 1990, Las Vegas, NV.

65. S. Hrg. 101-952, *supra* note 62, at 368. The Panel for a National Dialogue on Museum/Native American Relations: A Minority View. Undated document.

66. Memorandum from Loretta Neumann, Society for American Archaeology, to Jerry Sabloff, Pru Rice, Keith Kintigh, Bill Lovis, Mark Leone, Lynn Goldstein, Mark Lynott, and Bill Stini (Feb. [probably March] 2, 1990) (hereafter Neumann).

67. Bill McAllister, *Panel Calls for Legislation to Return Indian Remains*, Wash. Post (March 1, 1990).

68. Neumann, *supra* note 66. Also reported in Memorandum from Jane Buikstra to Eugene Sterud, Documents from No-Name Alliance (March 23, 1990). "[Inouye] has since encountered pressure from Indian groups and staff feel that he may try to move ahead this spring."

69. Neumann, *supra* note 66.

70. Dan Monroe, presentation to the Western Museums Conference, San Jose, CA (Oct. 26, 1990). From notes by James Nason.

71. Lisa Sharamitaro, *Service Organizations and the Path to Policy: the American Association of Museums and the case of the Native American Graves Protection and Repatriation Act (NAGPRA)*, Ohio State University, Arts Policy and Administration Program, Occasional Paper No. 14, at 6 (Oct. 14, 2000).

72. Minutes of SAA Executive Board Meeting no. 77, April 18, 1990, Las Vegas, NV.

73. Letter from Edward H. Able Jr., American Association of Museums, to Senator Daniel K. Inouye (April 5, 1990).

74. Some General Principles on Treatment of Disposition of Human Remains and Funerary Objects Synthesized from Policy Statements of Various Archaeological, Anthropological, Historic Preservation Organizations and Government Agencies, Draft (April 26, 1990).

75. Lurline McGregor of the Senate Select Committee staff later characterized the objections raised by the No-Name Alliance as "petty" and that the presentation as a whole was "amateurish." Memorandum from Gene Sterud, executive director, American Anthropological Association, to Lisa Jacobson, "Re: S. 1980 (Native American Cultural Patrimony)" (May 16, 1990).

76. Zell, *supra* note 59.

77. Interview with Eric Eberhard, Distinguished Indian Law Practitioner in Residence, Seattle University Law School (Jan. 2011).

78. S. 1980, 101st Cong. §(2) (May 1990).

79. S. 1980, 101st Cong. § (3)(a)(11) (May 1990). A one-word deletion meant that such items did not necessary have to have been "intentionally" placed with a deceased Native American.

80. S. 1980, 101st Cong. §(3)(a)(13) (May 1990).

81. S. 1980, 101st Cong. §(2)(11) (Nov. 21, 1989).

82. S. 1980, 101st Cong. §(3)(a)(13) (May 1990).

83. S. 1980, 101st Cong. §(3)(a)(5) (May 1990).

84. S. 1980, 101st Cong. §(3)(a)(7) (May 1990).

85. S. 1980, 101st Cong. §(3)(a)(6) (May 1990).

86. S. 1980, 101st Cong. §(3)(a)(10) (May 1990).

87. S. 1980, 101st Cong. §(4) (May 1990).

88. S. 1980, 101st Cong. §(4)(a), (Nov. 21, 1989).

89. S. 1980, 101st Cong. §(4)(a) (May 1990).

90. S. 1980, 101st Cong. §(4)(b) (May 1990).

91. S. 1980, 101st Cong. §(3)(a)(15) (May 1990).

92. S. 1980, 101st Cong. §(3)(a)(8) (May 1990).

93. S. 1980, 101st Cong. §(4)(b) (May 1990).

94. S. 1980, 101st Cong. §(4)(c)(3)(A) (May 1990).

95. S. 1980, 101st Cong. §(4)(d)(1)(A) (May 1990).

96. S. 1980, 101st Cong. §(4)(d)(1)(B) (May 1990).

97. S. 1980, 101st Cong. §(4)(d)(2) (May 1990).

98. S. 1980, 101st Cong. §(4)(e) (May 1990).

99. S. 1980, 101st Cong. §(5)(a)(1) (May 1990).

100. S. 1980, 101st Cong. §(5)(a)(2)(D) (May 1990).

101. S. 1980, 101st Cong. §(5)(a)(2)(B) (May 1990).

102. S. 1980, 101st Cong. §(5)(a)(5) (May 1990).

103. S. 1980, 101st Cong. §(5)(a)(3) (May 1990).

104. S. 1980, 101st Cong. §(5)(a)(4) (May 1990).

105. S. 1980, 101st Cong. §(5)(a)(6) (May 1990).

106. S. 1980, 101st Cong. §(5)(b) (May 1990).

107. S. 1980, 101st Cong. §(5)(c)(1) (May 1990).

108. S. 1980, 101st Cong. §(5)(c)(3) (May 1990).

109. S. 1980, 101st Cong. §(5)(c)(4) (May 1990).

110. S. 1980, 101st Cong. §(5)(c)(5) (May 1990).

111. S. 1980, 101st Cong. §(5)(a)(3)(D) (May 1990).

112. S. 1980, 101st Cong. §(6)(a)(4) (May 1990).

113. Keith Kintigh, Unauthorized Tentative Draft SAA Comments on Staff Draft of S. 1980 Substitute (May 4, 1990).

114. S. 1980, 101st Cong. §(6)(a)(3)(D) (May 1990).

115. Protection of Native American Graves and the Repatriation of Human Remains and Sacred Objects: Hearing on H.R. 1381, H.R. 1646 and H.R. 5237 before the House Committee on Interior and Insular Affairs, 101st Cong. 62 (1990), at 317.

116. S. Hrg. 101-952, *supra* note 62, at 29.

117. Letter from Jerry Rogers, National Park Service, to Walter Echo-Hawk, Native American Rights Fund (Feb. 28, 1990).

118. Memorandum from associate director, Cultural Resources, to director (March 7, 1990).

119. Memorandum from associate director, Cultural Resources, to director (March 7, 1990).

120. Crespi notes of telephone conversation with Jerry Rogers (March 7, 1990).

121. Topics Announced by Secretary Lujan on 20 March 1990. Prepared by Francis P. McManamon, Archeological Assistance Division, National Park Service (March 22, 1990).

122. Paul R. Wieck, *U.S. Government to Return Skeletal Remains to Tribes*, Albuquerque Journal (March 20, 1990).

123. Laurence Jolidon, *Interior Secretary Shows Concern*, USA Today (March 21, 1990).

124. Note from Chief Anthropologist Doug Scovill to Jerry Rogers, Testimony on S. 1980 (Inouye) and S. 1021 (McCain) (April 30, 1990). "Suggest you reconsider request to testify on subject legislation. Looks like a no-win proposition. . . . If I understand you correctly, you do not want to testify against these bills. As they are currently written, if we are to testify, we should testify against them."

125. S. Hrg. 101-952, *supra* note 62, at 562. Administration comments on the proposed substitute amendment for S. 1980 were not included in the hearing report. An unsigned report on S. 1980, dated July 2, 1990, states that "in general, the NPS favors the legislation with changes to the bill which are specified below." In response to one of the findings, the report comments stated that "it is the position of the Federal government that it does not own human remains. The government has stewardship responsibilities for human remains and associated funerary objects, which are held in trust for culturally affiliated groups who can establish rights to their ownership." The National Park Service objected to inclusion of sacred objects and cultural patrimony within the purview of the bill and argued that federal land managers should continue to act as stewards of human remains and associated funerary objects found on federal lands. The NPS expected to complete an inventory of the estimated 3,500 human remains in its collections by January 1991.

126. This policy revision was never completed.

127. S. Hrg. 101-952, *supra* note 62, at 78.

128. S. Hrg. 101-952, *supra* note 62, at 32.

129. S. Hrg. 101-952, *supra* note 62, at 44. Jerry Flute, assistant director of the Association of American Indian Affairs, later introduced the 1890 Wounded Knee Massacre as another example of a double standard, emphasizing that over thirty Medals of Honor were given to members of the 7th Cavalry for killing defenseless men, women, and children. His suggestion that award of these medals be posthumously revoked drew pointed response from McCain. "Let me tell you, that is a waste of time, because I don't see that we're going to revisit history in that fashion. Perhaps it should have been done otherwise, but I certainly would not support such an action" (S. Hrg. 101-952, *supra* note 62, at 75).

130. S. Hrg. 101-952, *supra* note 62, at 31.

131. S. Hrg. 101-952, *supra* note 62, at 31.

132. S. Hrg. 101-952, *supra* note 62, at 32.

133. S. Hrg. 101-952, *supra* note 62, at 34.

134. S. Hrg. 101-952, *supra* note 62, at 33.

135. S. Hrg. 101-952, *supra* note 62, at 34. Rogers was accompanied by Francis McManamon, departmental consulting archeologist with the NPS. In a May 21, 1990, memorandum, McManamon stated that Rogers "fielded the questions following his statement very skillfully. I think that the committee was left with the clear understanding that the NPS wants to work with its staff, and others on all sides of the issue, to reach a mutually acceptable solution."

136. S. Hrg. 101-952, *supra* note 62, at 34.

137. S. Hrg. 101-952, *supra* note 62, at 37.

138. S. Hrg. 101-952, *supra* note 62, at 38.

139. S. Hrg. 101-952, *supra* note 62, at 38.

140. S. Hrg. 101-952, *supra* note 62, at 39.

141. S. Hrg. 101-952, *supra* note 62, at 40.

142. S. Hrg. 101-952, *supra* note 62, at 119.
143. S. Hrg. 101-952, *supra* note 62, at 41.
144. S. Hrg. 101-952, *supra* note 62, at 124.
145. S. Hrg. 101-952, *supra* note 62, at 126.
146. S. Hrg. 101-952, *supra* note 62, at 127.
147. S. Hrg. 101-952, *supra* note 62, at 128.
148. S. Hrg. 101-952, *supra* note 62, at 367.
149. S. Hrg. 101-952, *supra* note 62, at 81.
150. S. Hrg. 101-952, *supra* note 62, at 417.
151. S. Hrg. 101-952, *supra* note 62, at 83.
152. S. Hrg. 101-952, *supra* note 62, at 417.
153. S. Hrg. 101-952, *supra* note 62, at 50.
154. S. Hrg. 101-952, *supra* note 62, at 417.
155. S. Hrg. 101-952, *supra* note 62, at 50.
156. S. Hrg. 101-952, *supra* note 62, at 198.
157. S. Hrg. 101-952, *supra* note 62, at 198.
158. S. Hrg. 101-952, *supra* note 62, at 48.
159. S. Hrg. 101-952, *supra* note 62, at 50.
160. S. Hrg. 101-952, *supra* note 62, at 79.
161. S. Hrg. 101-952, *supra* note 62, at 79.
162. S. Hrg. 101-952, *supra* note 62, at 76.
163. S. Hrg. 101-952, *supra* note 62, at 77.
164. S. Hrg. 101-952, *supra* note 62, at 78.
165. S. Hrg. 101-952, *supra* note 62, at 51.
166. S. Hrg. 101-952, *supra* note 62, at 51.
167. S. Hrg. 101-952, *supra* note 62, at 58.
168. S. Hrg. 101-952, *supra* note 62, at 61.
169. S. Hrg. 101-952, *supra* note 62, at 85.
170. Zuni Tribal Council Resolution M70-90-L017 (Nov. 16, 1989).
171. S. Hrg. 101-952, *supra* note 62, 89.
172. S. Hrg. 101-952, *supra* note 62, 90.
173. S. Hrg. 101-952, *supra* note 62, at 94.
174. S. Hrg. 101-952, *supra* note 62, 94.
175. S. Hrg. 101-952, *supra* note 62, at 95.
176. S. Hrg. 101-952, *supra* note 62, at 91.
177. S. Hrg. 101-952, *supra* note 62, at 63.
178. Discussions revolved partly around whether the human remains should be reburied in New Mexico or repatriated to either Texas (where the Confederate brigade was formed) or Alabama, Virginia, and Tennessee, where most of those who died were originally from. Peter Eichstaedt, *Confederate Remains Found at Glorieta Not from Texas*, Santa Fe New Mexican (Sept. 30, 1987).
179. S. Hrg. 101-952, *supra* note 62, at 65.
180. S. Hrg. 101-952, *supra* note 62, at 66.
181. S. Hrg. 101-952, *supra* note 62, at 66.
182. S. Hrg. 101-952, *supra* note 62, at 73.
183. S. Hrg. 101-952, *supra* note 62, at 68.
184. S. Hrg. 101-952, *supra* note 62, at 69.

185. S. Hrg. 101-952, *supra* note 62, at 69.

186. S. Hrg. 101-952, *supra* note 62, at 71.

187. S. Hrg. 101-952, *supra* note 62, at 572.

188. S. Hrg. 101-952, *supra* note 62, at 82.

189. Roger G. Rose, *Reconciling the Past: Two Basketry Ka'ai and the Legendary Liloa and Lonoikamakahiki* ix (Bishop Museum Press, 1992).

190. "Inventory of Human Skeletal Remains from Mokapu Peninsula," Elizabeth Tatar, principal investigator, Bishop Museum, Jan. 1994.

191. Memorandum from Lauryn Guttenplan Grant to participants in the Repatriation Issues Forum (June 14, 1990).

192. Letter from Elaine Heumann Gurian, deputy assistant secretary for Museums, Smithsonian Institution, to Walter Echo-Hawk, Native American Rights Fund (June 12, 1990).

193. Fax from Walter Echo-Hawk to Sarah Ridley, Henry Sockbeson, and Jack Trope (June 12, 1990).

194. Memorandum from Jack Trope to Gary Kimble, "Smithsonian meeting" (no date).

195. Fax from Walter Echo-Hawk to Jerry Flute, Gary Kimble, Gay Kingman, Sarah Ridley, Henry Sockbeson, and Jack Trope, "Report on Bunky's Meeting with Smithsonian and AAM Representatives on June 20, 1990" (June 21, 1990).

196. Draft letter from Smithsonian Secretary Robert M. Adams to Senator Daniel Inouye (June 4, 1990).

Chapter 6: A Defining Moment

1. As late as July 3, 1990, House committee staffer Marie Howard was unhappy with the version of the bill prepared by the committee's legislative counsel and there was some speculation that the bill would not be introduced prior to the hearing scheduled for July 17, 1990. Memorandum from Henry Sockbeson to Walter Echo-Hawk (July 3, 1990).

2. H.R. 5237, 101st Cong. §(1) (July 10, 1990).

3. S. 1980, 101st Cong. §(1) (May 1990 draft).

4. H.R. 5237, 101st Cong. §(2)(3) (July 10, 1990).

5. H.R. 5237, 101st Cong. §(2)(9) (July 10, 1990).

6. U.S. Const., Art. IV, §3, cl. 2.

7. *South Dakota v. Dole*, 107 S. Ct. 2793, 2796 (1987), cited in H.R. Rept. No. 101-877, at 26 (1990).

8. H.R. 1646, 101st Cong. § (3)(1) (March 23, 1989); S. 1021, 101st Cong. §(3)(1) (May 17, 1989); S. 1980, 101st Cong. §(3)(1) (Nov. 21, 1989); S. 1980, 101st Cong. §(3)(1) (May 1990).

9. H.R. 5237, 101st Cong. §(2)(11) (July 10, 1990).

10. H.R. 5237, 101st Cong. §(2)(5) (July 10, 1990).

11. H.R. 5237, 101st Cong. §(2)(14) (July 10, 1990).

12. H.R. 5237, 101st Cong. §(2)(6) (July 10, 1990).

13. H.R. 5237, 101st Cong. §(2)(7) (July 10, 1990). "Any Indian tribe, band, nation, or other organized group or community, including any Alaska Native village or

regional or village corporation as defined in or established pursuant to the Alaska Native Claims Settlement Act which is recognized as eligible for the special programs and services provided by the United States to Indians because of their status as Indians," 25 U.S.C. §440b(4)(e) (1990).

14. H.R. 5237, 101st Cong. §(2)(13) (July 10, 1990).
15. H.R. 5237, 101st Cong. §(2)(6) (July 10, 1990).
16. H.R. 5237, 101st Cong. §(2)(4) (July 10, 1990).
17. H.R. 5237, 101st Cong. §(2)(15) (July 10, 1990).
18. H.R. 5237, 101st Cong. §(3)(a) (July 10, 1990).
19. S. 1980, 101st Cong. §(3)(9) (May 1990).
20. H.R. 5237, 101st Cong. §(2)(2) (July 10, 1990).
21. H.R. 1646, 101st Cong. §(4) (March 23, 1989).
22. S. 1021, 101st Cong. §(5) (May 17, 1989).
23. S. 1980, 101st Cong. §(4) (May 1990).
24. H.R. 5237, 101st Cong. §(3)(b) (July 10, 1990).
25. H.R. 5237, 101st Cong. §(3)(c) (July 10, 1990).
26. H.R. 5237, 101st Cong. §(3)(d) (July 10, 1990).
27. H.R. 5237, 101st Cong. §(3)(e) (July 10, 1990).
28. S. 1980, 101st Cong. §(3)(a)(13) (May 1990).
29. H.R. 5237, 101st Cong. §(4) (July 10, 1990).
30. H.R. 5237, 101st Cong. §(5)(a) (July 10, 1990).
31. H.R. 5237, 101st Cong. §(5)(e) (July 10, 1990).
32. H.R. 5237, 101st Cong. §(5)(b)(1)(A) (July 10, 1990).
33. H.R. 5237, 101st Cong. §(5)(b)(1)(B) (July 10, 1990)
34. H.R. 5237, 101st Cong. §(5)(b)(2) (July 10, 1990).
35. H.R. 5237, 101st Cong. §(5)(b)(1)(B) (July 10, 1990).
36. H.R. 5237, 101st Cong. §(5)(c) (July 10, 1990).
37. H.R. 5237, 101st Cong. §(5)(d) (July 10, 1990).
38. H.R. 5237, 101st Cong. §(5)(d)(2) (July 10, 1990).
39. H.R. 5237, 101st Cong. §(5)(d)(3) (July 10, 1990).
40. H.R. 5237, 101st Cong. §(6)(a)(1) (July 10, 1990).
41. H.R. 5237, 101st Cong. §(6)(a)(2) (July 10, 1990).
42. H.R. 5237, 101st Cong. §(2)(1) (July 10, 1990).
43. H.R. 5237, 101st Cong. §(6)(a)(3) (July 10, 1990).
44. H.R. 5237, 101st Cong. §(6)(a)(4) (July 10, 1990).
45. H.R. 5237, 101st Cong. §(6)(b) (July 10, 1990).
46. H.R. 5237, 101st Cong. §(6)(c)(1) (July 10, 1990).
47. H.R. 5237, 101st Cong. §(6)(d) (July 10, 1990).
48. H.R. 5237, 101st Cong. §(6)(c)(2) (July 10, 1990).
49. H.R. 5237, 101st Cong. §(6)(e) (July 10, 1990).
50. H.R. 5237, 101st Cong. §(f) (July 10, 1990).
51. H.R. 5237, 101st Cong. §(7) (July 10, 1990).
52. H.R. 5237, 101st Cong. §(7) (July 10, 1990).
53. H.R. 5237, 101st Cong. §(7)(b)(2) (July 10, 1990).
54. H.R. 5237, 101st Cong. §(7)(c)(1) (July 10, 1990).
55. H.R. 5237, 101st Cong. §(7)(c)(2) (July 10, 1990).
56. H.R. 5237, 101st Cong. §(7)(c)(3) (July 10, 1990).

57. H.R. 5237, 101st Cong. §(7)(c)(4) (July 10, 1990).
58. H.R. 5237, 101st Cong. §(7)(c)(5) (July 10, 1990).
59. H.R. 5237, 101st Cong. §(7)(c)(6) (July 10, 1990).
60. H.R. 5237, 101st Cong. §(7)(g) (July 10, 1990).
61. H.R. 5237, 101st Cong. §(7)(c)(7) (July 10, 1990).
62. H.R. 5237, 101st Cong. §(7)(d) (July 10, 1990).
63. H.R. 5237, 101st Cong. §(7)(f) (July 10, 1990).
64. H.R. 5237, 101st Cong. §(7)(e) (July 10, 1990).
65. H.R. 5237, 101st Cong. §(8) (July 10, 1990).
66. H.R. 5237, 101st Cong. §(9)(1) (July 10, 1990).
67. H.R. 5237, 101st Cong. §(9)(2) (July 10, 1990).
68. H.R. 5237, 101st Cong. §(9)(3) (July 10, 1990).
69. H.R. 5237, 101st Cong. §(9)(4) (July 10, 1990).
70. H.R. 5237, 101st Cong. §(10) (July 10, 1990).
71. H.R. 5237, 101st Cong. §(11) (July 10, 1990).

72. The cosponsors were Daniel Akaka from Hawaii, Helen Delich Bentley from Maryland, James Bilbray from Nevada, Jack Buechner from Missouri, Albert Busta-mante from Texas, Cardiss Collins from Illinois, Ron de Lugo from the Virgin Islands, Ronald Dellums from California, Walter Fauntroy from the District of Columbia, Hamilton Fish from New York, Jamie Fuster from Puerto Rico, Dennis Hertel from Michigan, Ben Jones from Georgia, Matthew Martinez from California, Jim McDer-mott from Washington, Wayne Owens from Utah, Donald Payne from New Jersey, Charles Rangel from New York, Arthur Ravenel from South Carolina, and Henry Waxman from California.

73. The cosponsors were Charles Bennett from Florida, Ben Nighthorse Camp-bell from Colorado, Anthony Coelho from California, Ron de Lugo from the Virgin Islands, Ronald Dellums from California, Byron Dorgan from North Dakota, Eni Fa-leomavaega from America Samoa, Walter Fauntroy from the District of Columbia, Martin Frost from Texas, Sam Gejdenson from Connecticut, William Hughes from New Jersey, Matthew Martinez from California, Jim McDermott from Washington, Bruce Morrison from Connecticut, Robert Mrazek from New York, Major Owens from New York, Charles Rangel from New York, Robert Roe from New Jersey, Law-rence Smith from Florida, John Spratt from South Carolina, Gerry Studds from Mas-sachusetts, Patt Williams from Montana, and Don Young from Alaska.

74. Protection of Native American Graves and the Repatriation of Human Re-mains and Sacred Objects (H.R 1381, H.R. 1646, and H.R. 5237): Hearing before the House Committee on Interior and Insular Affairs, 101st Congress (hereafter H.R. Hrg. 101-62), at 1.

75. H.R. Hrg. 101-62, *supra* note 74, at 45. The year before, Campbell had at-tended a town meeting at which participant had suggested that the government should license individuals to "mine" Indian remains and the collect royalties on the results. "I thought that was outlandish." Campbell explained, "but this guy was serious." Native American Graves Protection and Repatriation Act (P.L. 101-601): Funding Hearing Before the Subcommittee on Interior, House Committee on Appropriations, 101st Congress, at 7.

76. H.R. Hrg. 101-62, *supra* note 74, at 46.

77. Testimony prepared for National Park Service Regional Director John Cook

was not approved by the Office of Management and Budget. A draft of that testimony did not address H.R. 5237, and it identified H.R. 1646 as better and more comprehensive than H.R. 1381. The draft testimony recommended deleting the specific deadlines for inventory completion in H.R. 1646 and adding a section establishing a review committee to advise the secretary on issues related to implementation of the bill. Jerry Rogers, the National Park Service associate director for Cultural Resources had previously informed his staff that he would not testify if it was to oppose the proposed legislation. See Note from Chief Anthropologist Doug Scovill to Jerry Rogers, Testimony on S. 1980 (Inouye) and S. 1021 (McCain) (Apr. 30, 1990).

78. H.R. Hrg. 101-62, *supra* note 74, at 53 .

79. H.R. Hrg. 101-62, *supra* note 74, at 58. National Park Service: 3,500 bodies; Tennessee Valley Authority: 10,000 bodies; Bureau of Land Management: 109 bodies; Fish and Wildlife Service: 637 bodies; U.S. Air Force: 140+ bodies; U.S. Navy: 85 bodies.

80. H.R. Hrg. 101-62, *supra* note 74, at 55.

81. H.R. Hrg. 101-62, *supra* note 74, at 98.

82. H.R. Hrg. 101-62, *supra* note 74, at 106.

83. H.R. Hrg. 101-62, *supra* note 74, at 108.

84. H.R. Hrg. 101-62, *supra* note 74, at 109.

85. H.R. Hrg. 101-62, *supra* note 74, at 123.

86. H.R. Hrg. 101-62, *supra* note 74, at 130.

87. H.R. Hrg. 101-62, *supra* note 74, at 130.

88. H.R. Hrg. 101-62, *supra* note 74, at 131.

89. H.R. Hrg. 101-62, *supra* note 74, at 132.

90. H.R. Hrg. 101-62, *supra* note 74, at 132.

91. H.R. Hrg. 101-62, *supra* note 74, at 135.

92. H.R. Hrg. 101-62, *supra* note 74, at 135.

93. H.R. Hrg. 101-62, *supra* note 74, at 136.

94. H.R. Hrg. 101-62, *supra* note 74, at 137.

95. H.R. Hrg. 101-62, *supra* note 74, at 135.

96. H.R. Hrg. 101-62, *supra* note 74, at 153.

97. Wampum Belts Returned to the Onondaga Nation by Dean Snow, from Man in the Northeast, number 38, 1989, 109–117. H.R. Hrg. 101-62, *supra* note 74, at 217.

98. H.R. Hrg. 101-62, *supra* note 74, at 176.

99. H.R. Hrg. 101-62, *supra* note 74, at 231.

100. H.R. Hrg. 101-62, *supra* note 74, at 229.

101. H.R. Hrg. 101-62, *supra* note 74, at 229.

102. H.R. Hrg. 101-62, *supra* note 74, at 234.

103. H.R. Hrg. 101-62, *supra* note 74, at 235.

104. H.R. Hrg. 101-62, *supra* note 74, at 255.

105. H.R. Hrg. 101-62, *supra* note 74, at 255.

106. H.R. Hrg. 101-62, *supra* note 74, at 256.

107. Article II of the Uniform Commercial Code applies to the sale of "goods," meaning all things (including specially manufactured goods) that are movable at the time of identification to the contract for sale. UCC §2-105.

108. H.R. Hrg. 101-62, *supra* note 74, at 257.

109. H.R. Hrg. 101-62, *supra* note 74, at 258.

110. H.R. Hrg. 101-62, *supra* note 74, at 260.

111. Memorandum from Walter Echo-Hawk to interested parties, Testimony of Antique Tribal Art Dealers' Association against H.R. 5237 (July 20, 1990).

112. Interview with Marie Howard, House Committee on Natural Resources (Jan. 29, 1999).

113. H.R. Hrg. 101-62, *supra* note 74, at 259.

114. H.R. Hrg. 101-62, *supra* note 74, at 261.

115. H.R. Hrg. 101-62, *supra* note 74, at 188.

116. H.R. Hrg. 101-62, *supra* note 74, at 90.

117. H.R. Hrg. 101-62, *supra* note 74, at 281.

118. H.R. Hrg. 101-62, *supra* note 74, at 304.

119. H.R. Hrg. 101-62, *supra* note 74, at 79, 144, 182, and 245.

120. H.R. Hrg. 101-62, *supra* note 74, at 78.

121. H.R. Hrg. 101-62, *supra* note 74, at 246.

122. H.R. Hrg. 101-62, *supra* note 74, at 305.

123. H.R. Hrg. 101-62, *supra* note 74, at 144.

124. H.R. Hrg. 101-62, *supra* note 74, at 77.

125. H.R. Hrg. 101-62, *supra* note 74, at 315.

126. H.R. Hrg. 101-62, *supra* note 74, at 304.

127. H.R. Hrg. 101-62, *supra* note 74, at 140.

128. H.R. Hrg. 101-62, *supra* note 74, at 72.

129. H.R. Hrg. 101-62, *supra* note 74, at 141.

130. H.R. Hrg. 101-62, *supra* note 74, at 244.

131. H.R. Hrg. 101-62, *supra* note 74, at 142.

132. H.R. Hrg. 101-62, *supra* note 74, at 142.

133. H.R. Hrg. 101-62, *supra* note 74, at 145.

134. H.R. Hrg. 101-62, *supra* note 74, at 145.

135. H.R. Hrg. 101-62, *supra* note 74, at 141.

136. H.R. Hrg. 101-62, *supra* note 74, at 92.

137. H.R. Hrg. 101-62, *supra* note 74, at 141.

138. H.R. Hrg. 101-62, *supra* note 74, at 283.

139. H.R. Hrg. 101-62, *supra* note 74, at 92.

140. H.R. Hrg. 101-62, *supra* note 74, at 71.

141. H.R. Hrg. 101-62, *supra* note 74, at 245.

142. H.R. Hrg. 101-62, *supra* note 74, at 305.

143. H.R. Hrg. 101-62, *supra* note 74, at 68.

144. H.R. Hrg. 101-62, *supra* note 74, at 141.

145. H.R. Hrg. 101-62, *supra* note 74, at 92.

146. H.R. Hrg. 101-62, *supra* note 74, at 92.

147. H.R. Hrg. 101-62, *supra* note 74, at 188.

148. H.R. Hrg. 101-62, *supra* note 74, at 74.

149. H.R. Hrg. 101-62, *supra* note 74, at 74.

150. H.R. Hrg. 101-62, *supra* note 74, at 69.

151. H.R. Hrg. 101-62, *supra* note 74, at 311.

152. H.R. Hrg. 101-62, *supra* note 74, at 311.

153. H.R. Hrg. 101-62, *supra* note 74, at 312.

154. H.R. Hrg. 101-62, *supra* note 74, at 77.

155. H.R. Hrg. 101-62, *supra* note 74, at 182.

156. H.R. Hrg. 101-62, *supra* note 74, at 308.

157. H.R. Hrg. 101-62, *supra* note 74, at 96.

158. H.R. Hrg. 101-62, *supra* note 74, at 75.

159. H.R. Hrg. 101-62, *supra* note 74, at 309.

160. H.R. Hrg. 101-62, *supra* note 74, at 143.

161. H.R. Hrg. 101-62, *supra* note 74, at 315.

162. H.R. Hrg. 101-62, *supra* note 74, at 75.

163. H.R. Hrg. 101-62, *supra* note 74, at 97.

164. Memorandum from Rick West to Bob Adams and Margaret Gaynor (July 25, 1990a).

165. Memorandum from Rick West to Bob Adams and Margaret Gaynor (July 25, 1990b).

166. H.R. 4739, 101st Cong. (May 8, 1990).

167. H.R. 4739, 101st Cong. (July 27, 1990).

168. Memorandum from Loretta Neumann, lobbyist, Society for American Archaeology, to Frank McManamon, departmental consulting archeologist, National Park Service (July 31, 1990, 10:39 a.m.).

169. Memorandum from Loretta Neumann, lobbyist, Society for American Archaeology, to Frank McManamon, departmental consulting archeologist, National Park Service (July 31, 1990, 12:59 p.m.)

170. S. Rept. 101-473, at 18 (1990).

171. Letter from Bruce C. Navarro, deputy assistant attorney general, U.S. Dept. of Justice, to Senator Daniel Inouye (Aug. 1, 1990), in S. Rept. 101-473, at 21 (1990).

172. This interpretation of the Antiquities Act is not consistent with that articulated by the Department of the Interior.

173. Letter from Harry McPherson to Daniel Inouye (Aug. 3, 1990).

174. Memorandum from Loretta Neumann, lobbyist, Society for American Archaeology, to Bill Lovis and Hester Davis (Aug. 15, 1990).

175. H.R. 4739, 101st Cong. (July 27, 1990).

176. Memorandum from J. E. King, Carnegie Museum of Natural History, to Philip Thompson, Museum of Northern Arizona (Aug. 29, 1990).

177. Memorandum from Walter Echo-Hawk to interested parties, Support Letters for the Bennett Repatriation Amendment (Aug. 15, 1990).

Chapter 7: The Biggest Thing We Have Ever Done

1. Letter from Walter Echo-Hawk, attorney, Native American Rights Fund, to Senator Wyche Fowler Jr. (Aug. 20, 1990).

2. Interview with Jack Trope, executive director, Association for American Indian Affairs, in Rockville, Md. (Sept. 9, 2010).

3. Email from Keith Kintigh to SAA Task Force on Reburial and Repatriation (Aug. 31, 1990).

4. Fax from Keith Kintigh, Society for American Archaeology, to Walter Echo-Hawk, Native American Rights Fund (Aug. 6, 1990).

5. Fax from Walter Echo-Hawk, Native American Rights Fund, to Jack Trope, Association for American Indian Affairs (Aug. 7, 1990).

6. Email from Keith Kintigh to SAA Task Force on Reburial and Repatriation (Aug. 31, 1990).

7. H.R. 5237, 101st Cong. §(2)(2) (July 10, 1990).

8. S. 1980, 101st Cong. §(4)(a)(2)(C) (Nov. 28, 1989).

9. The Indian Claims Commission did not consider any claims in Hawaii and only a few in Alaska.

10. Memorandum from Keith Kintigh, Gay Kingman, Walter Echo-Hawk, Henry Sockbeson, and Jack Trope to Steve Heeley and Lurline McGregor, Senate Select Committee on Indian Affairs (Sept. 12, 1990).

11. Fax memorandum from Walter Echo-Hawk, attorney, Native American Rights Fund to Dan Monroe, Marti Sullivan, and Suzan Harjo (Sept. 12, 1990).

12. SAA followed up with a September 19 phone call and September 20 memo endorsing the agreement, while unilaterally urging Howard to consider amending the grant provisions to specifically fund the documentation of items being repatriated. Memorandum from Keith Kintigh to Marie Howard (Sept. 20, 1990).

13. Email from Keith Kintigh to SAA Task Force on Reburial and Repatriation (Sept. 6, 1990).

14. Memorandum from Aubrey Hendricks and Shirley Powell to Committee on Public Archaeology (COPA) Representatives (Sept. 17, 1990).

15. Memorandum from Aubrey Hendricks and Shirley Powell to Committee on Public Archaeology (COPA) Representatives (Sept. 17, 1990). "Bennett has threatened to reintroduce his amendment in the Senate Conference Committee. This may be prevented if people contact their member(s) of the Committee on Armed Services as soon as possible."

16. Letter from Robert W. Page, assistant secretary of the Army (Civil Works) and C. Edward Dickey, acting principal deputy assistant secretary (Civil Works) to Udall (Aug. 31, 1990). In H.R. Rept. No. 101-877, at 23 (1990).

17. Letter from Bruce Navarro, deputy assistant attorney general, to Udall (Sept. 17, 1990). In H.R. Rept. No. 101-877, at 25 (1990).

18. Letter from Robert D. Reichauer to Daniel K. Inouye (Sept. 21, 1990), in S. Rept. No. 101-473, at 18 (1990). A similar letter from Reichauer to Morris Udall regarding H.R. 5237 was sent on October 15, in H.R Rept. No. 101-877, at 21 (1990).

19. H.R. 5237, 101st Cong. (Sept. 24, 1990).

20. S. 1980, 101st Cong. (Sept. 26, 1990).

21. S. 1980, 101st Cong. §(2) (Sept. 26, 1990). The SAA negotiators preferred omitting the findings section. "Findings have little legal affect, yet there was much nitpicking and ill will over the Inouye findings. [Udall's version] avoids unnecessary arguments." Email from Loretta Neumann to Keith Kintigh (Sept. 25, 1990).

22. S. 1980, 101st Cong. §(14) (Sept. 26, 1990).

23. H.R. 5237, 101st Cong. §(2)(4) (Sept. 24, 1990).

24. S. 1980, 101st Cong. §(3)(13) (Sept. 26, 1990).

25. H.R. 5237, 101st Cong. §(2)(3)(B) (Sept. 24, 1990), and S. 1980, 101st Cong. §(3)(11) (Sept. 26, 1990).

26. H.R. 5237, 101st Cong. §(3)(C) (Sept. 24, 1990).

27. H.R. 5237, 101st Cong. §(2)(6) (Sept. 24, 1990).

28. S. 1980, 101st Cong. §(3)(5) (Sept. 26, 1990).

29. S. 1980, 101st Cong. §(3)(5) (Sept. 26, 1990).

30. S. 1980, 101st Cong. §(3)(6) (Sept. 26, 1990).

31. S. 1980, 101st Cong. §(3)(9) (Sept. 26, 1990).

32. H.R. 5237, 101st Cong. §(2)(2) (Sept. 24, 1990).

33. "The definition of 'cultural affiliation' has been changed to read as requested by SAA and NARF—it retains the essential thread that SAA wanted (continuity of group identity) while not alleviating the Indian fears that it would put them in a legal straight jacket ('continuity' has been held, apparently to mean an unbroken chain, even if only for a short time." Email from Loretta Neumann to Keith Kintigh (Sept. 25, 1990).

34. S. 1980, 101st Cong. §(3)(1) (Sept. 26, 1990).

35. H.R. 5237, 101st Cong. §(2)(10) (Sept. 24, 1990).

36. H.R. 5237, 101st Cong. §(2)(14) (Sept. 24, 1990), and S. 1980, 101st Cong. §(3)(7) (Sept. 26, 1990).

37. Despite the earlier agreement with the Native organizations, the SAA privately opposed the aboriginal land provision. "As we have before, we object to linking ownership to the aboriginal lands, in the absence of cultural affiliation. While we understand the desire to assert more broadly Native ownership over Native American remains and cultural items, we fear that no matter how it is implemented, this provision will create a procedural nightmare and result in a morass of nonsensical and conflicting claims. On the balance we feel that, rather than turn such items over to unrelated groups, it is preferable to keep such unaffiliated items within the public trust, for the public benefit, and subject to future claims for repatriation due to demonstration of cultural affiliation." SAA Comments on H.R. 5237 Draft, prepared by Vin Steponaitis (Oct. 9, 1990).

38. S. 1980, 101st Cong. §(5)(b)(1) (Sept. 26, 1990).

39. H.R. 5237, 101st Cong. §(3)(d)(1) (Sept. 24, 1990).

40. H.R. 5237, 101st Cong. §(3)(e) (Sept. 24, 1990).

41. H.R. 5237, 101st Cong. §(4) (July 10, 1990).

42. H.R. 5237, 101st Cong. §(4) (Sept. 24, 1990), and S. 1980, 101st Cong. §(6) (Sept. 26, 1990).

43. S. 1980, 101st Cong. §(3)(13) and (3)(15) (Sept. 26, 1990).

44. H.R. 5237, 101st Cong. §(6)(b)(Sept. 24, 1990), and S. 1980, 101st Cong. §(8)(b) (Sept. 26, 1990). The SAA opposed this provision. "This subsection unintentionally embodies the anti-scientific notion that one can determine, in advance, that the outcome of a study (i.e. a piece of research) will be of major benefit to the United States. It is in the nature of scientific research that one does not know what the outcome, or the benefits of the outcome, will be before doing the research (otherwise the research need not be done)." SAA Comments on H.R. 5237 Draft, prepared by Vin Steponaitis (Oct. 9, 1990).

45. S. 1980, 101st Cong. §(9)(b)(1) (Sept. 26, 1990).

46. S. 1980, 101st Cong. §(9)(c)(2) (Sept. 26, 1990).

47. H.R. 5237, 101st Cong. §(7)(c)(4) (Sept. 24, 1990), and S. 1980, 101st Cong. §(9)(c)(4) (Sept. 26, 1990).

48. S. 1980, 101st Cong. §(11)(a)(5) (Sept. 26, 1990).

49. Interview with Eric Eberhard, Distinguished Indian Law Practitioner in Residence, Seattle University Law School (Jan. 2011) (hereafter Eberhard).

50. Note from Val Canouts to Frank McManamon (undated). Memorandum from Loretta Neumann to No-Name Alliance (Sept. 19, 1990).

51. In August 1990, the University of California issued a review of current policies and procedures for university collections of human remains and associated funerary objects. The report concluded that the university's acquisition, maintenance, preservation, and access practices were largely consistent with state law and professional museum standards. Report of University of California Joint Academic Senate–Administration Committee on Human Skeletal Remain, University Office of the President (Aug. 1990).

52. Interview with Marie Howard, House Committee on Natural Resources (Jan. 29, 1999) (hereafter Howard). On Sept. 25, 1990, California Governor George Deukmajian had vetoed a bill that would have required California museums, universities, and other state-funded institutions to inventory their archeological collections and return human remains and grave artifacts to their most likely descendants. Leslie Berger, *Governor Sides with School in Bone Debate*, Los Angeles Times, Sept. 27, 1990, at A-3.

53. The four phases of AAM reaction to repatriation were outlined by Dan Monroe in a presentation to the Western Museums Conference, San Jose, California (Oct. 26, 1990). From notes by James Nason.

54. *AAM Policy Regarding the Repatriation of Native American Ceremonial Objects and Human Remains*, Aviso (March 1988), at 4–5. Also *AAM Policy Regarding the Repatriation of Native American Ceremonial Objects and Human Remains: Objectives and Process* (March 1, 1988).

55. Notes from Repatriation Meeting (June 20, 1990). Memorandum from Elaine Heumann Gurian, Smithsonian Institution, to Ed Able, Robert M. Adams, Sandy Boyd, Walter Echo-Hawk, Margaret Gaynor, Lauryn Guttenplan Grant, Suzan Harjo, Duane King, Dan Monroe, Geoff, Frank Talbot, and Rick West (July 19, 1990).

56. Lisa Sharamitaro, *Service Organizations and the Path to Policy: The American Association of Museums and the Case of the Native American Graves Protection and Repatriation Act (NAGPRA)*. Ohio State University, Arts Policy and Administration Program, Occasional Paper 14 (Oct. 14, 2000).

57. Memorandum from Dan Monroe to American Museum of Natural History, Arizona State Museum, Bishop Museum, Denver Art Museum, Denver Museum of Natural History, Field Museum, Fine Arts Museum of San Francisco, Harvard University, Museum of New Mexico, Museum of Northern Arizona, Natural History Museum of Los Angeles County, Rochester Museum and Science Center, and University of Pennsylvania (Sept. 17, 1990).

58. Letter from Dan L. Monroe to AAM Executive Committee (Oct. 5, 1990).

59. Letter from Dan Monroe to AAM Government Affairs (Sept. 28, 1990).

60. Memorandum from Dan L. Monroe to AAM Executive Committee (Oct. 5, 1990).

61. Proposed Amendments to H.R. 5237 in order to meet AAM Concerns (undated).

62. Letter from Dan Monroe to AAM Government Affairs (Oct. 5, 1990).

63. Memorandum from Dan L. Monroe to AAM Executive Committee (Oct. 5, 1990).

64. Memorandum from Marie Howard to interested staff regarding agreement between Indian organizations and American Association of Museums (undated).

65. 136 Cong. Reg. H10990 (daily ed., Oct. 22, 1990). The NARF and the AAIA had provided House staff with "bottom-line positions" on the ATADA proposals. Memorandum from Walter Echo-Hawk, Henry Sockbeson, and Jack Trope to Marie Howard, NARF and AAIA position on ATADA Amendments to H.R. 5237 (Sept. 13, 1990). Memorandum from Walter Echo-Hawk and Henry Sockbeson to Judy Chapman, H.R. 5237—Review Committee Composition (Sept. 14, 1990).

66. Letter from Scott Sewell, deputy assistant secretary, to Udall (Oct. 2, 1990). In H.R. Rept. No. 101-877, at 29 (1990).

67. Several edited drafts of this letter are located in the files of the Office of Management and Budget. The original draft from the Department of the Interior stated that "we support enactment of H.R. 5237 if amended as suggested." Another draft stated, "we oppose enactment of H.R. 5237 at this time and urge that legislation concerning sacred objects and cultural patrimony be postponed."

68. Memorandum from Walter Echo-Hawk and Henry Sockbeson, Native American Rights Fund, and Jack Trope, Association for American Indian Affairs, to Cathy Wilson, Marie Howard, and Kim Craven, House Resources Committee staff (Oct. 3, 1990).

69. H.R. 5237, 101st Cong. §(5)(b)(1)(C) (Sept. 24, 1990).

70. H.R. 5237, 101st Cong. §(5)(a) (Oct. 10, 1990).

71. H.R. 5237, 101st Cong. §(6)(a) (Oct. 10, 1990).

72. H.R. 5237, 101st Cong. §(6)(b)(1) (Oct. 10, 1990).

73. H.R. 5237, 101st Cong. §(2)(3)(A) and (2)(3)(B) (Oct. 10, 1990).

74. H.R. 5237, 101st Cong. §(2)(2)(B) (Sept. 24, 1990).

75. H.R. 5237, 101st Cong. §(2)(2)(C) (Oct. 10, 1990).

76. H.R. Rept. No. 101-877, at 14 (1990).

77. H.R. 5237, 101st Cong. §(3)(a)(2)(C)(ii) (Oct. 10, 1990).

78. H.R. 5237, 101st Cong. §(3)(b) (Oct. 10, 1990).

79. H.R. 5237, 101st Cong. §(2)(4) (Oct. 10, 1990). Actually referred to P.L. 101-185.

80. H.R. Rept. No. 101-877, at 14 (1990).

81. H.R. 5237, 101st Cong. §(7)(e) (Sept. 24, 1990).

82. H.R. 5237, 101st Cong. §(8)(a)(1) (Oct. 10, 1990).

83. H.R. 5237, 101st Cong. §(8)(a)(2) (Oct. 10, 1990).

84. H.R. 5237, 101st Cong. §(8)(a)(1) (Oct. 10, 1990).

85. H.R. 5237, 101st Cong. §(8)(a)(3) (Oct. 10, 1990).

86. H.R. 5237, 101st Cong. §(7)(f) (Oct. 10, 1990).

87. H.R. 5237, 101st Cong. §(12) (Oct. 10, 1990).

88. H.R. Rept. No. 101-877, at 14 (1990).

89. Letter from James Reid, Antique Tribal Art Dealers Association, to Representative Bill Richardson (Oct. 9, 1990).

90. Memorandum from Loretta Neumann to the No-Name Alliance (Oct. 10, 1990). "Note that that this association hides behind the guise of legitimate anthropological and archaeological concerns in order to address their views."

91. H.R. 5237, 101st Cong. Markup (Oct. 10, 1990), transcript. Library of Congress.

92. Fax from Keith Kintigh to Walter Echo-Hawk, Henry Sockbeson, Jack Trope, Geoffrey Platt regarding joint support of H.R. 5237 (Oct. 11, 1990).

93. Letter from Edward H. Able Jr. to whom it may concern (Oct. 12, 1990).

94. Representatives Ben Campbell, Pat Williams from Montana, and James Scheuer from New York were now listed as cosponsors.

95. H.R. Rept. No. 101-877, at 9 (1990).

96. H.R. Rept. No. 101-877, at 14 (1990).

97. H.R. Rept. No. 101-877, at 8 (1990).

98. H.R. Rept. No. 101-877, at 9 (1990).

99. H.R. Rept. No. 101-877, at 10 (1990).

100. H.R. Rept. No. 101-877, at 15 (1990).

101. H.R. Rept. No. 101-877, at 15 (1990).

102. H.R. Rept. No. 101-877, at 15 (1990).

103. H.R. Rept. No. 101-877, at 16 (1990).

104. H.R. Rept. No. 101-877, at 16 (1990).

105. H.R. Rept. No. 101-877, at 16 (1990).

106. H.R. Rept. No. 101-877, at 16 (1990).

107. Letter from Morton Halperin, American Civil Liberties Union (Oct. 17, 1990).

108. Fax memorandum from Walter Echo-Hawk and Henry Sockbeson, Native American Rights Fund, and Jack Trope, Association for American Indian Affairs, to Steve Heeley and Lurline McGregor, Senate Select Committee on Indian Affairs staff (Oct. 18, 1990).

109. Memorandum from Shirley Powell and Aubrey Hendricks to COPA Representatives, Recent Legislative Activity (Nov. 1, 1990). Fax from Jack Trope, Association for American Indian Affairs to Henry [Sockbeson] titled "floor amendments S. 1980" (Oct. 18, 1990).

110. Fax from Walter Echo-Hawk, Native American Rights Fund, to Marie Howard, House Committee in Interior and Insular Affairs (Oct. 20, 1990).

111. Additional changes to H.R. 5237 were still being requested as the bill was considered by the House. A "desk copy" dated Friday, Oct. 19, included a handwritten definition of Indian tribe using the language from Section 4 of the Indian Self Determination and Education Assistance Act, language excluding the Smithsonian Institution from provisions of the bill, and deletion of lands conveyed to Alaska Native corporations from the excavation and discovery provisions. These provisions were introduced as amendments by the Senate the following Thursday.

112. 136 Cong. Reg. H10988 (daily ed., Oct. 22, 1990).

113. Fax from Dan Monroe, Oregon Art Institute, to Marty Sullivan (Oct. 22, 1990).

114. Fax from Geoffry Platt Jr., American Association of Museums, to Marie Howard, "re. differences between H.R. 5237 and S. 1980 (as per. Amendments released on 18 Oct.)" (Oct. 22, 1990).

115. Statement of Administrative Policy, H.R. 5237—Native American Graves Protection and Repatriation Act (Oct. 20, 1990). A handwritten note reads "released to Hill 10/22/1990."

116. Eberhard, *supra* note 49.

117. Amendment 3171, in 136 Cong. Reg. S18245 (daily ed., Oct. 25, 1990).

118. H.R. 5237, 101st Cong. §(2)(4) (Oct. 22, 1990), in 136 Cong. Reg. H10985 (daily ed., Oct. 22, 1990).

119. H.R. 5237, 101st Cong. §(2)(8) (Oct. 22, 1990), in 136 Cong. Reg. H10985 (daily ed., Oct. 22, 1990).

120. Eberhard, *supra* note 49.

121. Amendment 3172, in 136 Cong. Reg. H18245 (daily ed., Oct. 22, 1990).

122. H.R. 5237, 101st Cong. §(2)(7) (Oct. 22, 1990), in 136 Cong. Reg. H10985 (daily ed., Oct. 22, 1990).

123. 25 U.S.C. §450b (e).

124. Subject to a determination by the secretary of the Interior, 205 named Native villages were eligible for land benefits under 43 U.S.C. §1610 (b)(1), and another 11 were eligible under 43 U.S.C. §1615.

125. 43 U.S.C. §1611, 1613.

126. James D. Linxwiler, *The Alaska Native Claims Settlement Act: The First Twenty Years*, Paper 2, 38th Annual Rocky Mountain Law Institute, at 33 (1992), http://www.lbblawyers.com/ANCSA%20Paper%20with%20Table%20of%20Contents%201992.pdf (accessed April 7, 2011).

127. H.R. 5237, 101st Cong. §(2)(15) (Oct. 22, 1990), in 136 Cong. Reg. H10986 (daily ed., Oct. 22, 1990).

128. H.R. 5237, 101st Cong. §(3)(d)(1) (Oct. 22, 1990), in 136 Cong. Reg. H10986 (daily ed., Oct. 22, 1990).

129. 136 Cong. Reg. S18245 (daily ed., Oct. 25, 1990).

130. Eberhard, *supra* note 49.

131. 136 Cong. Reg. S18261 (daily ed., Oct. 25, 1990).

132. Eberhard, *supra* note 49.

133. 136 Cong. Reg. S17173 (daily ed., Oct. 26, 1990).

134. 136 Cong. Reg. S17174 (daily ed., Oct. 26, 1990).

135. 136 Cong. Reg. S17174 (daily ed., Oct. 26, 1990).

136. 136 Cong. Reg. S17173 (daily ed., Oct. 26, 1990). S. 3217, National Museum of the American Indian Amendments Act, 101st Cong. (Oct. 18, 1990). The bill included definitions and summary, inventory, notice, and repatriation provisions similar to those in H.R. 5237.

137. 136 Cong. Reg. S17173 (daily ed., Oct. 26, 1990).

138. 136 Cong. Rec. S17176 (daily ed., Oct. 26, 1990). The bill authorized the secretary of the Interior to delegate responsibility for determining the disposition of or control over inadvertently discovered cultural items to the appropriate secretary or agency head. 25 U.S.C. §3002(d)(3).

139. Wyoming state law prohibited the excavation of prehistoric ruins, relics, and archeological and paleontological deposits on public land without benefit of a permit issued by the Board of Land Commissioners. Wyo. Sta. 36-1-114, Protection of Prehistoric Ruins, in H. Marcus Price, *Disputing the Dead* (University of Missouri Press, 1991). The Archaeological Resources Protection Act specifically exempted from criminal penalty persons who removed arrowheads from the surface of federal lands. 16 U.S.C. §470ee (g).

140. 136 Cong. Rec. S17176 (daily ed., Oct. 26, 1990).

141. 136 Cong. Rec. S17176 (daily ed., Oct. 26, 1990).

142. 136 Cong. Rec. H12336 (daily ed., Oct. 27, 1990).

143. Howard, *supra* note 52.

144. 142 Cong. Rec. S8159 (daily ed., July 18, 1996).

145. Felicity Barringer, *Bush Weighs Bill on Tribal Remains*, N.Y. Times, Nov. 4, 1990, at sec. 1, pt., 1, p. 25.

146. Letter from Assistant Secretary of the Interior Constance B. Harriman to Richard G. Darman, Director, Office of Management and Budget (Nov. 9, 1990).

147. Memorandum for the President from Richard Darman, director, Office of Management and Budget (Nov. 14, 1990).

148. Letter from Secretary Clayton Yeutter, Department of Agriculture, to Richard Darman (Nov. 9, 1990). The OMB files contained an unsigned and undated memorandum, highly critical of the bill, that had been faxed from the Office of the Secretary of the Smithsonian Institution on October 19, 1990.

149. Letter from Assistant Secretary W. Lee Rawls, Department of Justice, to Richard Darman (Nov. 10, 1990).

150. White House Staffing Memorandum from Assistant to the President and Deputy to the Chief of Staff James Cicconi for action by Communications Director David Demarest, Counsel C. Boyden Gray, Presidential Assistant Ede Holiday, Legislative Affairs Director Frederick McClure, Assistant for Economic and Domestic Policy Roger Porter, and Council for Environmental Quality Chairman Michael Deland (Nov. 15, 1990). A handwritten note on the memorandum reads "Ok'd by phone 11/15/90."

151. 99th Congress: S. 2952, Native American Cultural Preservation Act. 100th Congress: S. 187, Native American Cultural Preservation Act/Native American Museum Claims Commission Act (three versions); S. 1722, National Museum of the American Indian Act (two versions); H.R. 3480, National Museum of the American Indian Act; H.R. 5411, Indian Remains Reburial Act; S. 2912, Comprehensive Preservation Act. 101st Congress: H.R. 1124, Indian Remains Reburial Act; H.R. 1381, Native American Burial Site Preservation Act; H.R. 1646, Native American Grave and Burial Protection Act; S. 978, National American Indian Museum Act; S. 1021, Native American Grave and Burial Protection Act; H.R. 2668, National American Indian Museum Act; S. 1579, Bill to amend the National Historic Preservation Act, Historic Sites Act, Archaeological Resources Protection Act, and Abandoned Shipwrecks Act (two versions); H.R. 3412, Bill to amend the National Historic Preservation Act, Historic Sites Act, Archaeological Resources Protection Act, and Abandoned Shipwrecks Act; H.R. 4739, proposed amendment to the National Defense Authorization Act for Fiscal Year 1991; S. 1980, Native American Repatriation and Cultural Patrimony Act (four versions); Pub. L. 101-185, National Museum of the American Indian Act; H.R. 5237, Native American Graves Protection and Repatriation Act (three versions); Pub. L. 101-601, Native American Graves Protection and Repatriation Act.

152. Interview with Jack Trope, executive director, Association for American Indian Affairs, in Rockville, MD (Sept. 9, 2010).

153. Geoffrey Platt Jr., *The Repatriation Law Ends One Journey—But Opens a New Road*. Museum News, Jan./Feb. 1991, at 91.

154. Minutes of the Society for American Archaeology Executive Board Meeting #79 (Nov. 18, 1990).

155. Keith W. Kintigh, *Surveying the Field—Repatriation We Can Live With*, Bulletin (Society for American Archaeology), Jan. 1990, at 2.

156. F. A. Calabrese, *Biocultural Immortality: The Future from the Past*, paper pre-

pared for the 6th Conference on Research and Resource Management in National Parks and Equivalent Reserves (Nov. 15, 1990).

157. Eberhard, *supra* note 49.

158. Howard, *supra* note 52.

159. 136 Cong. Rec. E3484 (daily ed., Oct. 22, 1990).

160. 136 Cong. Reg. S17173 (daily ed., Oct. 26, 1990).

161. Federal Courts Administration Act of 1992, Pub. L. No. 102-572, 106 Stat. 4516 (Oct. 29, 1992).

162. Violent Crime Control and Law Enforcement Act, Pub. L. No. 103-322, 108 Stat. 1796 (Sept. 13, 1994).

163. 104th Congress: S. 1983 (July 23, 1996), H.R. 4084 (Sept. 17, 1996). 105th Congress: S. 110 (Jan. 21, 1997), H.R. 749 (Feb. 13, 1997), H.R. 2893 (Nov. 7, 1997). 108th Congress: S. 2843 (Sept. 23, 2004). 109th Congress: S. 536 (Mar. 7, 2005), H.R. 6043 (Sept. 7, 2006). 110th Congress: S. 2087 (Sept. 25, 2007), H.R. 4027 (Oct. 31, 2007).

164. S. 3217, National Museum of the American Indian Amendments Act, 101st Cong. (Oct. 18, 1990).

165. S. 235, National Museum of the American Indian Amendments Act, 102nd Cong. (Jan. 17, 1991).

166. Native American Graves Protection and Repatriation Review Committee Report to Congress, 1993–1994 (1995).

167. S. Hrg. 104-399, at 24.

168. S. Hrg. 104-399, at 24.

169. S. 1970, 104th Cong. (July 18, 1996).

170. 142 Cong. Rec. S8157 (daily ed., July 18, 1996).

171. S. 1970, 104th Cong. § (2) (July 18, 1996).

172. 25 U.S.C. §3003(a) and (e).

173. 25 U.S.C. § 3003(a).

174. S. 1970, 104th Cong. §(4) (July 18, 1996).

175. 25 U.S.C. §3004.

176. 25 U.S.C. §3001(3).

177. S. 1970, 104th Cong. §(4) (July 18, 1996).

178. 25 U.S.C. §3005(c).

179. 25 U.S.C. §3005(e).

180. 25 U.S.C. §3005(b).

181. 25 U.S.C. §3005(f).

182. 25 U.S.C. §3004(b)(2).

183. S. 1970, 104th Cong. §(5) (July 18, 1996).

184. S. Rept. No. 104-350, at 3.

185. S. Rept. No. 104-350.

186. Pub. L. No. 104-278.

Chapter 8: Legislative History in Interpretive Context

1. William N. Eskridge Jr. and Philip P. Frickey, *Cases and Materials on Legislation, Statutes, and Public Policy* 881 (Thompson West, 1995) (hereafter Eskridge).

2. *Sutherland, Statutes and Statutory Construction* 45:3 (Norman J. Singer and

J. D. Shambie Singer, eds., 7th ed., Clark Boardman Callaghan, 2008) (hereafter Sutherland). This source provides a table of relevant cases for all jurisdictions.

3. Henry Friendly, Mr. Justice Frankfurter and the Reading of Statutes, in Friendly, *Benchmarks* 202 (1967). Cited in Eskridge, *supra* note 1, at 513.

4. Sutherland, *supra* note 2, at 46:6.

5. Sutherland, *supra* note 2, at 46:6.

6. Sutherland, *supra* note 2, at 46:1.

7. Sutherland, *supra* note 2, at 46:5.

8. Sutherland, *supra* note 2, at 45:2.

9. Sutherland, *supra* note 2, at 46:4.

10. Sutherland, *supra* note 2, at 46:6.

11. Sutherland, *supra* note 2, at 48:1.

12. S. 978, 101st Cong. (May 11, 1989); H.R. 2668, 101st Cong. (June 15, 1989).

13. S. Rept. No. 101-143 (1989).

14. 135 Cong. Rec. S12386–12398 (daily ed., Oct. 3, 1989).

15. H.R. Rept. No. 101-340 (1989).

16. 135 Cong. Rec. H8443–8456 (daily ed., Nov. 13, 1989).

17. H.R. Rept. No. 101-877 (1990).

18. Sutherland, *supra* note 2, at 48:14.

19. Sutherland, *supra* note 2, at 48:15.

20. Sutherland, *supra* note 2, at 48:16.

21. 135 Cong. Rec. S12397 (daily ed., Oct. 3, 1989).

22. 135 Cong. Rec. E3926 (daily ed., Nov. 17, 1989).

23. 135 Cong. Rec. E3803 (daily ed., Nov. 14, 1989).

24. 135 Cong. Rec. E3926 (daily ed., Nov. 17, 1989).

25. 135 Cong. Rec. E3923 (daily ed., Nov. 17, 1989).

26. 135 Cong. Rec. S5162 (daily ed., May 14, 1989).

27. 136 Cong. Rec. H10988 (daily ed., Oct. 22, 1990).

28. 136 Cong. Rec. H10989 (daily ed., Oct. 22, 1990).

29. 136 Cong. Rec. H10989 (daily ed., Oct. 22, 1990).

30. 136 Cong. Rec. H10990 (daily ed., Oct. 22, 1990).

31. 136 Cong. Rec. H10991 and H11487 (daily ed., Oct. 22, 1990).

32. 136 Cong. Rec. H10991 (daily ed., Oct. 22, 1990).

33. 136 Cong. Rec. S17173 and S17175 (daily ed., Oct. 26, 1990).

34. 136 Cong. Rec. S17174 (daily ed., Oct. 26, 1990).

35. 136 Cong. Rec. S17174 and S17175 (daily ed., Oct. 26, 1990).

36. 136 Cong. Rec. S17175 (daily ed., Oct. 26, 1990).

37. 136 Cong. Rec. S17175 (daily ed. Oct. 26, 1990).

38. 136 Cong. Rec. S17175 and S17176 (daily ed. Oct. 26, 1990).

39. 136 Cong. Rec. S17176 and S17177 (daily ed. Oct. 26, 1990).

40. Sutherland, *supra* note 2, at 48:4.

41. S. 978, 101st Cong. (May 11, 1989).

42. S. 978, 101st Cong. (May 17, 1989).

43. S. 978, 101st Cong. (Sept. 27, 1989).

44. S. 978, 101st Cong. (Oct. 3, 1989).

45. H.R. 5237, 101st Cong. (July 10, 1990)

46. H.R. 5237, 101st Cong. (Sept. 24, 1990)

47. H.R. 5237, 101st Cong. (Oct. 10, 1990, and Oct. 15, 1990).

48. H.R. 5237, 101st Cong. (Oct. 22, 1990).

49. H.R. 5237, 101st Cong. (Oct. 26, 1990).

50. H.R. 5237, 101st Cong. (Oct. 27, 1990).

51. Sutherland, *supra* note 2, at 48:10.

52. National Memorial Museum of the American Indian: Joint Hearing before the Senate Select Committee on Indian Affairs and the Senate Committee on Rules and Administration on S. 978 to Authorize the Establishment within the Smithsonian Institution of the National Museum of the American Indian and to Establish a Memorial to the American Indian, 101st Cong 79-93 (1989) (hereafter S. Hrg. 101-203).

53. S. Hrg. 101-203, *supra* note 52, at 57.

54. Establishment of the National Museum of the American Indian: Joint Hearings before the House Committee on the Interior and Insular Affairs, Committee on House Administration, and the Committee on Public Works and Transportation on H.R. 2668, National American Indian Museum Act, 101st Cong (1989) (hereafter H.R. Hrg. 101-53).

55. Protection of Native American Graves and the Repatriation of Human Remains and Sacred Objects: Hearing before the House Committee on Interior and Insular Affairs on H.R. 1381, Native American Burial Site Preservation Act, H.R. 1646, Native American Grave and Burial Protection Act, and H.R. 5237, Native American Grave Protection and Repatriation Act, 101st Cong (1990).

56. The act authorizes an appropriation of $25 million from the real property fund established pursuant to the Federal Property and Administrative Services Act of 1949 (40 U.S.C. 490) for the lease, repair, alteration, and construction of offices, an auditorium, and a loading dock at the Old U.S. Custom House in New York. The act also gives the board of regents discretion to establish programs in museum studies, management, and research in cooperation with colleges or universities recognized under the Tribally Controlled Community College Assistance Act (25 U.S.C. 1801(a)(4)).

57. 20 U.S.C. §80q-14 (8).

58. 20 U.S.C. §80q-10 (g).

59. 20 U.S.C. §80q-9a (a).

60. 25 U.S.C. §3001(5) and (7).

61. 25 U.S.C. §3001(15)(C).

62. 25 U.S.C. §3001(13).

63. 25 U.S.C. §3002(c)(1).

64. Sutherland, *supra* note 2, at 51:2.

65. Sutherland, *supra* note 2, at 51:5.

66. Sutherland, *supra* note 2, at 51:8.

67. Sutherland, *supra* note 2, at 50:1.

68. H.R. Hrg. 101-53, *supra* note 54, at 52 (testimony of Henry J. Sockbeson, senior staff attorney, Native American Rights Fund).

69. 20 U.S.C. §80q-9.

70. 20 U.S.C. §80q(6) and (7).

71. 25 U.S.C. §3001(4).

72. The Smithsonian Institution was explicitly included in the definition of federal agency in the July 10, 1990, and September 24, 1990, versions of H.R. 5237. In the October 10 and October 15, 1990, versions, the Smithsonian Institution was also in-

cluded in the definition of federal agency "except as may be inconsistent with the provisions of Public Law 101-185." The Smithsonian was finally excluded from the definition of federal agency by Senate amendment on October 26, 1990.

73. 43 CFR §10.2 (a)(1).

74. 25 U.S.C. §3003–3005. The Internal Revenue Service determined that it does not have sufficient control of cultural items that are seized and sold under authority of the Internal Revenue Code. Letter from Joyce E. Bauchner, assistant chief counsel—general litigation, Internal Revenue Service (Aug. 16, 1996).

75. 43 CFR §10, Final Rule, Preamble, 60 Fed. Reg. 62135 (Dec. 4, 1995).

76. 25 U.S.C. §3001(8).

77. The Smithsonian was explicitly excluded in the definition of museum in the July 10 and September 24, 1990, versions of H.R. 5237. Reference to the Smithsonian was removed from the definition of museum in the October 10 and October 15, 1990, versions. The explicit exclusion of the Smithsonian Institution was again added to the definition of museum by Senate amendment on October 26, 1990.

78. H.R. 5237, 101st Cong. §(2)(9) (July 10, 1990), and H.R. 5237, 101st Cong. §(2)(8) (Sept. 24, 1990).

79. For example, an individual farmer with a personal collection of Native American items would not be required to comply with the NAGPRA's collection provisions, even if he or she received a federal subsidy or grant, whereas an incorporated farm would be required to comply if it has a similar collection and received federal funds.

80. 136 Cong. Rec. H11487 (daily ed., Oct. 22, 1990).

81. 43 CFR §10.2(a)(3)(i).

82. 43 CFR §10.2(a)(3)(ii).

83. 43 CFR §10, Final Rule, Preamble, 60 Fed. Reg. 62135 (Dec. 4, 1995).

84. 25 U.S.C. §3002(d)(1).

85. 25 U.S.C. §3002(d)(1).

86. 25 U.S.C. §3002(b).

87. 25 U.S.C. §3002(a) and (d)(2).

88. 25 U.S.C. §3002(d)(3).

89. 136 Cong. Rec. S17176 (daily ed., Oct. 26, 1990). "The bill requires the party discovering a native American cultural item to provide notice to the Secretary of this particular Federal department with authority over those Federal lands. The Secretary of the Interior will have responsibility to determine the ownership of cultural items discovered on Federal lands."

90. 20 U.S.C. §80q-9(c) and §80q-11(a)(3). The 1996 amendments to the NMAI Act extended the repatriation provisions to unassociated funerary objects, sacred objects, and objects of cultural patrimony. 20 U.S.C. §80q-9(b).

91. 20 U.S.C. §80q-14(8).

92. 25 U.S.C. §450b(e).

93. H. Rpt. 101-340, Pt. 1, 16, and Pt. 2, 26.

94. 20 U.S.C. §80q-11(a)(2).

95. H.R. Rept. No. 101-340, 101 Cong., 1st Sess., Pt. I (1989), at 16; H.R. Rept. No. 101-340, 101 Cong., 1st Sess., Pt. II (1989), at 26.

96. National Museum of the American Indian Policy Statement on Native American Human Remains and Cultural Items.

97. Gillian Flynn and Thomas Killion, *Guidelines for Repatriation*, National Museum of Natural History, Smithsonian Institution (1997).

98. *How can a non-federally recognized tribe participate in the repatriation process at the National Museum of Natural History?*, http://anthropology.si.edu/repatriation/faq/#req07 (accessed April 7, 2011).

99. H.R. Rept. No. 101-340, 101 Cong., 1st Sess., Pt. I (1989), at 16; H.R. Rept. No. 101-340, 101 Cong., 1st Sess., Pt. II (1989), at 26.

100. Nancy B. Rosoff, *Integrating Native Views into Museum Procedures: Hope and Practice at the National Museum of the American Indian*, Museum Anthropology, 22, no. 1, at 35 (1998).

101. 25 U.S.C. §3002(a).

102. 43 CFR §10.2(b)(1).

103. 43 CFR §10, Final Rule, Preamble, 60 Fed. Reg. 62136 (Dec. 4, 1995).

104. 43 U.S.C. §1601 et seq.

105. 43 CFR §10.2(b)(2).

106. *Abenaki Nation of Mississquoi v. Hughes*, 805 F. Supp. 234 (D. Vt. Oct. 22, 1992).

107. 36 CFR §800.5(e)(1).

108. 36 CFR §800.2(g).

109. 53 Fed. Reg. 52829 (1988).

110. *Abenaki Nation of Mississquoi v. Hughes*, 805 F. Supp. 234, 250 (D. Vt. Oct. 22, 1992).

111. 25 CFR §83 (1992). "Indian group or group means any Indian or Alaska Native aggregation within the continental United States that the Secretary of the Interior does not acknowledge to be an Indian tribe."

112. *Abenaki Nation of Mississquoi v. Hughes*, 805 F. Supp. 234, 251 (D. Vt. Oct. 22, 1992). The court ultimately held that the plaintiffs had failed to sustain any of their claims and entered judgment for the defendants. The District Court opinion was affirmed on appeal. 990 F.2d 729 (2nd Cir. April 20, 1993).

113. 43 CFR §10.2(b)(2). "Indian tribe means any tribe, band, nation, or other organized Indian group or community of Indians, including any Alaska Native village or corporation as defined in or established by the Alaska Native Claims Settlement Act (43 U.S.C. 1601 et seq.), which is recognized as eligible for the special programs and services provided by the United States to Indians because of their status as Indians. The Secretary will distribute a list of Indian tribes for the purposes of carrying out this statute through the Departmental Consulting Archeologist."

114. 60 Fed. Reg. 62136 (Dec. 4, 1995).

115. 60 Fed. Reg. 62136 (Dec. 4, 1995).

116. Memorandum from Edith R. Blackwell, associate solicitor, and Barry N. Roth, associate solicitor, to Sherry Hutt, List of Indian tribes for the purposes of carrying out the Native American Graves Protection and Repatriation Act (NAGPRA) (March 18, 2011).

117. Native American Graves Protection and Repatriation Act Regulations—Definition of "Indian Tribe," Interim final rule with request for comments, 76 Fed. Reg. 39007–39009 (July 5, 2011).

118. S. 2952, 99th Cong. (Oct. 18, 1986).

119. S. 2952, 99th Cong. (Oct. 18, 1986); S. 187, 100th Cong. (Jan. 6, 1987).

120. H.R. Rept. No. 101-340, pt. 1, at 16 (1989). On November 13, 1989, the House of Representatives struck all of the Senate language and replaced it with the text from H.R. 2668. The House committee report directly addresses the language of the final bill.

121. 25 U.S.C. §3010.

122. 60 Fed. Reg. 62136 (Dec. 4, 1995).

123. *Idrogo v. United States Army*, 18 F. Supp. 2d 25, 27 (D. DC Aug. 6, 1998). "Americans for Repatriation of Geronimo is not an organization that falls within the ambit of NAGPRA's reach." *Muwekma Tribe v. Babbitt*, 133 F. Supp. 2d 42, 44 (D. DC Jan. 16, 2001). "Thus, although a number of museums possess cultural objects and remains of the Muwekma people, the Tribe cannot demand their repatriation until it receives federal acknowledgment." *Romero v. Becken*, 256 F.3d 349, 354 (5th Cir. July 16, 2001). "Based on Castro's answers, the court found that the complexity of the case was limited by the fact that Castro lacked standing to assert many of his claims because of his acknowledgment that the Lipan Apache Band of Texas is not a federally-recognized tribe." *Maynor v. United States*, Civil No. 03 CV 1559 (D. DC July 8, 2005). "Federally recognized tribal status is required for a tribe to bring land or cultural claims. 25 U.S.C.S. §§3001, 3004, and 3005. "The Tuscarora Nation of North Carolina does not appear on the *Federal Register's* list of tribes entitled to receive services from the U.S. Department of the Interior."

124. 43 CFR §10.9(e)(6) (2009).

125. 43 CFR §10.11 (c)(2)(ii)(A).

126. 43 CFR §10.2 (b)(3).

127. S. 1980 §(3)(6)(C), Native American Graves Protection and Repatriation Act (Sept. 10, 1990).

128. *Rice v. Cayetano*, 528 U.S. 495 (2000).

129. 20 U.S.C. §80q-14(7).

130. 20 U.S.C. §80q-3.

131. U.S. Const. Art I, 8, cl. 3.

132. 20 U.S.C. §80q-14(11).

133. 25 U.S.C. §3001(9).

134. S. 1989 §(2)(1). "The term 'Native American' means an Indian, Alaska Native, or Native Hawaiian."

135. H.R. 5237, 101st Cong. §(2)(11), Native American Graves Protection and Repatriation Act (July 10, 1990).

136. 60 Fed. Reg. 62137 (Dec. 4, 1995).

137. 43 CFR §10.2(d).

138. *Notice of Intent to Repatriate*, Tri-City Herald (Sept. 17, 1996), at D1.

139. *Bonnichsen v. Harrell*, CV96-1481-JE, Complaint (Oct. 16, 1996).

140. *Bonnichsen v. United States, Dep't of the Army*, 969 F. Supp. 628, 654 (June 27, 1997).

141. Letter from Francis P. McManamon, departmental consulting archeologist, National Park Service, to Lieutenant Colonel Donald Curtis Jr., U.S. Army Corps of Engineers—Walla Walla District (Dec. 23, 1997).

142. Interagency Agreement between the Department of the Army and the Department of the Interior on the Delegation of Responsibilities under Section 3 of the Native American Graves Protection and Repatriation Act Pertaining to Human Re-

mains Discovered Near the City of Kennewick, Washington. Jayson L. Spiegel, acting assistant secretary of the Army for Manpower and Reserve Affairs, and Donald J. Barry, acting assistant secretary of the Interior for Fish and Wildlife and Parks (March 24, 1998).

143. Memorandum from Francis McManamon, departmental consulting archeologist, National Park Service, to Donald J. Barry, acting assistant secretary of the Interior for Fish and Wildlife and Parks, Determination that the Kennewick Human Skeletal Remains Are "Native American" for the Purposes of the Native American Graves Protection and Repatriation Act (NAGPRA) (Jan. 11, 2000).

144. Letter from Secretary of the Interior Bruce Babbitt to Secretary of the Army Louis Caldera Regarding Disposition of the Kennewick Human Remains (Sept. 21, 2000).

145. *Bonnichsen v. Babbitt, 217 F. Supp. 2d 1116.*

146. *Bonnichsen v. Babbitt, 217 F. Supp. 2d 1116, 1136.*

147. 20 U.S.C. §80q(6) and (7).

148. 43 CFR §10.2(d)(1).

149. For example, small scalp locks were commonly placed with the deceased as part of traditional Hawaiian burial customs. These would not be considered human remains under NAGPRA because they were given freely. They may fit the definition of funerary object because they are exclusively made for burial purposes. See 61 Fed. Reg. 16264–16265 (April 12, 1996).

150. 43 CFR §10, Final Rule, Preamble, 60 Fed. Reg. 62137 (Dec. 4, 1995).

151. 20 U.S.C. §80q-14(4).

152. 25 U.S.C. §3001(2)(3) and (2)(4).

153. 25 U.S.C. §3001(3)(A) and (3)(B).

154. 25 U.S.C. §3001(3)(B).

155. 25 U.S.C. §3001(3)(A).

156. 67 Fed. Reg. 57623 (Sept. 11, 2002).

157. H.R. 5237, 101st Cong. §(2)(5) (July 10, 1990). H.R. 5237, 101st Cong. §(2) (5) (Sept. 24, 1990).

158. Proposed Amendments to H.R. 5237 in order to meet AAM Concerns (undated).

159. H.R. 5237, 101st Cong. §(3)(A) and (3)(B) (Oct. 10, 1990).

160. H.R Rept. No. 101-877, at 15 (1990).

161. 60 Fed. Reg. 62138 (Dec. 4, 1995). In 2002, the Minnesota Indian Affairs Council published a notice of inventory completion in which it determined the cultural affiliation of the 186 human remains and associated funerary objects to be with the Hopi Tribe of Arizona; Pueblo of Acoma, New Mexico; Pueblo of Isleta, New Mexico; Pueblo of Laguna, New Mexico; Pueblo of Pojoaque, New Mexico; Pueblo of San Ildefonso, New Mexico; Pueblo of Taos, New Mexico; and Zuni Tribe of the Zuni Reservation, New Mexico. 67 Fed. Reg. 57623 (Sept. 11, 2002).

162. 43 CFR 10.2 §(d)(2).

163. Pub. L. 101-185 §(11)(a). The repatriation of associated funerary objects and unassociated funerary objects were addressed in separate sections, which required that the unassociated funerary objects be linked to a specific burial site. Pub. L. 101-185 §(11)(d).

164. Pub. L. 101-278 §(3)(a)(4) and (4).

165. H.R. 5237, 101st Cong. §(2)(14) (July 10, 1990).

166. H.R. 5237, 101st Cong. §(2)(3)(c)(c) (Oct. 10, 1990).

167. H.R. Rept. 101-877, 101st Cong., at 14 (1990).

168. 43 CFR §10.2 (d)(3). "While many items, from ancient pottery sherds to arrowheads, might be imbued with sacredness in the eyes of an individual, these regulations are specifically limited to objects that were devoted to a traditional Native American religious ceremony or ritual and which have religious significance or function in the continued observance or renewal of such ceremony."

169. 60 Fed. Reg. 62138 (Dec. 4, 1995).

170. See H.R. 5237, 101st Cong. §(14) (July 10, 1990); H.R. 5237, 101st Cong. §(3)(B) (Sept. 24, 1990).

171. 64 Fed. Reg. 20021 (April 23, 1999), 64 Fed. Reg. 30355 (June 7, 1999).

172. 25 U.S.C. §3001(3)(D).

173. H.R. 5237, 101st Cong. §(2)(3)(C) (Sept. 24, 1990).

174. 20 U.S.C. §80q-9a(a).

175. 20 U.S.C. §80q-9(a)(1) and §80q-11(a)(1).

176. 20 U.S.C. §80q-9(a), (b), and (c).

177. H.R. Rept. 101-340, at 15.

178. 20 U.S.C. §80q-9 (d).

179. H.R. Rept. 101-340, at 15.

180. 20 U.S.C. §80q-9(e).

181. H.R. Rept. No. 101-340, at 16.

182. 20 U.S.C. §80q-11(a)(2).

183. 25 U.S.C. §3003 (a).

184. 25 U.S.C. §3003(e).

185. H.R. 5237, 101st Cong. §(5)(b)(1)(C) (July 10, 1990).

186. 25 U.S.C. §3003(b)(2).

187. 25 U.S.C. §3003(c).

188. 25 U.S.C. §3003(d).

189. 25 U.S.C. §3005(a)(1).

190. H.R. 5237, 101st Cong. §(5)(a).

191. H.R. Rept. 101-877, at 15.

192. 25 U.S.C. §3004(a).

193. 25 U.S.C. §3004(a).

194. 25 U.S.C. §3004(b)(1)(C).

195. 25 U.S.C. §3004(b)(1)(A).

196. 25 U.S.C. §3005(a)(2).

197. 20 U.S.C. §80q-9a(a).

198. *Smithsonian Institution: Much Work Still Needed to Identify and Repatriate Indian Human Remains and Objects.* U.S. Government Accountability Office, GAO-11-515 (May 2011).

199. *Smithsonian Institution: Much Work Still Needed to Identify and Repatriate Indian Human Remains and Objects*, at 40.

200. 25 U.S.C. §3005(4).

201. 25 U.S.C. §3005 (5) and 20 U.S.C. §80q-9a.

202. 20 U.S.C. §80q-10(a).

203. 25 U.S.C. §3006(c).

204. H.R. Rept. 101-340, at 16.

205. H.R. Rept. 101-877, at 16.

206. S. Rept. 101-473, at 11.

207. 20 U.S.C. §80q-9a (c) and 25 U.S.C. §3005(c).

208. *Black's Law Dictionary*, 6th ed., at 1325.

209. 25 U.S.C. §3001(13).

210. 25 U.S.C. §3001(13).

211. Letter from Bruce C. Navarro, deputy assistant attorney general, Department of Justice, to Representative Morris Udall (Sept. 17, 1990), in H.R. Rept. 101-877, at 25.

212. H.R. 5237, 101st Cong. §(2)(3) (Oct. 15, 1990).

213. H.R. Rept. 101-877, at 14.

214. 25 U.S.C. §3005(c).

215. 25 U.S.C. §194, derived from R.S. §2126, derived from act of June 30, 1834, ch. 161, §22, 4 Stat. 733. "In all trials about the right of property in which an Indian may be a party on one side, and a white person on the other, the burden of proof shall rest upon the white person, whenever the Indian shall make out a presumption of title in himself from the fact of previous possession or ownership."

216. H.R. 5237, 101st Congress, §(6)(c)(2) (July 10, 1990).

217. 136 Cong. Rec. S17176 (daily ed., October 26, 1990).

218. 25 U.S.C. §3005(b).

219. H.R. Rept. 101-877, at 15.

220. 25 U.S.C. §3005(a)(2).

221. See *Sandon v. Lewis*, No. 96-15295 (9th Cir., Feb. 20, 1998) (objection to cavity searches and drug testing); *Am. Fed'n Gov't Emps. v. Roberts*, 9 F.3d 1464, 1468 (9th Cir., 1993), (objection to the taking of urine samples); *United States v. Hammer*, 121 F. Supp. 2d 794, 802 (M.D. Pa., 2000) (holding that the religious convictions of a death row inmate and his request to not be subject to an autopsy must be given respect absent a compelling state interest and the interests of the state could be met in a less invasive manner by external examination); *State v. Biddings*, 550 N.E.2d 975, 980 (Ohio App., 1988) (holding that taking blood samples over religious objection may occur when the state has a compelling reason).

222. 25 U.S.C. §3005(e).

223. H.R. 5237, 101st Cong. §(7)(e).

224. H.R. Rept. 101-340, at 19.

225. 16 U.S.C. §470dd.

226. 16 U.S.C. §431-433.

227. 16 U.S.C. §469a-3(a).

228. 16 U.S.C. §470cc(b)(3).

229. 75 CFR 12402 (March 15, 2010). "The authority for part 10 is revised to read as follows: Authority: 25 U.S.C. 3001 et seq., *16 U.S.C. 470dd* (2), 25 U.S.C. 9."

230. H.R. 1381, 101st Cong. §(3)(b) (March 14, 1989).

231. *Statistical Abstract of the United States* (1993), at 220.

232. Secretary's 1997 Report to Congress on Federal Archeology, National Park Service. Bureau of Land Management: 264,000,000 acres; Forest Service: 190,586,313 acres; Fish and Wildlife Service: 92,666,000 acres; National Park Service: 83,233,318 acres.

233. *Statistical Abstract of the United States* (1993), at 220.

234. Department of Hawaiian Home Lands FY2001-2002 Annual Report, at 16.

235. 43 CFR §7.8 (1990).

236. *Kickapoo Traditional Tribe v. Chacon*, 46 F. Supp. 2d 644 (W.D.Tex., 1999).

237. *John Thorpe v. Borough of Jim Thorpe*, 3:10-CV-1317 (D.M.Pa., Feb. 4, 2011).

238. H.R. 5237, 101st Cong. §(3)(c)(2) and (3)(c)(4) (July 10, 1990).

239. H.R. Rpt. 101-877, at 24 (Letter from Robert W. Page, assistant secretary of the Army (Civil Works), to Representative Udall, Aug. 31, 1990). In fact, NAGPRA's consent requirement is similar to ARPA's requirement for tribal consent prior to excavation or removal of archeological resources on Indian lands. 16 U.S.C. §470cc(g)(2).

240. H.R. 5237, 101st Cong. §(3)(c)(2) (Oct. 10, 1990).

241. H.R. 5237, 101st Cong. §(3)(a)(2)(C) (July 10, 1990).

242. H.R. 5237, 101st Cong. §(3)(a)(2)(C) (Oct. 10, 1990).

243. H.R. 5237, 101st Cong. §(3)(a)(2)(C) (Oct. 20, 1990).

244. 60 Fed. Reg. 62140 (Dec. 4, 1995).

245. 43 CFR 10.11 and 75 Fed. Reg. 12389 (March 11, 2010).

246. H.R. Rept. 101-877, 101st Cong., at 14 (1990).

247. *Bonnichsen v. United States*, 217 F. Supp. 2d 1116, 1143, 1148 (D. Or., 2002). See S. Rept. 101-473, at 8 (claimant must show "a continuity of group identity from the earlier to the present day group"). See also S. Rept. 101-473, at 9 ("The requirement of continuity between present day Indian tribes and material from historic or prehistoric Indian tribes is intended to ensure that the claimant has a reasonable connection with the materials").

248. 12 Stat. 945, 11 Kappler 694.

249. 14 Ind. Cl. Comm. 14. (1964).

250. 16 Ind. Cl. Comm. 484.

251. *Bonnichsen v. United States*, 217 F. Supp. 2d 1116, 1143 (D. Or., 2002).

252. H.R. Rept. 101-877, 101st Cong. (1990), at 31. Misidentified in the court opinion as a Senate report.

253. 25 U.S.C. §70n and 70u.

254. 14 Ind. Cl. Com. 14, 166.

255. 136 Cong. Rec. S17176 (Oct. 26, 1990).

256. 43 CFR §10.4(b).

257. *Yankton Sioux Tribe v. United States Army Corps of Eng'rs*, 83 F. Supp. 2d 1047, 1057 (DC SD, 2000).

258. *Yankton Sioux Tribe v United States Army Corps of Eng'rs*, 194 F. Supp. 2d 977, 985 (DC SD, 2002).

259. H.R. Rept. 101-877, 101st Cong. (1990), at 8.

260. *Fallon Paiute-Shoshone Tribe v. U.S. Bureau of Land Management*, 455 F. *Supp. 2d* 1207, 1220 (D.Nv., 1996). The court also erroneously stated that the Native American Graves Protection and Repatriation Review Committee previously found that the Bureau of Land Management wholly failed to consult with the tribe. The review committee's findings do not address the adequacy of the agency's consultation effort. See *Native American Graves Protection and Repatriation Review Committee Findings and Recommendations Regarding Human Remains and Associated Funerary Objects from Spirit Cave in Nevada*, 67 Fed. Reg. 17463 (April 10, 2002).

261. H.R. 5237, 101st Cong. (Sept. 24, 1990).

262. *Stare decisis et non quieta movere*: to stand by decisions and not disturb the undisturbed.

263. *United States v. Corrow*, 941 F. Supp. 1553, 1562 (D.N.M., 1996); U.S. Ct. App., 10th Cir. (1997); cert. denied, 522 U.S. 1133, 118 S.Ct. 1089, 140 L.Ed.2d 146 (1998).

264. *Bonnichsen v. United States*, 367 F.3d 864, 873 (9th Cir., 2004).

265. *Conroy v. Aniskoff*, 507 U.S. 511, 519 (1993).

Index

About the Author

A cultural and legal anthropologist, C. Timothy McKeown has served since 1990 implementing federal Indian law with the U.S. Department of the Interior. He was involved in implementation of the Native American Graves Protection and Repatriation Act (NAGPRA) from 1991 to 2009, for which he drafted the implementing regulations; provided training to representatives of Indian tribes, Native Hawaiian organizations, museums, and federal agencies; and served as the secretary of the Interior's representative to the Native American Graves Protection and Repatriation Review Committee. He currently serves with a multidisciplinary team providing forensic analysis on tribal trust litigation in federal District Courts and the U.S. Court of Federal Claims. McKeown earned his doctorate in cultural anthropology from Northwestern University with a dissertation focusing on the future images of environmental scientists at the International Institute for Applied Systems Analysis in Laxenburg, Austria. He has also worked for the Institute for Alternative Futures, Navajo Nation, and Jicarilla Apache Tribe and as a consultant for the National Association of Tribal Historic Preservation Officers.